# THE PRESIDENCY IN MEXICAN POLITICS

# The Presidency in Mexican Politics

George Philip
*Reader in Latin American Politics*
*London School of Economics*
*and the London Institute of Latin American Studies*

St. Martin's Press    New York

© George Philip 1992

All rights reserved. For information, write:
Scholarly and Reference Division,
St. Martin's Press, Inc., 175 Fifth Avenue,
New York, N.Y. 10010

First published in the United States of America in 1992

Printed in Hong Kong

ISBN 0–312–06766–6

Library of Congress Cataloging-in-Publication Data
Philip, George D. E.
  The presidency in Mexican politics / George Philip.
    p.   cm.
  Includes bibliographical references and index.
  ISBN 0–312–06766–6
  1. Presidents—Mexico.   2. Mexico—Constitutional history.
  I. Title.
  JL1241.P53   1992
  354.7203'13—dc20                             91–21564
                                                  CIP

# Contents

*Preface* vii
1  Introduction: The Mexican Political System  1
2  Díaz Ordaz and the Student Massacre at Tlatelolco  19
3  From Counter-insurgency to Economic Crisis: The Echeverría Presidency  65
4  López Portillo: From Boom to Bust  97
5  De la Madrid: The Limits of Orthodoxy  133
6  Conclusion: The Presidency and Political Change  167
*Notes*  185
*References*  202
*Glossary and Abbreviations*  208
*Index*  210

# Preface

It is quite normal for researchers working on Mexico to complain at some length about the difficulties encountered in researching the inner workings of government in that country. The reasons have, however, changed considerably. Twenty or thirty years ago it was very difficult to find appropriate material for political research; it was not just that political activity was generally secret, but political discourse was heavily coded. Acute observers – diplomats for example – could follow events up to a point but their information was inevitably sketchy rather than comprehensive. Even good journalists were sometimes badly misled.

Today there is a problem of a different kind. There is far more material on Mexican politics, but the most readily available of this relates to the area of political society rather than to the innermost areas of the state. For a student of the Mexican presidency it is still difficult to find proof (even of a balance-of-probability kind) that would persuade a reader to accept that what an author believes went on was what actually happened. This is to some extent a problem for the study of the core executive in any country. It is hopeless to rely purely on the public record, and the press may at times be as misleading as it is helpful. On the other hand, why should a reader accept an author's version of anonymous, off-the-record interviews?

I can offer no solution to this problem. I have in fact talked at some length to a relatively small number of people closely connected with one or more of the four presidents discussed in this book. At times I heard things that seemed so important that it would be wrong not to mention them; where corroborative on-the-record evidence was lacking I have simply identified 'a source', but not the name. Where reliable on-the-record material has existed I have of course used it. There are also very many more people with whom I have discussed political questions in some detail, but without focusing so specifically on the presidential issue itself. Relying on interviews involves a danger not so much of factual error (I offer no excuses for any which may exist) but of a distorting perspective dependent on the nature of one's contacts. However the key judgements in this book are my own; it is for the reader to decide whether to trust them.

The aim of this study is far more than just to reconstruct events. It aims also to understand the Mexican presidential institution and, through it, something of the Mexican political system as a whole. The focus is on actual conflicts between various groups and individuals; I believe that these conflicts can be understood, for the most part, as resulting from the rational (or at any rate intelligible) behaviour of semi- or fully-organised interests. This is not to deny the importance of cultural factors in politics but the book does represent an attempt to get away from the cultural stereotypes which are all too often used as a substitute for serious analysis. Octavio Paz' *Labyrinths of Solitude*, despite its virtues, has unfortunately led some later analysts – both academic and journalist – into the bad habit of using *mestizaje*, or some similar general concept, as a depressingly promiscuous explanation to serve whatever may seem to need it. Meaningful conceptual relationships – those which truly convince and stand the test of time – need much more work and are built up more slowly.

I wish to thank the British Council, the London School of Economics and the Institute of Latin American Studies for their help in financing my various trips to Mexico. I am grateful also to Sarah Cameron, Norman Cox and Sir William Harding for their comments on earlier drafts of particular chapters and to Lloyds Bank for access to their library. I must also thank the very many people who, by arguing about politics with me, have helped to shape the ideas presented here. The responsibility for any mistakes in the work is entirely my own.

GEORGE PHILIP

# 1 Introduction: The Mexican Political System

The laws of thermodynamics are said to predict that the bumble bee cannot fly. There are no equivalent laws governing political systems but the continued survival of the Mexican system still surprises. Every few years a scholarly analysis will declare that Mexican politics is in crisis;[1] a former student of mine, apparently without irony, once wrote that 'the most consistent feature of Mexican politics is the crisis'. Yet the Mexican system, unusually for Latin America, has produced two generations of political stability; for most Mexicans, these years have not been especially unhappy. So why is a system which is apparently capable of working quite well so regularly denounced as fundamentally unviable?

One answer often given is that the system has led governments to adopt unsatisfactory policies. Critics do not always agree about which policies to denounce. However, in broad terms, left-wingers tend to argue that the system has betrayed its revolutionary and popular origins and carried out policies not in the best interests of the majority of Mexicans.[2] Economic liberals have argued, rather, that the system has degenerated into a set of lobbies and populist gestures; its policies, in other words, have been bad for Mexico's development because the system has no effective way of ordering popular input into government. It therefore oscillates between extremes of exclusionary repression and bursts of irrational 'populism' which please crowds but do serious economic damage.[3]

These criticisms are often quite perceptive. What is more difficult is to judge the difference between the ordinary imperfection of political life and an inherent (or somehow acquired) system-threatening syndrome. There is, in Adam Smith's words, 'a lot of ruin in a nation'. It is certainly true that Mexican governments have made some serious mistakes over the past twenty-five years. Yet to err is human, not especially Mexican. Mexican presidents have not sent troops to Vietnam or Afghanistan. They did not invent or participate in the Common Agricultural Policy. They did not invent 'incomes policies' leading to the near paralysis of the economy as a result of strike activity. They did not impose a poll tax. If the test of a good political system is its ability to protect society from the errors of its policymakers or to guarantee social justice in a civilised environment, then this is a test which no system can pass.

It is also true that the Mexican economy suffered during the 1980s from a combination of debt problems and lower oil prices so that the trend of slowly-improving living standards went sharply, if (one hopes) temporarily, into reverse. Yet the Mexican performance during the 1980s does not compare badly with that of Latin America as a whole. It was possible to make the case in 1982 that Mexico and perhaps Argentina had made more unforced errors of policy than most other Latin American countries; this assertion in respect of Mexico certainly cannot be sustained in 1990. Assessments of economic performance notoriously fluctuate, but if one takes a long view Mexico compares at least adequately with the Latin American average. While scholars who have portrayed the system as a simple alliance between political and economic power have proved poor judges of events, the apocalyptic writings of only a few years ago also now appear quite obsolete.[4]

Another line of criticism is that the system worked well enough in the past, but does not work so well now. An increasingly urban, middle-class and politically sophisticated population is less willing to tolerate the kind of political manipulation generally practised by the Institutional Revolutionary Party (PRI).[5] In many ways this line of attack also has much to commend it. What still needs to be asked, however, is whether or not the system is capable of adapting to changing conditions – and, if it is, then how. In the 1940s and early 1950s, the system underwent considerable change; the military lost its position in politics, the power of state governors was decisively reduced and the no re-election rule for presidents was firmly reinforced. There have also been major changes in the past twenty years. The media are far freer and more outspoken than in the late 1960s. There is a serious electoral opposition; the Church has become a more direct political actor and the trade union issue is now at or near the top of the political agenda. Some influential Mexicans are specifically familiar with Burke's statement that 'a political order without the means of at least some change is without the means of its own preservation'.

Virtually no senior Mexican politician would be unfamiliar with the logic of this argument. What is clear, however, is that the system has not responded *smoothly* to change; instead it has generally tried to block new political forces before reluctantly coming to terms with them. This has given an air of crisis to a number of recent events; indeed if one defines a crisis as a short period of conflict and tension, then the Mexican system is indeed crisis-generating. Yet these crises have not proved system-threatening. A balanced account of the system must accept that it has been crisis-resolving as well as crisis-producing. In this respect the Mexican system is not particularly unusual – and it has proved far more successful than some.

What, then, is the role of the presidency in this system? Several scholars have ventured answers.[6] The Mexican classics, generally the work of lawyers and historians, have argued that the system is highly presidential; one might almost be forgiven for thinking that the presidency was the system. More recent writers, who have tended to be pluralists or Marxists, have offered very different types of answer; the pluralists have tended to stress the power of particular groups and the role of bargaining and negotiation. Marxists have not really focused on the presidential institution at all, preferring to stress various 'isms' and the overpowering logic of capital accumulation.

In recent years there has been within the United States an increased willingness to realise that political institutions matter, and that there is far more to political life than the operation of informal processes or group and class activities.[7] In Mexico itself it is remarkable how, within the space of a few years, political scientists who would once have concentrated almost entirely on impersonal questions such as 'the role of the state' are once again concerned with institutions, personalities and political tactics.

In my own view both of these developments are highly positive. It should be possible to find ways of treating earlier legal-institutional approaches with a proper respect while making full use of the insights provided by 'process-based' writings of the more recent past. This work is intended as a step in this direction.

The argument here is that the Mexican system is indeed highly presidential. However its dynamic involves an interaction – sometimes co-operative, sometimes creatively diverse, sometimes destructively confrontational – between state power and various forms of societal power. On the societal side, the dynamic is provided by several factors – the importation of new ideas from abroad, the continued process of socio-economic change, economic boom and setback – which are in at least some respects inherently unpredictable. On the side of state power there is, more than anything else, the presidential institution. The rest of this introduction will outline some of the main features of Mexican political institutions. Readers who regard themselves as expert in the subject may prefer to move directly to the next chapter.

## THE MEXICAN PRESIDENCY

Mexican presidents serve for six years with no possibility of re-election. While some presidents have sought to exercise power after the end of their term of office, these attempts have not generally been successful. When in office, however, they are subject to few if any legal or constitutional constraints. A Mexican president can, literally, get away with murder, although it is fair to say that murderers do not generally become presidents. What is true, however, is that the principle of presidential authority extends the benefits of non-accountability (of what the Mexicans call *impunidad*) to far more junior figures than the president himself. The main thing that these juniors have to fear is the wrath of a future president.

Under these circumstances, the political calendar assumes considerable importance. Mexican presidential elections are held in the early July of the sixth presidential year and the new president is inaugurated in December. The outcome of these elections has generally been considered a formality (though less so in 1988 than before) and the crucial step has therefore been the nomination of the official presidential candidate of the PRI. This usually occurs in September or October of the pre-election year. Between this nomination and the inauguration of the new president come a difficult fourteen months. Some outgoing presidents have been content to depart quietly, but others have been determined to leave their mark upon events. The prospect of a rapid move from political pre-eminence to a state of at best semi-retirement is obviously a difficult one; what makes matters worse is that Mexican presidents are often selected young. Retirement generally comes in a man's early fifties; sometimes (as is scheduled in 1994 for example) in his mid-forties. Not everyone can contemplate so early a retirement from so eminent a career without a degree of trauma or bitterness. Moreover some presidents, not necessarily seeking a final-year drama, have one thrust upon them. Often the build-up of problems during the presidential term, and the general release of political inhibitions at its end, have left an outgoing president little choice but to react. There is therefore a high probability that political crises, should they occur, will take place at or near the end of a presidential term.

Until now at least, it has been the rule that the outgoing president chooses his successor. The successor has always been a senior member of the Mexican cabinet; this, however, need not mean very much since the president chooses his cabinet as well. Yet this presidential selection, the *destape*, is one of the high points of the Mexican political calendar. For several years before, senior government ministers will seek to catch the presidential eye; sometimes they will seek to undermine their rivals, although this is a dangerous game. Yet it is important for presidential aspirants to act with discretion; the obvious front-runner is chosen only rarely. In the end, presidents are reasonably free to choose whom they wish although they will try to keep people guessing for as long as possible in order both to secure their own power and to avoid any 'stop X' movement developing. They may also wish to test their senior ministers before selecting one for the highest office.

Robert Scott, thirty years ago, suggested a set of prerequisites for successful presidential aspirants; they should be in good health, energetic, and not 'violently ugly'. The should come from a modest middle-class background, have a good education, have demonstrated some administrative capacity, be neither devoutly Catholic nor aggressively atheist, and come from a major Mexican state.[9] This list, though generally anodyne, has not in fact proved much of a guide. President de la Madrid (1982–8) is a devout Catholic from the small state of Colima; his family's Revolutionary background was non-existent. Salinas de Gortari, the son of a Cabinet minister, did not come from a modest background; he has a foreign education and three Harvard degrees. Good health is obviously an unpredictable factor; obvious incapacitation would rule out a presidential candidate (and not only in Mexico), but physical fitness is by no means a major factor in selection. Nor is it clear that either Echeverría (1970–6) or López Portillo (1976–82) ever demonstrated serious administrative ability. Echeverría did not serve in any senior position outside *Gobernación*, though admittedly he did show talent in that particular role. López Portillo's ministerial career before he became president was far from distinguished. As to whether a presidential nominee can be 'violently ugly', the reader is advised to consult photographs. It is however one of the strengths of Mexican politics that plausible charismatic figures do not often reach the top.

In essence, therefore, the outgoing president chooses whom he wants. There is some suggestion that Echeverría sought to choose a cipher in a failed bid to exert influence after the end of his term – but this is far from being proved. Certainly in general terms there is little doubt that most outgoing presidents since 1952 have chosen the man they genuinely considered best for the job. Sometimes they subsequently came to believe that they had chosen badly; however, a choice, once made, is definitive and cannot be revoked.

What any president must try to do is ensure that, when his choice is made, senior political figures rally around the chosen figure. This did not really happen in 1987, when the PRI split seriously, or even in 1981, when two senior figures made very clear their unhappiness with de la Madrid. Efforts are always made just after the *destape* to project a mood of national unity. To facilitate this, it often happens that just before the *destape* an elder-statesman figure is given the job of running the official party. This is generally the signal that individuals and groups who have fallen into official disfavour are now welcome to rejoin the fold. At the same time, figures close to the outgoing president are often given appointments that will to some extent protect them from the vagaries of an incoming administration; state governorships and foreign embassies are often useful in this context and there is also the legislature.

However while the outgoing president will normally seek to create an element of continuity, an incoming figure will often introduce some discontinuity. The new president will need to show that he is his own boss; if his predecessor seeks to pressure him in any way, such pressures are likely to be resisted. The new president will place his own friends and allies in senior cabinet positions; there may be one or two people left over from the previous administration but not many. State governors do overlap presidential terms, but central governmental positions rarely do.

## POWER WITHIN THE PUBLIC SECTOR

The Mexican public sector is clientelist. The president chooses his cabinet and selects people to fill a number of other offices; senior figures in the government will also expect to be able to appoint their juniors, and so the process continues downward. This type of system generates groups (*camarillas*) who work together in order to share out such offices as become available. [10] It can generate inertia and inter-bureaucratic rivalry; it does not generally create any powerful 'bureaucratic' interest in the way that a professional civil service often can. The system is too amorphous.

Since the mid-1970s there has been a lot of discussion within Mexico about the rise of the so-called 'technocrats'.[11] A technocrat is defined as a person (usually a man) with a degree in economics or political science from a foreign (usually a US) university. His career pattern will involve work in federal government positions, usually in Mexico City, and will require trained expertise; it may not be part of his career to stand for elective office. Technocrats have, however, worked their way into the top reaches of the Mexican system and now (depending on the definition one uses) dominate it.

During the last twenty-five years there has been a considerable professionalisation at the senior level of government. In 1958 the British ambassador could report that 'the Mexican "cabinet" scarcely ever meets as a collective entity for the transaction of business'.[12] López Mateos introduced a cabinet committee on economic matters, but both he and Díaz Ordaz generally left economic policymaking to the Secretary of Finance, Ortiz Mena. He was, in effect, *the* government expert on questions of economic policy. Since 1970, however, the professional background of senior decision-makers has markedly broadened. In Salinas de Gortari's first cabinet (appointed December 1988), all of the main economics secretaries had master's or doctor's degrees in that subject from a major US university. The president himself has a doctorate and two master's degrees from Harvard. Additionally, two other senior secretaries had studied public administration at postgraduate level; one in Britain and the other in the USA. In terms of academic qualifications, Salinas's first cabinet is one of the strongest in the world.

It is debatable how far this change has really altered the character of the system. It certainly has altered the career advice that an ambitious young Mexican might be expected to receive

('Go north young man – and study economics!').[13] It has also removed the last obstacle to the recruitment of upper-class Mexican youth into the government; channels of social mobility, for those not fortunate enough to have access to private higher education, have been correspondingly curtailed. Furthermore a cabinet full of English-speaking economists with postgraduate qualifications is likely to look at the world somewhat differently from the less sophisticated machine politicians who held power in the 1950s and early 1960s. What is far less clear is that there is a genuine technocratic interest, as such, in the Mexican system.

What appears to have happened instead is that key political conflicts (high politics, if one may put it this way) are fought out in intra-bureaucratic battles. Computers serve as artillery, numbers as ammunition and the strategic objective is the presidential ear. Between 1970 and 1982 there was a definite monetarist vs structuralist division; after 1982 non-orthodox economists were kept firmly away from economics ministries. However the existence of broad agreement on basic economic principles has not prevented intra-bureaucratic conflict taking place since then.

Another development during the whole period under discussion has been the relative decline of the PRI and the local political élites which traditionally influenced the official parties. To some limited extent the PRI has lost ground to the various opposition parties. Far more important, however, has been its loss of power vis-à-vis the agencies of central government. The states and localities are heavily outspent by the federal agencies, and local political figures – however prominent – rarely make it to the top in Mexico City.[14] Political experience counts for too little, and educational qualifications for too much.

## LOW POLITICS:CORPORATISM AND PLURALISM

If one defines high politics as being about the making of public policy at national level, low politics can be seen as mainly involving competition for the resources of the state or, at any rate, the system. Although there are horizontally-based organisations, trade unions and peasant leagues, the authorities are generally suspicious of genuinely independent movements and normally seek to break them up. Although this is sometimes a question of force, it is done more often by providing selective inducements to people to defect from solidarity movements. It helps that there are official structures into which defectors may be integrated. While unofficial solidarity movements are rarely encouraged, however, Mexican politics do feature some powerful corporate structures. There are three labour confederations organised within the Confederación de Trabajo; the CROM and the CROC are not particularly important, but the CTM is by any standards a strong union. Much has been written about Mexican labour, but the topic remains complex and in some respects obscure.[15] It is unlikely that anybody would be so foolish as to present these Mexican labour organisations as militant, class-conscious vanguard associations; they are evidently accommodationist and moderate. On the other hand, scholars who have sought to portray them as simple instruments of social control and capital accumulation surely exaggerate in the other direction. There is labour influence within the Mexican system. While this may not be very great, part of the explanation for this lies in the fact that developing countries with labour surplus do not generally afford possibilities for strong and effective blue-collar unionism.

In fact Mexican labour is organised on a fairly typical Latin American pattern. Closed shop arrangements are legally valid in many places; a worker who loses his union card may also lose his job. In theory workers in unions affiliated to the PRI via one of its corporate members are required to turn out and vote for the party; such discipline is not generally enforced, but political loyalty is in theory part and parcel of union identity. The Ministry of Labour is given extensive powers to recognise unions and union leaderships; most industrial relations conflicts in unionised organisations end up being arbitrated by the ministry. One result is that labour contracts have tended toward a bureaucratic uniformity which has had relatively little relationship to an employer's ability to pay.[16] Most unionised workers earn considerably more than the legal minimum wage. There has, in other words, been a general tendency – typical of corporatist labour structures – for workers to be offered a degree of security in return for political loyalty. While evidently not in socialist Utopia, most workers are thereby far better off than they would have been under Mr Gradgrind – a fact of which left-wing critics of the system have not always been sufficiently aware. Moreover there are few Latin American countries in which any labour leader can be found with the political influence enjoyed over so long a period by the head of the CTM, Fidel Velázquez.

Velázquez himself is said to have attributed his success to the fact that he was content to act as a labour leader and had no further intellectual or political aspirations. In return, he has enjoyed a power of patronage which – during the last forty years – has been second to none.

If the CTM is one of the gateways into 'low politics', state governorships are another. State governors are effectively appointed by the president, in the sense that nomination by the PRI is generally tantamount to election. On just one occasion, in 1989, an opposition candidate for a state governorship has been successful. State governors effectively control their own state, although they are subject to removal by the centre (i.e. by the president) at any time and also have to co-operate with the local branches of government ministries. In January 1951 the CIA reported that:

> State governors are of two types – those that are selected and imposed as puppets of the national government and those who are selected through negotiation with the national government on the basis of strong local support.[17]

Today, however, genuine local support often carries little weight in the selection process; it is certainly something that a president can overlook whenever he wishes. This change reflects the centralisation of Mexican politics which has occurred since 1951 with respect both to government and (to a lesser degree) opposition.[18]

Rural politics in Mexico are almost infinitely complex, but it is generally accepted that the official peasant organisation, the CNC, is no longer a very significant factor in terms of political power. Far more important (though slowly declining in influence) in rural and to some extent also in urban areas, is the *cacique*.

The word *cacique* is a corruption of the Arawak word Kassequa.[19] Broadly speaking, it means 'boss' – in the Tammany Hall sense of the word. However a *cacique* is different from an American political boss in one crucial sense. American boss-politics revolves around the ability of a particular individual to operate a political machine in a consistent election-winning way. The basis of his power is elected office, and bosses have held power consistently over long periods through consistent re-election. In Mexico re-election is generally not permitted, so that elected office cannot serve as a main basis of boss rule. However because

Mexican elections are rarely competitive (though undoubtedly more often so now than in the past), a successful candidate does not have to be popular. An American political boss enjoys power and may occasionally resort to illegality; however he must retain a minimum level of popular support or his career will be over. To retain this support, he must be responsive to local feelings and values. A Mexican *cacique* is far closer to a position of power without responsibility; he need not be elected to anything and his nominees are unlikely to face any kind of serious electoral test. A *cacique* needs a kin group or local faction who will support him unconditionally, financial resources sufficient to buy a more extensive group of followers, and the support or at least benevolent neutrality of political figures senior to himself so that these will turn a blind eye to the *cacique*'s often-violent illegalities. He also needs to be acceptable to higher, more central, powers.

The system has tended in the past to maintain social control by co-opting and living with local *caciques*, withdrawing support only in cases where the *cacique* lost out in a power struggle at the top or where his rule proved so outrageous that serious local protest was engendered. This is not to say that all *caciques* are necessarily evil characters; it is rather that they all have had access to extra-legal sources of power with few channels of accountability. Virtually the only real safety valve was the possibility of popular appeal to the state governor or – in more extreme cases – the president.

## THE ECONOMY AND THE PRIVATE SECTOR

Although Mexican politics have some pronouncedly corporatist features, it is by no means wholly a corporatist system. To put the matter plainly, there is marginality among the poorest, corporatism among middle-income Mexicans, and increasing neo-pluralism for the upper-middle classes (including intellectuals) and the bourgeoisie. Neo-pluralism does provide relatively privileged groups with the necessary independence to criticise, and where necessary challenge, the state.[20] Thus universities are to a substantial degree autonomous of the government. The Church exists independently even though, in theory, it plays no active part in politics. Opposition parties are legal and operative, though prior to 1988 they were rarely allowed to win anything very serious.

Neo-pluralism also generally prevails in the private sector. While it is true that all companies have to join at least one of the three chambers of commerce set up by the system, these chambers do not in any very serious sense seek to control the membership.[21] Some attempts are made to exert influence – in the early 1980s a number of businessmen were firmly dissuaded from publicly supporting the National Action Party (PAN). However business has been sharply critical of the government at various times, and there are voluntary business associations which exist in addition to those which the state formally controls.[22] Business attitudes to the political system cover a wide range, from strong support to considerable hostility.

Business organisations are, of course, very much less important to business than labour unions are to individual workers. Business power comes from control of money far more than through access to organisation. The state can therefore hope to control business only if it is in a position to control the economy as a whole.

In fact, until the mid-1980s at any rate, the Mexican economy as a whole was run on lines which were more corporatist than liberal. Public ownership and investment, though rapidly expanded during 1970-82, was probably less important here than the state's regulatory power – over food prices, utility prices, imports, wages and a host of other variables.[23] The direction of policy was to channel resources away from exporting activities – agriculture prior to 1970, oil after 1975 – into import-substituting industrialisation. Some favoured areas of activity – for example the *maquiladora* exporters to the United States – were, however, given particularly favourable treatment and thereby exempted from this general bias of policy.

This 'model' of import-substituting industrialisation ran into difficulties during the period covered by this book. By the late 1960s it was becoming clear that agriculture was losing much of its dynamism. The government began to talk of encouraging manufacturing exports (with all that this shift implied for real wage rates, relative prices, spatial patterns of growth, etc.) but not enough was done. From the mid-1970s oil appeared to come to the rescue. Oil exports, and the foreign borrowing which they permitted, financed a boom which ended in crash in 1982. After 1982 the direction of policy has been to move toward a form of market-orientated capitalism. This move, however, was by no means complete at the end of 1988.

Import substituting industrialisation (ISI) is still a controversial topic. Critics argue that the consequences of protecting industry are economic distortion, opportunities for corruption and favouritism, and inefficiency. The policy favours those with friends in government or who know how to play the system rather than those who are most efficient at the job of producing what the customer actually wants. The policy does, however, have its defenders. Many Latin Americans have seen it as a means of introducing some of the efficiency of capitalism while avoiding (or at any rate postponing) some of the economic brutalities of a thoroughgoing liberalism. Few non-affluent societies have, as a matter of historical fact, been willing to put their trust in a wholly *laissez-faire* policy. Victorian Britain, which perhaps came nearest, found a number of ways to protect the haves (though not the have-nots) from the operation of market forces; to name only one, the British Empire provided, in Bright's words, 'a huge system of outdoor relief for the aristocracy'.

Import-substituting industrialisation, as practised in Mexico, gave new entrepreneurs the confidence to invest and larger companies the ability to build up their financial power and undertake more ambitious projects. The corporatism which ISI made possible had the effect of minimising the threat of class conflict from an expanding urban labour force. Even the 'marginals', who benefited least from these policies, did at least gain from a growing demand for goods and services produced in the informal sector – itself the result of steady economic growth on the part of the formal sector.

One could write a book on the tension between market liberalism and protective corporatism in Mexico during 1964–88. This, however, is a study of presidential power and it is necessary to turn from this very cursory examination of the economy to a discussion of the political system itself.

## THE HOBBESIAN BARGAIN

Any picture of key Mexican political actors brings out many of the authoritarian features of the Mexican system.[24] We have the all-powerful president, the foreign-educated technocrat, the official trade union leader, the state governor and the small town or rural *cacique*. None of these is subject to very much accountability except from above. What Mexico had in common with other post-revolutionary systems was that traditional ('aristocratic') conservative interests suffered major damage during the upheaval and its aftermath. The landowning class was weakened by a succession of upheavals and very largely destroyed under Cárdenas. The Church, though more resilient, was also weakened by the Revolution and by the victory of its political enemies. Mexican conservatism, therefore, is not the conservatism of tradition but the less secure right-wingery of 'order and progress'. It is a kind of conservatism which I call Hobbesian.

Hobbes's Leviathan came into being in order to bring an end to the state of nature which (in the myth) had existed until then; under the state of nature, man's existence had been 'solitary, poor, nasty, brutish and short'. Men were willing to give up their liberties to the sovereign in return for peace, physical protection and the (implied rather than spoken) right to private property. States of nature and Leviathans are of course metaphors, but the notion of a 'Hobbesian bargain' – the sacrifice of democratic rights in exchange for the promise of peace and prosperity – can be illuminating. Certainly the Mexican Revolution at times came close to being a 'state of nature' in the Hobbesian sense, and the period 1920–40 also featured considerable political upheaval. After all of this, it would be surprising if there was not élite and also some public support for a quieter if less principled pattern of politics.

A 'Hobbesian bargain' does not, of course, require the active support of all sectors of society; there is, instead, a subtle mixture of support, consent and imposition. In the Mexican case, support was based on a tacit alliance between traditional conservative interests – the Church, the capitalist class and what was left of the landowning interest – and the less ideologically committed of the revolutionary leaders. In a quieter period, many revolutionary generals enjoyed the prospect of being able to join the private sector and become rich.[25] The old establishment could meanwhile by acquiescence and friendship secure the protection which it could not hope to win by fighting the new order. Both élites forgot their principles and remembered their friends. While this bargain was obviously never formalised, the key date relating is surely 1940 when Cárdenas gave way to Avila Camacho. From then on, the key Hobbesian priorities – peace, order, economic progress – became the key principles of Mexico's new authoritarian conservatives.

What this meant was that the 'Revolution' abandoned its radicalism while its conservative former opponents accommodated themselves to it. The actual extent of convergence remained limited; private and public sector élites maintained general outlooks which were very different from each other. Business particularly retained a residual suspicion of the political system – which added fuel to private sector discontent in 1960, 1974–6 and 1982–3. Nevertheless Mexican conservatives, during the post-war decades, were sufficiently afraid of mobilisation and attracted by the prospect of order to accept a political regime which they distrusted and a number of public policies which they disliked. Meanwhile the revolutionaries, under pressure from their own more entrepreneurial generals and also from Washington, disguised the extent to which their orientation had changed by adopting the cold war ideology of development and anti-communism. This change of outlook did not immediately undermine the authority of the revolution, on the contrary, in the simple 'strong government' sense, the political élite further consolidated and centralised power.

The main enemy, against whom the Hobbesian bargain was struck, was political mobilisation in all of its various manifestations. Some of these manifestations (such as the Catholic peasantry of the *Bajío*) had few allies, either at the time or among later historians.[26] However the *Cardenista* coalition of workers, peasants and socialist intellectuals did pose a genuine counter-challenge. After 1940 this challenge gradually weakened as the socialists lost control of the state. What remained within the system was some kind of commitment to social democracy; this commitment was never overriding but should not be seen as rhetorical only. There remained also a left-wing opposition. The 'old' *Cardenista* left retained considerable force until the early 1960s; subsequently a new and rather different kind of left – not revolutionary socialist in the traditional sense – came to the fore. However unlike Hobbesian conservatism, which essentially did control the state between 1940 and 1970, revolutionary socialism after 1940 suffered from its lack of a firm base either within the Mexican state or Mexican society. Its hold over the working class or the peasantry was probably never more than tenuous.

If socialism was relatively weak in post-1940s Mexico, then liberalism was weaker still. It should be remembered that liberal ideas were influential in nineteenth-century Mexico and in the early years of the Revolution. Madero's battle-cry against Porfirio Díaz was *sufragio efectivo: no re-elección!* Moreover, post-1940s Mexico did have a system of elections, a legal opposition, a formally free press and statutes of university autonomy. These, however, did not influence anything very much because the authorities felt able to ignore the rules whenever they wished. The presidential election of 1940 was massively fraudulent; that of 1952 only somewhat less so.[27] Opponents of the system had certain formal legal rights which in the event mattered little because the authorities enforced the law selectively or not at all.

Mexico in 1965 can be said to be a facade democracy with an effective authoritarianism but also a tacit semi-pluralism. A wise Hobbesian despot does not actually seek bad relations with his most powerful subjects. There were, even in 1965, interests within the political system capable of challenging it; but these interests at that time did not see any need to do so. They were largely content with the status quo.

Most Mexicans are not particularly ideological. They are interested in whatever will improve their living standards and look to the state for the provision of such services – health, education, electricity, transport – as they cannot provide for themselves. They are 'socialist' in as far as they want collective provision of services which cannot otherwise be provided, 'liberal' in their hostility to overbearing state power, and 'Hobbesian' in their preference for economic progress in a context of reasonably strong government. In 1965 most Mexicans would have benefited from over a generation of positive *per capita* growth, slowly rising real incomes and several years of low inflation. These were scarcely conditions in which aggressive mass politics were to be expected.[28]

Yet the process of economic growth has a logic of its own. During the 1950s Mexico moved from being a society which was predominantly rural to one which was predominantly urban; it is now three-quarters urban. Statistics on social mobility and education level are less reliable, but there can be no doubt that the continuing post-war trend has been for the middle class to become both relatively and absolutely larger and the population as a whole better educated, longer lived and more sophisticated. These changes have little immediate impact on politics but, over a period of time, their effect can be enormous.[29] Mexico in 1965 was a quite different country from when the 'Hobbesian bargain' was struck; it has now changed very much more. The partial unravelling of this bargain as a result of these and other changes is an important part of our story.

# 2 Díaz Ordaz and the Student Massacre at Tlatelolco

In the eyes of most historians the Tlatelolco massacre of 2 October 1968, when scores (perhaps hundreds) of unarmed student demonstrators in a central square of Mexico City were shot dead by the military, was the central act of the Díaz Ordaz presidency. It was central both in terms of the numbers of dead, the symbolism of the location and the international publicity given to the event, and also in the (retrospectively) apparently predictable nature of the Díaz Ordaz government's response. This response, aside from its barbarism, was a classic demonstration of the power of the Mexican presidency. It led to a considerable reappraisal of the nature of the Mexican system.

Díaz Ordaz' critics from within the system – who, it must be said, were fewer in number at the time than they subsequently became – came to see this action as typical of the man and his regime but not at all typical of the Mexican system of government as a whole. Earlier presidents had certainly resorted to acts of repression, but (so the argument went) regime violence was often hidden and almost always mixed with some attempt to concialiate or co-opt. A good example of this kind of critique was quoted in *Latin America* on 11 September 1970. The article quoted 'political insiders' as saying that Díaz Ordaz:

> has endangered the system by being unable to manipulate it in a traditional way – through skill in manoeuvring, guile, blandishments, promises, some concessions and where necessary bribes, with force kept in the background as an ultimate threat to be used, if at all, only with the utmost discretion.

What these 'insiders' (for which one may read Echeverría and his close allies) were saying was that Díaz Ordaz had cost the system much of its public image, both at home and abroad. Until the massacre, it was possible for sympathetic observers to talk about 'emerging democracy' in Mexico and to play down the repressive forces that lurked never very far below the official surface. Tlatelolco did not really provoke a full scale legitimacy crisis – the basis of political order was never seriously in question – but it did shatter many fond illusions about the PRI and seriously damaged its credibility.

Díaz Ordaz later defended his action in terms of legitimate violence directed against a subversive threat. Conservatives, some of whom are still willing to offer at least a qualified defence of Díaz Ordaz, tended to feel that – allowing for an element of over-reaction in the official response – the repression of the student movement did not represent a serious departure from the normal way in which the system responded to threats; what was new was the challenge of the students and the changes in Mexican political society that, to some extent, lay behind it. An internal US government report noted that repressive 'tactics had always worked in the past and the government probably assumed they would be equally as effective again'.[1] A further observation sometimes made (not necessarily in defence of the government) was that the true significance of the Tlatelolco massacre lay less in the character of the state's response than in the identity of the victims. On this occasion, state violence was used against middle-class dissent; this triggered a hard-line response which featured scarcely, if at all, when the victims of violence were peasants, workers or the poor in other guises.

The later view of most intellectuals was, inevitably, much more radically critical of Díaz Ordaz. Aguilar Camin later referred to 'Díaz Ordaz' paranoia and his institutionalisation of violence . . . under Díaz Ordaz the the political system reached an extremity of rigidity and violence from which the system needed to draw back and adjust in order to guarantee its own survival'.[2] It is of course true that many present-day intellectuals were students in 1968 and so literally in the firing-line of government repression; it is scarcely surprising that they are unwilling now to be silent about what they were put through at the time. However the reaction of the international academic community was also very strong. It might have been stronger still if there had not been too many other examples of repressive violence directed against their own citizens by Latin American governments during the decade following 1968. Even so Evelyn Stevens's *Protest and Response in Mexico* which detailed the student movement and its repression, together with the work of other scholars in the early 1970s, led to a major shift in the way Mexican politics was perceived; Mexico came to be seen, not as an emerging democracy, but as an intolerant authoritarian system.[3]

A very great deal has been written about the events of 1968 themselves but almost all of it from the standpoint of the students.[4] Attempts to examine events from the viewpoint of the authorities are rare; we have Scherer's excellent though inevitably patchy investigative journalism, Cabrera's journalistic account (more sympathetic to Díaz Ordaz) and Zermeño's interesting but general reflections on the nature of the Mexican state. There is no biography of Díaz Ordaz, no state papers dealing with the period are yet available and no participant on the government side has written a serious set of memoirs. Nor is this vacuum likely to be filled soon. What follows, therefore, is based on insufficient sources, but an attempt to understand Díaz Ordaz is essential if one is to comprehend Mexican presidentialism.

## THE PRESIDENT'S PERSONALITY

Díaz Ordaz was born into a provincial middle-class, nominally Catholic, family in the state of Puebla. There was evidently an element of *mestizaje* in his background of which Díaz Ordaz was later reported to be sensitive. Yet there was nothing of the outcast, or nonconformist, about Díaz Ordaz – and still less about Puebla. Loaeza states that 'for many years, Pueblan society has been regarded as one of the most traditional in the country, in large measure thanks to the dominant presence of the Catholic Church'.[5] After graduating from the University of Puebla Díaz Ordaz' early career developed under the patronage of Maximino Avila Camacho, elder brother of Manuel Avila Camacho (President 1940–6); in the (perhaps rather colourful) words of a US journalist 'Maximino is everything that his brother is not – flamboyant, impulsive, immensely rich, a dictator with a great flair for the dramatic, a *caudillo* who made one of Mexico's most important states a kind of bizarre private preserve, and lined it with personality and gold'.[6] Despite Maximino's alleged flamboyance, however, he was an authoritarian figure who had a short way with dissidents; in provincial Mexican politics at the time this was not unusual.

Díaz Ordaz started his political career in the provincial government in Puebla after which, apparently narrowly failing to become governor, he went to the Federal District first as Deputy and then as Senator from his home state. He did not work in the federal bureaucracy until 1953. Virtually his only post in the bureaucracy was in *Gobernación* (government – better read as 'administration') of which he became Secretary during the López Mateos presidency (1958–64). He owed this promotion in part to his friendship with López Mateos himself – they were senators in the late 1940s and were part of a small group which met regularly to discuss the pressing issues of the day. Both men were critical of what they saw as the excessive personalism of Alemán. Díaz Ordaz was again disappointed in 1953 when Ruiz Cortines gave him a fairly junior posting in *Gorbernación*: he rose from Director to *Oficial Mayor* in 1954.

A lengthy stay in *Gobernación* marks a man for life. *Gobernación* has many functions in Mexican politics, but ultimately it is a form of political police organisation; it is the role of *Gobernación* to see that the presidential writ runs through civilian Mexico. In the 1950s, though not now, *Gobernación* was officially regarded as the senior ministry and as the coordinating body between the president and the rest of the cabinet. During the 1946–76 period it was quite normal for the secretary of *Gobernación* to be made President; of the five presidents who served between these dates, four had come from *Gobernación*. However this consistency misleads slightly. The only real 'Apostolic successions' were those of Díaz Ordaz and Echeverría. Miguel Alemán broke an earlier tradition when he was nominated in 1946, and Ruiz Cortines had served as Secretary for *Gobernación* for only three years when he was nominated in 1951. Neither was considered, at the time, to be the obvious front runner.[7]

The real *Gobernación* presidents, therefore, were Díaz Ordaz and Echeverría. For a decade or more before being nominated president they had both spent their time reading police and intelligence reports on potential subversion, checking the press for signs of disaffection, helping (with the PRI) to resolve local disputes over nomination to elected office and, on occasion, wielding the power of the centre over a recalcitrant or incompetent local office holder. Yet the secretary of *Gobernación* is not as powerful as this job description suggests; he holds office at the will of the president and must do what the president wants rather than what he himself wants to do; often the task is an uncomfortable one. Such a job might be expected to reinforce any authoritarian characteristics in a man and the absolute discretion and secrecy which the job requires must also take its toll.

Julio Scherer has suggested [8] that Díaz Ordaz was an excessively authoritarian figure (by the standards of place and time) even as secretary of *Gobernación*. It is impossible to examine this claim without taking a closer look at the events of 1959–63 (which will be considered in the next section). However there is no contemporary evidence to suggest that Díaz Ordaz, however strong his reputation for hard-line anti-communism, was either cruel or emotionally unstable before assuming the presidency. On 9 June 1964 Lazaro Cárdenas gave Díaz Ordaz his personal endorsement for the presidency; there is no doubt that this was a formal and essentially ritualistic act, but would Cárdenas have met and endorsed a man if he believed him to be a monster? The US Embassy, perhaps more likely in 1964 than now to look benignly on a potential tyrant, reported on 1 April that Díaz Ordaz 'most nearly represents the PRI's middle class managerial and technical groups'.[9] Contemporary critics of Díaz Ordaz considered him a man without marked characteristics of any kind; more of an *apparatchik* than an autocrat.

Anecdotal evidence (given retrospectively) does however suggest an authoritarian, rather cynical, human being much troubled by private fears. Many Mexican men who grew up in provincial middle-class families before the Second World War surely emerged with a cast of mind that, in our own more relaxed age, would appear patriarchal. Sons rebelling against the values of their fathers were as much a feature of the Mexican 1968 as of their contemporary movements in Western Europe; in social as much as political terms, Mexico had its share of narrow intolerance. Publication in Mexico of Oscar Lewis's (admittedly disturbing) *Children of Sanchez* was possible only after a major controversy.[10]

Díaz Ordaz was a quieter and more retiring figure than most. He avoided the traditional male vices; he did not smoke; he rarely drank; unusually for a Mexican politician, he regularly retired early to bed (to sleep) – which caused amused comment from some of his contemporaries.[11] Though far from humourless, he seems to have been something of a puritan. One source recalls that when the US astronaut Neil Armstrong was invited to Mexico, a party was held in his honour at the presidential palace. Martínez

Domínguez, then head of the PRI and a man whose private life was always interesting, arrived with three ladies who asked for Armstrong's autograph; the interpreter, preparing to comply, asked who the ladies were. Díaz Ordaz answered: *'son tres putas'*. One observer, more sympathetic than most, described Díaz Ordaz as 'a hanging judge'; he was, in other words, a man who disciplined himself more than most men do and was quite prepared to discipline others if they behaved in ways to which he objected. He could be quite dismissive of people whom he did not respect. Scherer tells the story of when he (Scherer) went to interview Papa Doc Duvalier: Duvalier had objected to what he claimed was a lack of courtesy shown him by the Mexicans and the Mexican Foreign Ministry duly prepared an apology. Díaz Ordaz vetoed the apology. He explained to Scherer 'Duvalier is the son of a whore; do you think I care what a son of a whore thinks?'[12]

Perhaps because of a rooted cynicism, Díaz Ordaz had few friends. (Later, in bitter old age, he told one senior Mexican official that he had none.) He alienated the journalist Julio Scherer (prepared at one point to befriend him) by giving him a bribe of $100 and insisting that he accept it. Scherer also remembered Díaz Ordaz as 'a bag of nerves' and, in early presidential days, a man obsessed by fear of failure.[13] Certainly, when president, Díaz Ordaz was not really close to anybody; he thought, and acted, alone.

Compared with López Mateos, and indeed Echeverría, Díaz Ordaz was an uncharismatic individual and not a man greatly liked by the general public. It did not help that he was by no means good-looking. He is said to have resented his lack of popularity, particularly since many things seemed to be going well for Mexico at the time; there was economic growth, low inflation and an apparent continuity in rising prosperity. At any rate until 1968 the reasons for Díaz Ordaz' relative unpopularity could only have been personal – a fact of which Díaz Ordaz, certainly no fool, would have been fully aware. It was around this time that the president of a neighbouring country is said to have asked his chief adviser why he was not more popular and received the reply 'let's face it Mr President; you are just not a very likeable man'.[14] Power and achieved ambition might have mellowed another individual; they did not have this effect on Díaz Ordaz.

Another figure remembers Díaz Ordaz as being an intelligent man (an evaluation borne out by records of his discussions with President Johnson and others) who understood the need to control his own naturally violent temperament. He was fond of quoting the French novel *Clochemerle* to illustrate the point that violence, however apparently trivial, has a tendency to get out of control. Under the pressure of the presidency and the frustrations thereby engendered, his restraint weakened and natural violence came to the fore. That Díaz Ordaz had a bad temper is apparently borne out by an article that appeared, many years later, in *Excelsior*.[15] This asserted that he, as a rising figure in *Gobernación*, was sent to the Yucatán in 1954 to oversee the removal of governor Marentes and his replacement by a figure more to the liking of Presidente Ruiz Cortines. Díaz Ordaz found himself facing a gathering of Marentes supporters; one of them told him that there would be blood in the streets if Marentes fell. 'If people are injured, we will tend them,' replied Díaz Ordaz, 'if there are dead we will bury them. That is all I have to say.' He then walked out.

Even if the anecdote is apocryphal, or at least improved with the telling, Díaz Ordaz was a man who seems to have deserved his authoritarian reputation. However, he was also a product of his time and a man whose exaggerated faith in strong and inflexible government was, in part, a response to the reawakening of old fears as a result of the Cuban Revolution. To this aspect, we now turn.

## PRELUDE TO DÍAZ ORDAZ: MEXICAN POLITICS AND THE CUBAN REVOLUTION

In many ways the key fact of Mexican politics between 1940 and 1964 was the decline of the 'revolutionary coalition' which had formed in the 1930s under Cárdenas. This coalition was broadly socialist though never communist in any iron curtain sense. Its key beliefs were in land reform, strong trade unionism and economic nationalism; above all there was the belief in an interventionist state, sympathetic to the demands of workers, peasants and intellectuals, unsympathetic to the Church, business and, subject to inevitable considerations of power, the United States.

As early as 1940 there were signs of a right-wing reaction against this coalition.[16] When he ensured the presidential nomination for Avila Camacho (President 1940–46) Cárdenas indicated willingness to support a candidate who, it was supposed, would seek a series of compromises with the right and present the consequences as a triumph for national unity. What neither Cárdenas nor his left-wing supporters (and sometimes competitors) could have foreseen in 1940 was that President Alemán would, under conditions of international cold war, align Mexico firmly with the US position abroad and with Mexican capitalism at home. Alemán's own excesses triggered off a limited move back towards the left during 1952–4, but President Ruiz Cortines soon returned to an essentially pro-US and pro-capitalist line; he was personally friendlier towards Cárdenas and in other respects more moderate and careful than Alemán but the essential thrust of his policy was not greatly different.

Despite occasional expressions of irritation about particular disagreements, the general viewpoint of the US Embassy at this time was – in the words of Ambassador White – 'President Ruiz Cortines is definitely not socialistic and we must work closely with him. He is our greatest hope because only he can change socialistic and hostile policies of Cabinet Ministers and he has done so'.[17] As this quotation suggests, the left's loss of influence up to the late 1950s was relative rather than absolute. Even Alemán found it desirable to avoid confronting the left on every issue and Ruiz Cortines was seen by contemporaries as middle-of-the-road rather than conservative. He was careful to balance his essentially pro-capitalist policies with the occasional gesture in a different direction. Moreover Ruiz Cortines, probably quite sincerely, worried that the pattern of economic development which Mexico was successfully pursuing had some negative implications for the distribution of income. He later evaluated his performance in the presidency as 'reasonable (*regular*); I didn't abuse my power but didn't do everything I should have done. The rich became richer.'[18]

In order to evaluate the strategies adopted by the Mexican left it is helpful to look at some of its sub-divisions. It is fair to say that some Mexican left-wingers were, by the late 1950s, notably unambitious. A noteworthy member of the collaborationist left was Lombardo Toledano. During the cold war years Lombardo sought to compensate for his loss of influence within the Mexican labour movement by looking for an international role within Latin America. Here he was more active than successful. He did run for the presidency in 1952, more because it gave him a platform than because he seriously expected to win; subsequently his own party, the Partido Popular, was given official recognition and Lombardo ran it in a style which was more familial than comradely. At the party Congress in 1955 he gave all of the top positions to his family and friends and continued to involve himself in conflict with other figures on the left. (It was said of the late President Ceausescu of Romania that he believed in Socialism in one family.) In the early 1960s it was widely reported that Lombardo had accepted a government subsidy for his party.

Although it would be hard to present Lombardo as a revolutionary hero, his attitude was not simply cynical. It stemmed also from scepticism about the ability of the left to remain a serious force in opposition to a system which, it must be said, both Cárdenas and Lombardo had done so much to create. Until Fidel Castro proved otherwise, in 1958–9, many Marxists believed that Leninist revolution was not an option in Latin America both because of the region's relative underdevelopment and because of US influence.

Another factor is that orthodox communism, at least until the late 1950s, was far more involved with attempting to support and protect the Soviet Union than in promoting revolution in countries such as Mexico. It was a French Socialist in the 1950s who described his national Communist Party as being 'not so much on the Left as in the East'. It was very much in the Soviet interest at this time that the Mexican government remained relaxed about any communist threat; the Soviet Embassy in Mexico was an active one. According to a US Navy intelligence report in 1958, it 'has approximately 60 personnel and is larger than the embassy in Buenos Aires or the legation in Montevideo. It reportedly controls all Bloc maritime and military espionage in the area and is the principal dissemination center for all of Latin America'.[19] Communist policy in Latin America during the 1950s was to encourage anti-Americanism (not a particularly difficult task with the Mexican intelligentsia at any rate) and to seek alliance with the 'progressive national bourgeoisie' to bring about social reforms. The left wing of the PRI was, in this sense, a natural ally of the communists and sleeping insurrectionary dogs could be left to rest in peace.

Where the left was less collaborationist, it faced an uphill battle and enjoyed little popular appeal. At an ideological level Mexico was (as it remains) a Catholic country in which the Church benefited hugely from its enforced distance from direct political power. In the 1950s the Catholic Church was socially conservative, morally orthodox and strongly opposed to communism and indeed Marxism in any form. For those Mexicans who did not have conservative or Catholic sympathies, the Revolutionary nationalism espoused by the government (with however much or little sincerity) still had a considerable appeal. Direct electoral attack on the PRI was hopeless, even discounting the likelihood of ballot rigging in the event of there being a serious challenge.

Thus in 1958 the left could not agree on whether to put up a presidential candidate against López Mateos. Lombardo wanted the left to support López Mateos 'rather than to advertise their weakness in the Presidential ballot'.[20] The official Communist Party, however, did want to propose a candidate but found it difficult to get anybody suitable. The man on whom they finally settled was (in the incredulous words of the British Ambassador) 'seventy-four years old . . . He is not and never has been a member of the PCM [Communist Party] and he is a professing Roman Catholic . . . In terms of practical politics this nomination is a joke.'[21] In the end, the communist candidate received too few votes in the federal district to be worth tabulating separately; he could not have got as many as 400. Lombardo's Popular Party, which did contest congressional elections, did little better.

It is admittedly true that few people on the left took electoral opposition seriously. An alternative strategy, with more serious chance of success, was to try to penetrate the PRI's mass organisations. The left had controlled the CTM and some powerful non-CTM unions until Alemán comprehensively defeated the syndicalist left during 1948–9. The difficulty here was that union structures had become progressively less independent since 1940 and far more controlled by the state. As has been pointed out elsewhere,[22] state control of labour in particular was facilitated by closed shop agreements (so that a member expelled from a union for indiscipline would also lose his job) and by the extensive powers of the Ministry of Labour to recognise or not a particular union leadership. Nevertheless workers in some powerfully unionised operations – notably the railway workers and the schoolteachers – began during 1958 to show serious signs of discontent. The motivation may have been 'political' to some extent, but relative deprivation was probably a more important motive; the Mexican economy grew rapidly during the 1950s but the growth was accompanied by inflation. Tight official control over union structures in many cases prevented workers' wages even keeping up with inflation, let alone enjoying the fruits of growing prosperity.

Nineteen fifty-eight was a year of labour unrest. Dissident movements developed in a number of unions. The pattern was similar in several cases.[23] Initial workers' demands for higher wages were refused or met with limited offers. These were then rejected by dissident leaders who threatened strike action if better offers were not made. The leaders then either decided, or were encouraged, to take their grievances to the President who often proved conciliatory or at least willing to offer a compromise. The dissident leadership then sought and occasionally won recognition from the Ministry of Labour. There is reason to believe that the government genuinely wished to show a friendlier attitude toward labour, recognising that wages had earlier fallen behind and also wanting the popularity that generous wage settlements might bring.

When faced by what they regarded as a political threat, however, the authorities clamped down. The repression of the railway workers' union in 1959 and the imprisonment of its leadership was a much-discussed feature of the López Mateos presidency.[24] So also was the demobilisation of various independent peasant movements which showed themselves in the late 1950s.[25] Much more could be said about these incidents. What is of most interest to the issue of presidential power is the seemingly commonplace observation that the Mexican state both could and did coerce dissent by means up to and including assassination. This partially bears out the contention that the state's reaction to the 1968 student movement was not really out of character. It also suggests that the state was not easily harmed by a policy of overt challenge from trade union and peasant radicalism; this was also a point made by the collaborationist left.

There was, however, a further strategy which some people on the left were in a position to undertake. This involved trying to build connections between the overtly oppositional left and left-wing supporters of the system. As we have seen, the PRI does not reject potential supporters on ideological grounds; below the topmost reaches of government the system actually welcomes support from people of widely varying political viewpoints. Provided that they accept official disciplines, which are as much a matter of form and ritual as of belief, left-wingers (and right-wingers also) can play an active part in the Mexican government. (This generalisation is however less true today than it was before 1982.) Although no person with a history of known left-wing sympathy has reached the presidency since 1940, left-wingers have on a number of occasions reached cabinet position and they have traditionally been strong in the foreign ministry. There was, of course, a clear difference of emphasis between that part of the left which chose to remain within the system and that which formally declared itself Marxist; at the same time there was, and remains, a considerable degree of cooperation between the two. Moreover there has generally been a certain amount of division and rivalry on the Mexican left (as in the left in other parts of the non-communist world) motivated in part by ideological dispute of various kinds and in part by petty rivalries and jealousies. Yet the degree of disunity should not be exaggerated. During the late 1950s the undisputed leader of the left within the system was ex-President Cárdenas.

Lazaro Cárdenas has often been cited as the figure who emphatically proved that ex-presidents do wield real power in Mexican national politics. I discuss this assessment further below but do not wholly accept it. What is certain is that Cárdenas played an active role after stepping down from the presidency in 1940. During the 'national unity' period of Mexico's involvement in the Second World War Cárdenas served for several years as Minister of Defence. He played little direct role during the presidency of Alemán but appears to have been active in seeking to block any possibility of Alemán standing for re-election.[26] Cárdenas seems to have encouraged the alternative presidential candidacy of General Henríquez but to have switched his support to Ruiz Cortines once it was clear that he, and not Alemán, would be the official candidate. Henríquez did induce a significant part of the PRI to break away from the system, but the 1952 presidential election results were rigged against him: this was the last major split in the PRI prior to 1988.[27]

In the 1950s Cárdenas played an active part in foreign affairs, supporting fellow-travelling causes generally and being rewarded with the Stalin Prize in 1955. It is, however, not clear that Cárdenas exerted very much influence over Mexican foreign policy during this time. Certainly US Ambassador White had few problems in explaining the US point of view during the Guatemalan crisis of 1954. White later reported that 'at my third conference with President Ruiz Cortines on this subject he told me that he had instructed the Foreign Office to change its policy with respect to Guatemala' and to move toward support of the United States.[28]

In 1957, as the succession to Ruiz Cortines was coming under discussion, Cárdenas travelled around Mexico making speeches supportive of Revolutionary unity. It is not, however, clear that Cárdenas' undoubted visibility was matched by real influence. The British Ambassador took the opposite view: 'with the field to himself for a while General Cárdenas will increase the list of his enemies which is already long'.[29] There is in fact good evidence that Cárdenas did not influence the *destape* and, indeed, that he was not happy with the selection of López Mateos.[30]

The event that really galvanised the Mexican left was the Cuban revolution. This certainly was a momentous event in the whole hemisphere; Mexico was by no means alone in being affected by the fallout. At the beginning in Mexico as elsewhere, the revolution attracted support across a fairly wide political spectrum but as the Marxist-Leninist character of the Castro regime became increasingly evident so opinion polarised between a supportive minority and a hostile majority.

Cárdenas was an early and enthusiastic supporter of the revolution, visiting Cuba in 1959 and 1960. President López Mateos was a good deal more circumspect but initially made clear his qualified sympathy with Castro and his refusal to join the US administration's efforts to pressurise and isolate Cuba.[31] Ultimately, however, the effect of Cárdenas' efforts to use the Cuba question to mobilise the left was the opposite of what he intended; hostility to the Cuban revolution, as well as some related issues,[32] provided a catalyst for the most effective right-wing mobilisation in Mexico since the early 1940s. It is to the character of Mexican conservatism during this period that we must now turn.

## THE RIGHT AND THE CUBAN REVOLUTION

The most outstanding feature of the Mexican right in the decade prior to the Cuban revolution was its quiescence. If Mexican conservatives had a motto, it would have been 'things are going our way – don't rock the boat'. Some sections of the right did show liberal principles during the 1920s; the Vasconcelos campaign of 1929 has been seen in retrospect as the lost moment of Mexican liberalism.[33] However Mexican liberals were disillusioned by defeat and alarmed by Cárdenismo; they subsequently settled relatively contentedly in the less threatening post-war environment. Economic growth was rapid; fortunes were being made and the middle class was becoming larger and more prosperous. Business got most of what it wanted from the state. The Church was tolerated and quietly gained strength. Moreover despite occasional differences on specific issues, the United States government was far from unhappy at the general direction of events within Mexico. Admittedly the PAN (which was founded in 1939 and legalised in 1943) continued to exist as an opposition force, but it relied as much on government sufferance as on its own support; the support which it had came not from the real élites but from political Catholics and from middle-class minorities who had missed out on the general economic progress. Adrian Lajous recently recalled a conversation with a veteran PRI activist in an area of the Federal District during the 1958 elections:

> I know this district . . . I used to set fire to the factories here in my Anarchist days . . . The PRI always wins in this district. The only people who live here are the rich and the poor and they both vote for us. The poor understand that the government favours them. The rich also, although they won't admit it; they vote for us with a guilty conscience. Only the lower middle class votes for the PAN . . . the only people who vote for the PAN are those who have come down in the world.[34]

The PAN did (and does) have a genuine base of social support, but it is an inherently limited one. The system realised full well that the PAN was not a serious threat and tried to keep it in the game in the role of a loyal opposition.[35] When the PAN did in fact boycott Congress (during 1958–64) in protest against electoral fraud, the government in 1963 decided to offer to introduce proportional representation into Congress; this virtually guaranteed that the PAN would have significant congressional representation after 1964. It is noteworthy that the PAN during 1960–2 was extremely virulent in its attacks on Cárdenas and the left.

What did indeed worry the right was precisely the perceived connection between the Cuban revolution, ex-President Cárdenas and the left within the system. Even if any connection between the Mexican left and López Mateos existed only in the minds of the right-wing opposition, the fears expressed on this point were no doubt sincere. When the right did begin to mobilise, it soon became clear that it could muster a far more impressive base of independent support than could the left. The provincial middle class in cities such as Monterrey, San Luis Potosí and Puebla could mount real demonstrations and, where permitted, a serious electoral challenge to the PRI.[36] President López Mateos once told the US ambassador: 'I am more afraid of the Catholic Church than of Communism. We can crack down on and control the Communists in Mexico but cannot do the same with the Church which in Mexico has a history of interference in political affairs.'[37] The right organised a range of front organisations during the early 1960s – the National Anti-Communist Party, the Mexican National Party, the Christian Family Movement, etc. at a national level and more local organisations such as the Co-ordinating Committee of Private Initiative set up in the state of Puebla and the Regional Anti-Communist Crusade in the state of Nuevo León.[38] Finally big business, in the form of Concamin, Concanaco and Coparmex, weighed in by asking – in a full-page advertisement published in all the major newspapers in Mexico in November 1960 – whether President López Mateos was aiming to introduce a form of socialism into Mexico.[39] Business spokesmen and the Catholic Church fully supported each other on 'moral' issues and on hostility to Castro's Cuba.

Right-wing opposition posed a particular problem for the Mexican authorities because of the nature of the political system itself. Policy, as we have seen, mostly favoured conservative interests; the structure of the state, however, did not. Neither business nor the Church had a formal role in policymaking; their access to the state was purely a matter of presidential discretion. Therein lay both a sense of status-deprivation and insecurity. As early as 1957 an intelligence report prepared for the US State Department predicted that 'commercial and industrial interests, now pressing for formal recognition as a sector of the PRI, will seek to increase their already considerable influence within the government'.[40] Efforts by business, and the Church, to improve upon their *de facto* acceptance within Mexican society were, however, strongly resisted by the left and even by more moderate elements within the system.[41] Over time, however, the growth of cities, the increasing internationalisation of capital and the increasing importance of the middle class might have been expected to create problems for the traditional way in which Mexico was governed. In the early 1960s the right had money, a significant degree of active popular support, undoubted organising ability and the implicit support of the United States government; the result was to reduce the freedom of action of the Mexican authorities in a way in which left-wing opposition did not.

Although the period of militant right-wing activity was relatively brief, it genuinely seems to have disconcerted and alarmed the Mexican authorities. Gonzalez Casanova, in his acclaimed study of *Democracy in Mexico*, concluded that 'the conditions for a Socialist Revolution are not present in Mexico. The conditions for a Fascist coup d'état, however, could appear'.[42] Events have proved this judgement to have been somewhat alarmist, though one should not underestimate fear of the Catholic right as a factor in official thinking during the 1960s and even afterwards. It does appear that Díaz Ordaz was given the presidential nomination at least partly because he was seen as being the man most in sympathy with, and so best able to head off, the resurgent Catholic right.[43] In a polemic against Díaz Ordaz that later became famous, the pro-communist journal *Politica* in 1963 declared that his candidacy 'smells of the sacristy'.[44].

## LÓPEZ MATEOS AND THE MEXICAN PRESIDENCY

López Mateos, caught in an increasingly aggressive polarisation between left and right, ultimately surmounted his difficulties. There were, however, a few awkward moments. By 1961 a serious problem of capital flight in reaction to fears of López Mateos' alleged radicalism, increased signs of middle-class mobilisation, and pressure from the US combined to push López Mateos much further to the right than he intended.

At first López Mateos appeared to vacillate; US Ambassador Mann even forecast a split within the PRI as a result of presidential indecisiveness.[45] In fact, however, he was carefully manoeuvring, moving to the right as far as was necessary while seeking to maintain a degree of credibility with the left. From the beginning of 1961 the Mexican government, while careful to avoid open commitment to the US line, began to distance itself from the Cuban revolution. The difference of outlook between López Mateos and Cárdenas (who were in fact never especially close) became increasingly obvious. In mid-1961 Cárdenas emerged as leader of a new organisation, the National Liberation Movement

(MLN), which was seen by its enemies as a communist front. It was, in fact, an attempt to bridge the gap between the 'inside left' and the more overtly Marxist opposition, in order to bring pressure upon the Mexican authorities to move to the left. The MLN's failure to influence the government turned out to be complete. Pro-Cuban demonstrations organised for April 1961 were suppressed. In September López Mateos promised that private enterprise would have a dominant role in the future economic development of Mexico. On 8 December all ex-presidents reiterated (as was required of them) their support for López Mateos and declared their willingness to serve in various administrative positions; this was seen as an attempt to re-establish the political order which some feared was becoming threatened. In January 1962 López Mateos distanced Mexico more than ever before from Castro's Cuba. In April 1962 he was able to please business interests by announcing that President Kennedy would shortly be visiting Mexico (the business associations were warmly supportive). Kennedy came in July and his arrival was widely seen as a watershed; subsequently Mexican policy shifted uncomplicatedly toward a traditional 'national unity' conservatism.

The MLN failed in other ways as well. From the viewpoint of the Marxist left, a key problem was Cárdenas's unwillingness to break publicly with the system and Lombardo's consistent willingness to accommodate. This enabled López Mateos to disrupt left-wing unity by calling for national unity whenever he felt the need to do so. Some observers in fact believed that Cárdenas would defect overtly from the PRI and would therefore split it; the United States embassy thought so at least for a part of 1962.[46] Instead Lombardo defected from the MLN in 1962; according to the official results the Popular Socialist Party (PPS) had suffered badly in the 1961 elections and Lombardo must therefore have wondered whether his party had any kind of future in the absence of a *modus vivendi* with the system. By defecting from the MLN the PPS acted to strengthen the system; according to a US State Department report in 1964:

> the PRI has working arrangement with Communist Vicente Lombardo Toledano and his PPS, which it partially subsidises. The government uses this agreement to obtain information on Communist activities and ensure the fragmentation of other Communist groups.[47]

Cárdenas did not return to the official fold with quite the same meekness but nevertheless, as on 9 June 1964, he endorsed Díaz Ordaz' presidential candidacy.

Cárdenas and Lombardo no doubt believed privately that the left did not have the strength necessary to force the issue against the government; it was better to remain in position and accept small concessions than risk losing everything on a single throw of the dice. The bitterness felt toward Lombardo by some other Marxists after his abandonment of the MLN was perhaps reflected in the 1964 *Yearbook of the Great Soviet Encyclopedia* which described Lombardo as a man 'who considers himself a "Marxist" but conducts an opportunistic policy'.[48] From the government's point of view, this disunity on the left was extremely helpful.

Only a small minority of the far left seriously believed in the possibility of armed action. Some sections of the independent peasant confederation, the CCI, were apparently contemplating a *guerrilla*[49] but they do not seem to have been typical. The official murder of Ruben Jaramillo in May 1962 served as a reminder of what overt rebels might expect. Some of the left wanted to try a more clearly electoral strategy. However this, too, could easily be blocked by the government. Attempts were made during 1963 to put together an electoral front – the FEP – but these were aborted by the government's refusal to offer it electoral recognition. [50] Meanwhile the state's ability to control official organisations was stronger than ever. The defeat of the radical labour leaders in 1959 was followed at the end of the López Mateos *sexenio* by the co-opting of the 'independent' peasants' confederation and its incorporation into the existing official structures. For the left as a whole, therefore, the aftermath of the Cuban revolution was little better than disastrous. Although López Mateos was willing to make the occasional left-wing gesture at the level of public policy, the left's efforts to increase its political power failed almost completely; it found itself in a far weaker position in 1964 than it had in 1959. For many (though not all) the result was a retreat into quiescence or dogmatism. What the 1968 student leaders found on the left was mainly a vacuum,[51] and the new left would be (as in other countries) primarily a middle-class left, rather than a left intent on penetrating and 'subverting' Mexico's corporate structure.

The right, meanwhile, also calmed down but more from a sense of triumph than defeat. A huge anti-communist demonstration in

Monterrey in February 1962, led by the Garza Sada family, had a considerable impact in the rest of Mexico. In December 1962 López Mateos proposed a law of proportional representation which virtually guaranteed PAN a significant role in Congress; PAN supported the law enthusiastically. Finally the nomination of Díaz Ordaz in 1963 gave them little cause for protest.

Apart from the outcome itself, several conclusions can be drawn about the political conflicts that occurred under López Mateos. One is that ex-President Cárdenas suffered a clear-cut defeat in his attempts to move Mexican politics to the left. While it is true that ex-President Alemán sought to counter Cárdenas by setting up the right-wing *Frente Civica*, a major lesson (which Echeverría, many years later, apparently did not learn) seems to be that ex-presidential power in Mexico is inherently limited. Cárdenas drew strength from a variety of sources, all of which ultimately proved inadequate for him. Prior to 1958 there was, as we have seen, ample margin for regional *caciquismo* to exert power within particular states; local power was a more serious matter in 1958 than in 1988 and ex-presidents who wished to do so could continue to enjoy local influence. The Avila Camacho family in Puebla provides a case similar to the Cárdenas family in Michoacán. Even so, one scholar has argued that local Cárdenismo, considered as a movement, lost strength after 1940 despite the fact that one of Cárdenas's brothers served as governor during the 1950s.[52] What is beyond question is that López Mateos was able to appoint a non-Cárdenista to be governor of Michoacán in 1962 precisely in order to reduce the impact of Cárdenismo.[53]

Cárdenas was never prevented from seeking international contacts and carrying out a personal foreign policy, provided it was understood that he represented mainly himself and not necessarily the Mexican government. As we have seen, he did so actively. However, according to Agee, the CIA was allowed to tap his telephone during the early 1960s which suggests that official policy was both more devious and more conservative than it seemed.[54] Finally it may be that Cárdenas, as ex-president, had a symbolic role which could be made active in the event of an actual crisis within the Mexican political system itself. Thus when it appeared that President Alemán was himself about to break the rules of the game by allowing himself to be considered for presidential re-nomination, strong opposition from an ex-president was helpful to the system and carried weight.[55] However while Cárdenas could help block a re-election attempt on the part of Alemán (an unconstitutional act), he could not prevent both Alemán and Ruiz Cortines (and still more López Mateos) choosing successors whom he himself did not welcome. Ultimately, moreover, Cárdenas was too much of a loyalist to wish full-scale confrontation with the system.

Cárdenas also, obviously, carried weight when the top political authorities did not object to what he was trying to do. In retrospect Cárdenas' apparent role in getting Fidel Castro released from prison, where he had been held by the Mexican authorities shortly before he began his expedition against Batista, had far greater significance than was realised at the time.[56]

However when Cárdenas attempted to return to an overt national political role the result was a failure. Ex-presidents were free to try to work within the system but could not be allowed to mobilise against it. Working within the system, moreover, meant accepting various binding constraints of which the most important was that the decision of the president of the day was final. This meant that, in practice, Cárdenas was largely powerless to alter the general rightward trend of Mexican politics during the years 1940–70 – at best he succeeded in slowing it down a little.

A second general conclusion is that the semi-polarisation of Mexican society in 1961 and 1962 was quite clearly between right and left (as the terms have traditionally been understood) and not between society and the state. The slogan of the right was *Cristianismo si! Comunismo no!* while that of the left was 'Revolutionary unity'. One reason why the conflict threatened to become so intense was that each side sought to enlist the help of the state against the other. One observer has seen the emergence of a militant right during this period as a sign that the middle class was prepared to join the true establishment (big business and the Church) in a campaign to defend the post-war social order against the renewed threat of Cárdenista socialism.[57] In this view, only some of the working class and peasantry may have been class-conscious during this period but most of the middle and upper classes assuredly were. The right, understood in both class and value terms, took on the Cárdenista left and won. Their reward was President Díaz Ordaz.

The fact that political conflict was fought out between right and left, and to some extent in class terms, suggests that there is some plausibility in the notion that the Mexican state in the aftermath of the Cuban revolution behaved in a way which was in some sense Bonapartist. It may have 'objectively' favoured the right (by supporting conditions for capitalist economic development) but it 'subjectively' sought to stand above both interests in order to give just rewards to each. However the notion of Bonapartism is rather too economistic to do full justice to the situation. The conflict here was less about income distribution than about the symbolism of the revolution and the distribution of political power.

López Mateos did attempt some left-wing gestures to counter-balance his general drift to the right; apart from his non-aligned foreign policy and nationalisation of the electric power industry – itself a careful balancing act [58] – there was the workers' profit-sharing legislation of 1962. Although this has sometimes been seen as a sop thrown by an authoritarian state to a tamed union leadership,[59] there is some evidence that the government was genuinely concerned about potentially hostile employer-reactions and went as far with this law as it dared.[60] This 'subjective' stance gave the López Mateos government an international credibility which its policies did not wholly warrant.

Finally it can be seen that the events of the early 1960s ended in victory for the system. The PRI did not split. Lombardo and Cárdenas eventually declared their support for Díaz Ordaz. Meanwhile the private sector ended reconciled to, and contented with, the presidency of López Mateos despite the doubts which had earlier been expressed. Its counter-mobilisation therefore remained within the limits of the 'Hobbesian bargain': it did not challenge the system as such, and restricted its opposition to what it saw as left-wing efforts to subvert it. Once the left had been defeated, the right returned to its customary quiescence. In April 1964 the State Department reported that 'government policies have promoted confidence of the private sector, one of the most dynamic in Latin America. Unlike most election years 1964 is not expected to see a slowdown in economic activity'.[61]

Although the López Mateos presidency was a triumph for the system (which in 1964 was stronger than it would be in any subsequent election year), it was less clearly a triumph for López Mateos himself. He had taken office with a desire to reduce levels of inequality within the country and to increase the popularity of the government among the lower classes. In an early speech he defined himself as being 'on the extreme Left, within the Constitution'. Assuredly he did not mean by those words what Cárdenas would have meant, but equally he did not intend to be just another man of the right. Yet his presidency saw acts of strong repression – the murder of Jaramillo, the imprisonment of Vallejo and Campa, the crushing of the railway workers – and an economic policy that ended up almost uncomplicatedly pro-capitalist. Ortiz Mena, Finance Minister under López Mateos as well as Díaz Ordaz, developed the main concepts of 'stabilising development' during this period. López Mateos did avoid pressure to break completely with Cuba but by 1964 Mexican–Cuban relations were more symbolic than important – except as a conduit for espionage and secret diplomacy. This was not so much what López Mateos wanted as what he felt he could not avoid.

## NATIONAL AND LOCAL POLITICS UNDER DÍAZ ORDAZ

When Díaz Ordaz became president at the end of 1964, therefore, the system had come through a period of considerable political turbulence at the national level. During the first few years of the Díaz Ordaz presidency, however, more attention was given to local politics and to the interaction between local and national power.

Mexican authorities have, from the days of the Spanish Empire, seen local and regional government fundamentally as providing an opportunity for patronage. Nomination to senior office was often the result of loyal service and, frequently, an opportunity for the person so chosen to make money.[62] During the post-revolutionary years the central authority was sufficiently weak to need to use its power of patronage merely to confirm in office local power-holders, *caciques*, who were in a position to mobilise resources (money, often armed men) in support of their own candidates. The political climate was generally lawless. In return for ritual acknowledgement of the powers of central government, regional power-holders were allowed extensive local autonomy.

Gradually, however, the power of the central government grew. The expansion of the bureaucratic agencies of central government after 1945 often brought federal ministries into conflict with local interests.[63] Under such circumstances the balance of forces overwhelmingly favoured the federal interests; local governments were kept short of money and power.[64] Local political resistance did occur but rarely succeeded; the central government sometimes responded with direct force, more often by a policy of divide and rule. At times indeed the federal government sought to combine its centralising objectives by allying itself with popular discontent against a powerful *cacique* who had proved too unpopular and independent; the emergence of Navismo in San Luis Potosí would be an example here. By the early 1960s local power was generally seen as subordinate to national power.

Actual patronage, as opposed to the increasingly-centralised control over bureaucratic resources, was mainly organised by *Gobernación* and the PRI: it involved balancing several competing systems of logic – including local feeling, interest-group pressure and national priorities. A certain number of Congressional seats, for example, were allocated to the 'mass' organisations – the CTM, CNC, etc. – as a reward for loyalty to the system. Local candidates were also selected centrally although there was generally a myth that local assemblies actually chose them. In 1958 the British Embassy noted that 'the party's President, General Olachea, was indiscreet enough to hand over to the local delegates in full view of the assembled journalists the sealed envelopes contining the names they were to vote for'.[65]

Several kinds of objection were commonly made by dissidents to this type of arrangement. The first was that the type of politics involved was unprincipled and therefore constituted a betrayal of the ideas involved in the Mexican revolution. Instead of there being any kind of battle of ideas, competition within the PRI generally involved rival groups of Mexican office-holders (or would-be office-holders) formed into *camarillas* on personal criteria. The role played by these *camarillas* left no room for ideological politics; those with strong-principled views were more likely to find trouble than success. The PRI and the mass organisations, therefore, could not develop an identity different to that required of them by the top political authorities.

The PRI was, by 1960 if not earlier, an instrument of rule rather than a means of exerting pressure – and not even an especially important instrument when considered alongside the trade unions, peasant leagues and federal bureaucracy.

The second objection was that candidates for public office were selected with little or no thought to their attractiveness to the electorate in question. It was usually assumed that nomination was tantamount to election. In much of the country, and particularly in rural areas, such an assumption was obviously warranted. However there were a small number of medium-sized towns – notably Mérida, Ciudad Juárez, Hermosillo, Enseñada, Chihuahua and San Luis Potosí – in which local middle-class movements generally led by the PAN could occasionally provide an electoral challenge to the PRI. However it was generally the case that even here the entry of competitive politics was blocked by the use of the PRI machine, by ballot-rigging, or, in more difficult cases, by violent repression.

Those who objected most strongly to these arrangements were typically younger members of the middle class. The fact of these disaffections was not especially new. The British ambassador's Annual Report for 1951 noted that:

> The general public is apathetic about the elections; they realise these are rigged and leave politics to the professional politicians and to businessmen who know on which side their bread is buttered. But there is a sign among the younger people particularly of a desire to clean things up and to break the monopoly of the official party. This is as yet only a glimmer of light but, for the hopeful, it is the writing on the wall.[67]

These lines could surely have been written in 1970 and even perhaps in 1988. They were, of course, not the writing on the wall but they do indicate a degree of middle-class alienation which is a constant element of the whole post-war period.

A very good example of the kind of issue at stake is provided by the *Navista* movement in San Luis Potosí in and after 1958.[68] Dr Salvador Nava, one of four brothers who had trained as physicians, led a challenge in 1958 to the mayoral candidate imposed by the regional *cacique* Gonzalo Santos. Santos had controlled Potosíno politics for fully a generation and become very rich in the process. During this time he had made a number of enemies; one of these was Adolfo López Mateos to whom Santos had been opposed at the time of the Presidential *destape* in 1958. The federal government was known to be unhappy at the independence shown by Santos; Ruiz Cortines had offered to make him ambassador to Guatemala but did not push things further when Santos indignantly refused.[69]

Urban middle-class opposition to Santos was clearly on the increase during the 1950s. Once López Mateos' election to the presidency was secured, the momentum of protest increased sharply. Insensitively-handled attempts to repress a student riot further aggravated matters and the pressure of citizen opposition appears to have persuaded the government in Mexico City to make concessions. Some PRI representatives did in fact support the dissidents. It also seems to have suited López Mateos to identify himself with a reform candidate – who was an independent, not a representative of an opposition party. Dr Nava was declared elected mayor of San Luis Potosí and the governor (a Santos placeman) resigned shortly afterwards. However while an independent candidate for mayor was acceptable, Nava's attempt to win the PRI nomination to become governor was rejected; when Nava sought the governorship as an independent, the vote was rigged against him and protest was suppressed.[70]

It may be that the Catholic, anti-Castro, agitation played a part in the authorities' decision to withdraw tolerance from *Navismo*. The official winner of the 1961 elections, López Dávila, played an active part in seeking to block efforts to spread the Monterrey-based protests.[71] Certainly official propaganda against Nava during 1961 accused him (in effect) of political Catholicism. What is certain is that López Dávila and his successors were far more closely controlled by *Gobernación* than Santos had been, although (as we shall see) the authorities continued to have serious problems in that state.

A final objection made to those local political arrangements concerned the evident fact of growing centralisation. This centralisation was not wholly exploitative. Escalante shows that the federal government, while determinedly controlling Yucateco politics, was funnelling resources into the state to protect it from the worst consequences of the decline of the henequen industry.[72] Octavio Paz' description of the Mexican state as a 'philanthropic ogre' gives some indication of the ham-handed paternalism that could sometimes be found in at least the poorer regions of Mexico. Wealthier states such as Baja California and Nuevo León may have lost wealth as well as power although they clearly benefited from the growth of the 1940–82 period which the PRI's system of political control helped facilitate. In any case opposition politicians have at times been able to take advantage of local resentment of Mexico

City and locals have sometimes used the opposition to 'send a message' rather than expressing any real determination to challenge the regime.

Naturally the government saw the issue of centralisation in a very different way than the protesters. Almost all senior government figures have believed that centralisation including, if necessary, the imposition of state governors upon recalcitrant regions was a factor making for efficiency, economic growth and modernisation generally. Figures such as Díaz Ordaz would also have attached great importance to the maintenance of political order as an end in itself. Older members of the middle class had lived through thirty years of upheaval and social revolution and found it more than enough. The Hobbesian logic was widely accepted; the system guaranteed minimum rights to almost all Mexicans (the right to live in peace, to enjoy religious freedom and to make a living) and could not afford to promise more. Serious dissent, even when directed against admitted abuses, threatened renewed upheaval and civil war and was therefore unacceptable.

Díaz Ordaz was a man of provincial origins who was generally respectful of provincial authority. At first, however, it seemed as though he intended to shake up the PRI when he appointed Carlos Madrazo to the Presidency of the party. Madrazo had made his way up through the Chamber of Deputies, the federal bureaucracy and the governorship of Tabasco, and decided (apparently on his own initiative) to open up the PRI by encouraging primary elections and other forms of popular participation. The PRI, in other words, was to be reformed from a patronage party into a members party.[73]

This reform proved divisive and brought Madrazo into conflict with several state governors who made their objections known through *Gobernación*. In a showdown, Díaz Ordaz backed the provincial authorities and Madrazo resigned. According to one source Díaz Ordaz never intended that any of Madrazo's reforms should actually happen; when he appointed Madrazo to the PRI, it was not with the intention of shaking it up in any way and Díaz Ordaz was no less surprised than anyone alse at Madrazo's reformist enthusiasm. 'It was my fault', Díaz Ordaz said later. 'Carlos was an activist by temperament and I gave him a position where there was nothing to be done. I should have sent him to the provinces to build roads and bridges.'

The reasons for Madrazo's failure are instructive. His key concept was to introduce a system of primaries into the PRI. This would mean that the party member, deprived of a serious vote at national elections because of the predominance of the PRI, would still express a real preference in candidate selection. Moreover, Madrazo believed, giving PRI members this right would encourage active membership of the PRI. This would both strengthen the PRI as a party and make it more representative of what active (inevitably mainly middle-class) citizens wanted. Corruption and abuse of power locally would thereby be checked.

However problems with this concept were not slow to emerge. Ugalde found that in Enseñada, one of the municipalities chosen for the pilot scheme, conflict tended to occur between sections of the official party rather than, as had been the intention between individual candidates, judged on their merits.[74] Meanwhile some observers believed that the effect of the reforms would be to strengthen the PRI in Mexico City, which would control the intra-party electorate (by deciding who was and who was not a party militant, and therefore eligible to vote in primaries) and count the votes, and to weaken the power of the state governors. Anything which strengthened the central PRI would naturally strengthen Madrazo himself.

There was also a more general problem. One of the features of genuinely competitive politics is that there are losers as well as winners. Losers whose campaigns are motivated by principle can always console themselves that they helped to educate the public or influence the course of events; losers whose motives are fundamentally careerist simply lose. Many, probably most, people active within the PRI are (as we have seen) motivated more by the hope of patronage than by political principles. (Incidentally this is not a point necessarily being made in a negative spirit; misguided idealists have generally harmed the world more than honest careerists.) *Gobernación*, and the PRI itself, have shown clear understanding of this fact; within the overall patronage machine there are consolation prizes for individual losers (provided they accept defeat in a disciplined manner) and there is some effort to provide checks and balances at any rate between the organisational oligarchies which make up the PRI. A primary system would, in the eyes of some of its critics, simply enable winners to settle scores with losers. This fear was expressed by the CROC in

Enseñada and, after its representative lost the primary municipal elections, there was evidence that its fears may have been justified. An additional concern was that a really divisive primary election might, in those towns where the PAN had real presence, lead to the defection of losers and the weakening of the PRI – exactly the opposite result to that intended by Madrazo.

There is also the consideration that free elections are, inevitably, settled according to the political appeal of the rival candidates – not their *curricula vitarum*. However, appointment to local political office (to which election is a formality) is an important way for state governors and leaders of the organised blocs within the PRI to reward loyalty and public service. Difficulties quickly emerged in both Sonora and Sinaloa when it became clear that there was conflict between the governors' desire to appoint loyalists to municipal office and Madrazo's desire for a competitive election between rival candidates. This was the issue which led to direct conflict between these state governors and Madrazo.

Following Madrazo's resignation in late 1965, it soon became very clear that Díaz Ordaz, even more than Ruiz Cortines and López Mateos, fully intended to let sleeping dogs lie. State governors were selected centrally and allowed to act as viceroys in local politics. A sense of Díaz Ordaz' style is provided by the (friendly) record of Carlos Loret de Mola who was made governor of the state of Yucatán during 1969.

Loret de Mola had been Federal Deputy and then Senator of the state; it was reasonable to suppose that he might be a candidate for governor. After he was awarded the position, he asked President Díaz Ordaz to what his success was due. 'I considered you a good candidate and in the final months I made a definitive choice'.[75] Later Díaz Ordaz advised him 'be a conscientious and hard-working governor and don't come to see me again ever'.

Left-wingers who hoped to rise in the PRI by encouraging political dissent in the hope of being co-opted or alternatively by seeking to make use of Madrazo's reforms were generally left out in the cold. The *yucateco* Cervera Pacheco was blacklisted by Díaz Ordaz for his involvement in local disturbances (though this did not prevent him rising later to become a member of President Salinas's Cabinet). Similarly the Cárdenista Natalio Vázquez was passed over for the governorship of Michoacán in favour of Carlos Galvez Betancourt, who had previously worked in *Gobernación*.

The choice, early in 1967, of Faustino Felix Serna (a wealthy local landowner) as candidate for the governorship of Sonora proved locally controversial and contributed greatly to the victory by the PAN in elections in the state capital Hermosillo later in that year. However only one governor was replaced during the Díaz Ordaz *sexenio* – by far the lowest figure of all recent Mexican presidents.[76]

A feature of local politics during the Díaz Ordaz presidency was that the PAN was staging one of its periodic revivals. It has been said that US Ambassador Mann sought to strengthen the PAN during his period in Mexico (1961–4).[77] More important, with the election as party chairman of Adolfo Christleib Ibarrola in 1962, the PAN acquired only its second leader of genuine national quality. Catholicism also began to undergo major change beginning with the Second Vatican Council (1962) – a change reflected in Latin America with the rise of Christian Democracy. Despite these changes PAN remained relatively conservative, but it did move away from the uncomplicated pro-clerical reaction of *Cristianismo si! Comunismo no!* to a line which was more critical of the government and more aware of Mexico's own problems. PAN was further strengthened by López Mateos' electoral reform which gave it twenty deputies in the Chamber; it had never previously had more than six. For what they are worth, presidential election results between 1952 and 1970 show a slow but definite increase in the PAN's share of the vote – from 7.82 per cent to 13.98 per cent.[78]

The PAN had always polled well in local elections in some municipalities but found that the system had no compunction about rigging seriously-contested ballots. During the Díaz Ordaz government, however, the PAN actually did win some municipalities. The most noteworthy victories were in Merida and Hermosillo in 1967; in both cases the PAN capitalised on a local mood of disaffection in states with a tradition of resentment towards Mexico City. In both cases the centre, including Díaz Ordaz himself, handled the resulting tensions very clumsily; even a PAN spokesman admitted that, in Hermosillo, 'it is clear that the PAN did not win . . . the PRI lost'.[79]

The PAN victories led to a tightening of ranks within the PRI. Díaz Ordaz appointed Martínez Domínguez, who had the reputation of being a skilful hard-liner and a man close to the President, to lead the PRI. Public money was also poured into politically strategic areas. The PRI then returned to its customary position of victor in almost all significant local elections. Opponents of the PRI believed that this was done fraudulently, and there is evidence that this was sometimes the case, but fraud did not seem to be the problem that it became in the 1980s.[80] What is clear is that the PRI concentrated its forces on opposition targets and used its very considerable muscle; there was to be no move toward a serious two-party system and another political safety-valve was closed.

## THE STUDENT MOVEMENT

The 'Mexican 1968' therefore emerged into a system in which it was difficult, if not impossible, for articulate left-wing youth to find any constitutional form of self-expression. For those familiar with '1968' movements in other countries it will not be news that in Mexico, as elsewhere, there was a marked tension between the 'old' left (generally led by the Communist Party) and the new youth- and student-led movements. We have already discussed some of the reasons for this, noting that the old left had suffered a severe defeat during 1958–64. Some of its members had been severely repressed and those remaining at liberty were naturally not over-eager to attract the attentions of the security police. Díaz Ordaz certainly maintained a generally repressive security climate even before the student movement developed. Asked to comment on preparations for the visit of President Johnson to Mexico in mid-1966, the CIA produced two reports which provided a considerable insight into the Mexican security situation at that time.[81]

The first report began by pointing out that 'the security forces in Mexico City are experienced and effective in controlling demonstrations'. It went on to point out that, although many left-wingers remained at liberty, 'the Mexican government maintains some surveillance over the activities of these various extremist and exile groups.' Moreover, 'Mexican authorities customarily use detention, coercion and other warnings to keep potential troublemakers in line'.

The second report made a very similar assessment:

Top government leaders are strong, determined men, conversant with the uses of power. Security forces are tough and well trained; when so ordered they carry out missions without overmuch regard for legalisms.

Specifically, faced with the Johnson visit in 1966,

> the security authorities let it be known that they wanted to talk with 48 leaders of various small leftist political groupings likely to take part in anti-US demonstrations. Forty seven of these individuals promptly appeared and were informed in no uncertain terms that they would be held personally responsible for any unseemly activities by their memberships.

The report then went on to compare security in Mexico with that in other Latin American countries; the most impressive South American country in this regard was Chile, but Mexico had the edge.

> The Chilean police are as good or better than the Mexicans in most functions. But they do not have an equivalent intelligence capability and in some activities might be hampered by legal considerations and traditional respect for the rights of the individual.

In fact the authorities rarely needed to adopt illegal measures against opponents. The 'law of social dissolution' was a catch-all measure which provided up to ten years' imprisonment for those convicted; this provided the legal basis for the imprisonment of Vallejo and Campa after the railway workers' strikes of 1959. Constitutionally and legally presidential power in Mexico is virtually absolute.[82]

If all of this were not enough, the left continued to reflect the splits which had developed in the early 1960s. Lombardo had finally been awarded a few congressional seats by the PRI, despite the fact that the PPS did not in fact reach the number of votes necessary to enjoy the advantages of proportional representation. His support of the government was at this stage almost complete – possibly accounted for by the the government's agreement to subsidise a PPS-controlled Workers' University. Lombardo even declared his opposition to demonstrations mounted against the US involvement in Vietnam [83] although some such demonstrations did in fact occur. The Communist Party, although a little more independent (of the Mexican government at any rate) than Lombardo, was not in a good position to attract radical youth either. Young radicals found the Communist Party leadership ageing, dogmatic and liable to expel any activist for adventurism.[84]

In addition to this atmosphere of political repression, the atmosphere of control extended across a range of social and intellectual activities; personal liberty did not rank high among the priorities of the PRI, the mass organisations or, indeed, the old left.

Within this generally repressive atmosphere, however, student radicalism did enjoy a degree of immunity which was greater in the capital city than in the provinces. UNAM (the National Autonomous University of Mexico), because of its central location and prestige, had a relative immunity within the university sector. Disturbances at the National Polytechnic and at some provincial universities had been met by the sending in of troops; the army was sent in to the University of Morelia in October 1966 and the University of Sonora in March 1967.

The mobility and relative invisibility of student leaders (particularly in a movement such as that of 1968 which was deliberately unstructured) also gave them considerable advantages over more visible and vulnerable workers' and peasant leaders. Many of the leaders of the 1968 movement had earlier participated in other activities. Heberto Castillo had been a member of the MLN, and figures such as Gilberto Guevara Niebla had participated in regional protests. There had also been a student movement at UNAM in 1966 which led to the resignation of the rector. Student life certainly provided a window for political activity that broader Mexican society, on the whole, did not.[85] Moreover, in Mexico as elsewhere, student protest was often articulate, uninhibited and – in the eyes of many – outrageous.

International factors were also obviously important in 1968. Much of the explanation for what happened in Mexico in that year relates to attempts to replicate what was going on, or had gone on, in France, Czechoslovakia and the United States. Díaz Ordaz evidently believed that some international conspiracy was afoot and apparently sent Moises Navarro as emissary to Paris to find out whether the French authorities had any serious information on

Franco–Mexican student links. Some very limited connections were found involving Trotskyist groups but these did not even begin to explain what was happening in Mexico. To try to explain this, we must look at the character of educated Mexican youth.

One radicalising factor behind the student protests was that the co-optation process was not working as well as it once had. As Camp has shown,[86] the UNAM was an important base for recruitment into the political élite during the 1920s and 1930s. During that period, many of the students were sons of the anti-revolutionary wealthy and consequently conservative; those students who did, however, show an interest in joining the system were generally encouraged to do so. UNAM academics were often actively involved in élite recruitment. We know less about recruitment during the 1940s and 1950s but, by the mid-1960s, children of the establishment were in many cases already attending private universities and studying abroad. UNAM was beginning to lose its primacy, while Díaz Ordaz' personal preference for provincial universities (he himself had graduated from Puebla) was also a sore point.

In a sense education problems in Mexico were typical of those faced by those developing countries which, since 1945, managed a degree of economic progress. The first development is that infant mortality rates tend to fall, sometimes sharply. Families in poor countries typically aim to have large numbers of children as a kind of old age insurance; when infant and child mortality rates fall, the population not only increases but becomes younger. This puts considerable pressure on the educational facilities of the country involved. The second development is that educational facilities improve somewhat as a growing middle class retains its access to the education system. The Mexican public education system is not especially impressive but the number of those leaving secondary and preparatory schools increased considerably during the growth years of the 1950s and 1960s. There were therefore many more potential students wishing to enter university.

In Mexico the percentage of the 15–19 age-group attending educational courses rose from 6 to 13 between 1940 and 1960. Most of this secondary and tertiary education took place in the cities and particularly in the Federal District. Thus in 1960 only 14 per cent of the 15–19 age-group lived in the Federal District (DF) but the DF nevertheless accounted for 40 per cent of all secondary school students. At the level of higher education the proportion of the 20–24 age-cohort attending university rose from 1.3 per cent to 2.7 per cent between 1940 and 1960; in absolute terms (i.e. adding it to the growth of the population) this represented quadrupling over a twenty-year period. Moreover, during the sixties 65 per cent of all university students attended courses in Mexico City.[87]

To be a university student at UNAM in 1965 was still to be relatively privileged although, with university enrolment at some 100 000, it was far from being any guarantee of élite status (as it had been in the 1920s). In addition to this increase in numbers was the further problem that private universities were just beginning to become attractive to children of the very wealthy who could thereby sidestep the 'massifaction' and political turbulence of the state institutions; this trend continued during the 1970s and 1980s.[88] From the early 1960s emphasis began to be placed on postgraduate education either abroad or in the private university sector. The Colegio de México began offering master's degree courses in economics in 1965. Moreover, even the relative privilege which still attached, to some extent at least, to study at UNAM, was far less of a factor for students in the various preparatory schools which had grown up in Mexico City after 1950.

This expansion in the size of the student population did nothing to improve the quality of the education provided. Even if the state had made available the money to keep up with the increase in student numbers (and it did not [89]), there would have been difficulties in finding qualified teachers to cover the increasing demand. Nor was there the political will to enforce admission standards; partly for ideological reasons and partly due to the political realities, no serious attempt was made to control entry into the universities. The quality of the education provided inevitably tended to decline.

Finally governments in some developing countries deliberately expanded their bureaucracies in order to provide employment for graduates of the public universities. This provided a degree of both security for graduating students and control by the government over student activities. We shall see below that the Echeverría government did attempt a policy of this kind, but under Díaz Ordaz (and Ortiz Mena) it was government policy to hold back the growth in public spending as far as this could reasonably be done. It was a key element of 'stabilising development' that taxes were kept low (to encourage enterprise) and the budget deficit kept within bounds (to avoid inflation, devaluation and capital flight).

## Díaz Ordaz and the Student Massacre

This imposed severe constraints on what the government could offer to graduating students and, indeed, to the universities themselves.

The UNAM in early 1968, therefore, fulfilled virtually all of the criteria of relative deprivation theory. Students who studied there regarded themselves as upwardly mobile; their expectations had been increased both by the general increase in Mexican per-capita income over the previous generation and by the achievement of university entry by the students themselves. Many, though not all, of these students would have come from families where parents did not have degrees. However while UNAM still had some intellectual *cachet* the value of a UNAM education had declined in relative terms and, measured according to the admittedly crude yardstick of government expenditure per student, declined further during 1966–8. The social value of a degree was tending to decline as the direct result of the expansion of secondary and higher education. Moreover the tradition of student political activism itself proved damaging to teaching in some key disciplines such as economics[90] and the vicious circle thus tended to close; student protest reduced the opportunities for social mobility, the closing down of which, in turn, made student protest more likely.

The student protests began on 26 July 1968 when a large pro-Castro demonstration took place. On 29 July there was a further demonstration which turned violent; a number of students were killed by police. Matters then escalated as students began to demand the dismissal of those in the security forces held responsible for the deaths. Notably large marches were held on 1 and 27 August. On 1 September Díaz Ordaz made a relatively conciliatory speech which, however, did not succeed in heading off the students' activities. The culmination of a further series of marches and demonstrations was the massacre of Tlatelolco on 2 October in which several hundred people died when troops fired on an essentially unarmed demonstration.

There can be little doubt that Díaz Ordaz believed he was the target of a conspiracy. From his point of view the student movement had a number of ominous characteristics. The most overt was the threat to the Olympic Games, which were scheduled to open in Mexico on 12 October. Whatever other failings Díaz Ordaz might have had, there can be no doubt of his patriotism. He did, it is true, pursue a consistently pro-US policy during his administration but he saw this as a matter of necessity rather than choice. He once told Scherer that 'there is not a true Mexican who does not wish to settle accounts with the United States. It is our obsession and we must always remember to repeat our grievances so as not to forget them'.[91] Mexico's success in bidding for the Olympic Games, the first to be held in a developing country, was for Díaz Ordaz (and others of his generation) the chance to raise the national flag with pride. The threatened disruption of these games by student activists (whom Díaz Ordaz did not understand and, if such a thing were possible, would have hated even more if he had) was unwelcome indeed. While the student movement was almost entirely non-violent, the authorities would also have been concerned about the danger of a *guerrilla* rising. Left insurgencies were either in progress or threatened or recently terminated in most of Latin America. Mexico did not yet face an actual insurgency of note although some minor activities seem to have taken place even before October 1968; Cabañas had apparently already begun some kind of operation in the state of Guerrero and there had also been some preparation for urban guerrilla activity.[92]

Another factor of psychological importance was the intensity of the insult directed against Díaz Ordaz himself. Traditionally Mexican presidents have been afforded a degree of respect bordering on veneration. Díaz Ordaz was, however, addressed in a very different light by the rebellious students. Aguilar Camin later recalled the 'sacrilegious mood' which prevailed when, during the demonstration of 27 August, one student painted on the gates of the presidential palace the words *'Chango cabron, al paredon'*[93]. When Díaz Ordaz in an effort to conciliate said that he offered his hand to the students he received from some of them the reply that the hand would first have to be submitted to the paraffin test to make sure that it had not recently been holding a firearm. Díaz Ordaz would scarcely have been human if he had not wanted revenge for this kind of treatment.

Finally there was fear that the student movement might spread. Some attempts were made by radical students to win support among the peasantry, but this had very little impact indeed. There was, however, more connection with some dissident trade union members; the students' demand that Vallejo and Campa be freed (which was also something that the Mexican Communist Party very much wanted) appears to have had an impact. One student leader recalled that:

One could document a great number of conflicts during this period; teachers' strikes, stoppages in the hospitals, railway workers' strikes; there were meetings in San Lazaro . . . On 2 October, when the massacre began, a railway workers' contingent was arriving at Tlatelolco.[94]

A note of caution may be in order here however. It must be said that the students of 1968 (and again not only in Mexico) were in many case naively optimistic about their prospects of winning popularity in wider society. Within Mexico the strong opposition expressed to the student movement on the part of Gómez Villanueva (of the CNC), Fidel Velázquez, and (on a more muted scale) Cárdenas was almost certainly sincere and not just an attempt to curry favour with Díaz Ordaz. The Church and the PAN were in some ways more sympathetic to the student movement, or at least the feelings that lay behind it, than was the old left which shared with the authorities a belief in discipline, respect for procedures and for what they would have regarded as decent standards of behaviour. Just as student unrest strengthened the candidacies of Richard Nixon in the US and Georges Pompidou in France, so there were many Mexicans who would have been willing to support a decisive anti-student response by their own political authorities.

The facts so far presented about the student movement and the official response lie on the public record. One source, which I cannot name but believe reliable, goes very much further and suggests that Díaz Ordaz suffered something of a temporary nervous breakdown during this period. According to this source, Díaz Ordaz became obsessed with the notion that he was facing some kind of armed threat and to have placed his trust in ever-closer liaison with the military. He apparently went so far as to believe that his telephone might be tapped. Rather than telephone his defence minister, García Barragán, he sought face-to-face meetings with him. However it was obvious that the whole of the president's time could not be taken up in meetings with his defence minister. Instead it was agreed that each man would nominate a confidant; the two men would meet daily and discuss whether there was new information of sufficient value to justify a meeting; Díaz Ordaz nominated López Portillo and García Barragán nominated his son. In this somewhat bizarre way were orders from the presidency passed on to the military.

Only partial corroboration is possible from other evidence. Agee reports that, in late September, the CIA station chief in Mexico City – after one of his regular meetings with Díaz Ordaz – 'got the strong impression that the president is confused and disoriented'.[95] Aguilar Camin later referred in print to Díaz Ordaz' paranoia.[96] This was not to say that Díaz Ordaz necessarily acted out of character: it was just that, under conditions of stress, an already authoritarian president became more so.

The Mexican political élite responded to the upsurge of protest in three different ways. A few individuals, not many, called for conciliation. Octavio Paz, then ambassador in India, wrote a memo to Díaz Ordaz calling for a dialogue with the students; he then resigned following the Tlatelolco massacre.[97] More directly involved was Javier Barros Sierra, the rector of UNAM. Barros Sierra was quick to condemn police violence following the July demonstrations and the invasion of university autonomy by the army which took over two preparatory colleges on 29 July 1968. On 1 August Barros Sierra himself led a march in defence of university autonomy; the itinerary was carefully prepared so as to avoid the danger of confrontation with the security forces.

Barros Sierra came under heavy and sustained attack from the Díaz Ordaz administration. He was publicly criticised during September by two PRIista deputies (one of whom had earlier worked very closely with Díaz Ordaz) and subjected to other forms of pressure. On 23 September Barros Sierra tried to resign from his position, but his resignation was not accepted. In his 'resignation' speech he asserted:

> I am being made the object of a campaign of personal attacks, calumnies, lies and defamation. It is certainly true that the attacks are coming from junior figures without moral authority, but in Mexico we all know from where the ultimate authority comes.[98]

He told one source that he was surprised one September day to have been telephoned by Díaz Ordaz himself. 'Listen, *hijo de la chingada,* I know that there is a window in the Presidential palace from which, at a certain time and a certain angle, an assassin could shoot me. Well console yourself with this thought. I have given orders. Within half an hour of my death, you will be lying dead yourself!'

It seems clear that Barros Sierra did enjoy some support from figures who, while themselves keen to remain in the background, were far from happy at what was happening. Barros Sierra had been close to López Mateos: he had never liked Díaz Ordaz who was a rival for the succession. Other figures close to López Mateos such as Humberto Romero and Manuel Moreno Sánchez, also disliked Díaz Ordaz.[100] Moreover on 20 September the PAN congressional representatives called for the withdrawal of government troops from the UNAM. On 23 September the Junta da Gobierno of UNAM, as we have seen, refused to accept Barros Sierra's resignation.

Some other authorities wanted to negotiate with the students without making major concessions. De la Vega Domínguez sought to maintain a dialogue of sorts, but there were inevitable difficulties. One was that, without any serious support from the President, they had little to offer, although there is a suggestion that the government was willing to abolish the 'law of social dissolution' which was one key student demand: in fact this law was abolished in 1969. [101] However the students did not especially wish to negotiate either.

In order to negotiate, the students would have had to create some kind of hierarchy or at least a small group with representative powers. They would have had to formulate a feasible set of demands and decide which of these they wished to insist upon and which were expendable. Any concessions made by any of the movement would have proved unpopular with the other students, and might have led to the discrediting of any moderate student. The position of serious student negotiators would have been an unenviable one. According to one student leader, it was very difficult for the students to maintain any kind of consensus even as things stood.[102] Much the same point could be made about any government negotiator. All that happened was that there were a number of face-to-face meetings between government figures and students which did not succeed in resolving anything.[103]

The third strategy, the one adopted by Díaz Ordaz, was to call in the army, put down a demonstration, and undertake a vigorous repression of those student leaders who managed to escape the original massacre. After the military action the authorities managed, apparently by the threat of torture, to persuade two of the arrested student leaders to 'confess' publicly that the student movement had been preparing armed conflict against the government.

It is nevertheless not certain that the authorities ever intended the repression to become a massacre in which foreign journalists and uninvolved civilians were also hit. Troops appeared to believe that they were being fired on from the top of some of the high-rise buildings at Tlatelolco. They certainly fired back at the top of these buildings. A senior figure in the foreign ministry received a flesh wound while standing near the window of the 14th floor of the ministry building. Once panic breaks out, even highly trained troops can fire indiscriminately. The Mexican army certainly did so. After the massacre, the government told the diplomats of friendly countries that some repression, including the detention and arrest of known student leaders, had been intended but that more blood had been shed than planned. If this is what had indeed happened, it would explain why the authorities sought to develop a more specialist kind of unofficial riot police – an attempt which aborted after the Corpus Christi massacre of June 1971.

In military terms Díaz Ordaz' repression could have made sense. In coercive terms the student movement was indeed defeated. However in ideological terms, partly because of the degree of violence unleashed, it was the government that lost.

There was immediate damage to Mexico's international reputation, not so much in the eyes of foreign governments (Washington, as we have seen, had few illusions about the nature of the Mexican system while Castro needed a semblance of friendship with Mexico too badly to risk an open break) but rather in the defection of intellectuals, journalists and others who in the past had tended to portray Mexico in a relatively favourable light. Changes in the international intellectual climate tend to occur slowly but with a good deal of effect in the longer run. Within Mexico also, a great deal of damage was done to the way in which the politically-aware viewed their own society. The informal grape-vine worked even though the media were largely controlled.

Moreover the repression itself existed in a moral vacuum. Previous presidents such as López Mateos had known how to temper repression with other, more conciliatory, policies and to make it look as if they were defending ideas rather than simply position. Díaz Ordaz offered merely order without law or justice; order for the sake of order as Porfirio Díaz had once done. As we have seen, the Mexican system has had many of the characteristics of a Hobbesian despotism and many Mexicans no doubt supported Díaz Ordaz out of conviction rather than just convenience. Yet the

Mexican system does need ideas (however devalued these might later become in some practical contexts) because it is constantly seeking to renew itself and can only hope to do so when new values are brought into play. It has therefore happened that many of the 'losers' in revolutionary conflicts have been posthumously treated as heroes and that many of the ideas adopted by the official party have come from their (physically) defeated opponents.

It is not, of course, entirely clear that the students of 1968 had a coherent view of the world that could be effectively summed up in a simple slogan. Their demand for freedom was in obvious ways at odds with their association (often at arms' length) with orthodox Stalinist Communism. In Mexico, however, there was no shortage of intellectuals seeking to put the student protest in the most sympathetic light possible. What did it actually stand for? 'Liberty' said Octavio Paz; 'democratic freedoms' said Heberto Castillo; 'equality' said a latterly-sympathetic Echeverría. 'Subversion' said Díaz Ordaz, but this interpretation of the Tlatelolco massacre went to the grave with him.

## DÍAZ ORDAZ AND THE RIGHT

'Power tends to corrupt' said Lord Acton 'and absolute power corrupts absolutely.' The image of a half-crazed old autocrat using military force against his own unarmed people – the image of Deng or Li Peng in June 1989 – is an obvious one to apply to Díaz Ordaz in 1968. Yet, as we have seen, this is not the only possible interpretation of what happened and not the one most widely accepted at the time.

The political system closed ranks behind Díaz Ordaz in 1968; it is difficult to see what else it could have done. At least a Mexican presidency lasts for a finite period and has a definite ending date; after October 1968 Díaz Ordaz did not have impossibly long to go. It would be wrong to imagine, however, that the upper levels of the Mexican government were entirely composed of well-intentioned liberals appalled at the massacre but unable to think of any way of protesting. On the contrary Díaz Ordaz did have much genuine support for his course of action – not just unthinking loyalty.

Since those who supported the military action have chosen not to go on the record, one has to make a guess at how they would have presented their argument. Their essential point – a point made relentlessly by senior Mexican figures to whoever will listen [104] – would have been that Mexican stability was fragile. It was evident that Mexico did face the threat of some kind of insurgency in 1968 – almost every other Latin American country did at some point during the decade after the Cuban revolution. Those countries which suffered the worst problems (at any rate among the more developed Latin American republics) were often those in which the government's initial response to insurgency was weak and hesitant – consider Uruguay, Argentina and Allende's Chile. Tlatelolco did not prevent an insurgency in Mexico and it may have influenced some protesters in the direction of insurrection, but it would also have helped persuade some wavering radicals that it was not worth challenging the Mexican state; in this sense Díaz Ordaz' repression and Echeverría's opening could perhaps be seen as complementary. Moreover if Mexico had faced a more serious insurgency after 1968 than it actually did, it would have been less insulated from foreign intervention; the country's economic vulnerability to political violence hardly needs to be stressed.

Not all readers will find this line of argument convincing. What it surely leaves out of account is the closing-down of political channels in the decade prior to 1968. Even if the use made by Ruiz Cortines and López Mateos of Mexico's revolutionary tradition and credentials was largely a pretence, it was at any rate an important and skilfully-conducted pretence. Cárdenas, Lombardo and even Castro were part of the Mexican state's insurance policy against truly unpredictable disturbances from below; the premium which had to be paid on this policy was surely not excessive. It was only to be expected that a rapidly growing and urbanising society such as was Mexico in the 1960s would at some point demand new channels of expression and participation. What was less expected was the Díaz Ordaz government's lack of interest in providing them.

Another possible interpretation, also exculpatory of the system to some extent, was that the regime was not excessively powerful but rather not powerful enough. This was the line taken by Echeverría and implicit in much intellectual discussion of Mexico after 1970. This argument also is worth considering.

Granted, let it be said, that the system did become excessively rigid and exclusionary during the 1960s; whose fault was that? López Mateos moved to the right after 1960 because he came under intense pressure from the US government, the Church and Mexican business to do so. It was a right wing panic in the aftermath of the Cuban revolution which upset the delicate equilibrium previously existing between left and right in Mexico. In their view it was the privileged, not the president, who were to blame. Echeverría obviously believed this and felt in 1970 that the system had become dangerously unbalanced; in order to re-balance it and regain lost state autonomy, it would be necessary to weaken the right.

This is a difficult argument to evaluate in the absence of fuller evidence. However there is no suggestion that Díaz Ordaz was ever particularly close to business or the right. On the contrary, during 1968 when some business interests were pushing for a more direct influence on government, [105] the government rejected all such pressures. On 8 March 1968 Martínez Domínguez (of all people) stated: 'there is a minority which tends to concentrate economic power in its hands. This is unjust, but the injustice would be disastrously aggravated if that minority were also to monopolise political power'.[106] In addition to Martínez Domínguez' statement, Reyes Heroles (at that time Director of Pemex) attacked the private sector in his report on 18 March 1968 and then launched a further, direct, verbal attack on ex-President Alemán on 5 August 1969.

What may well have contributed to this tension was business disquiet at a new law, proposed in 1967, which slightly strengthened labour's position. Some private sector representatives let it be known that they were unhappy with this law; their concerns were not so much with the unions themselves as with the labour bureaucracy which was given effective power over some companies as well as over the labour force. Entrepreneurs tended to see the CTM trade union confederation in particular as a Trojan horse of government.[107]

One source indicates that Díaz Ordaz never dealt very much with the economy or the private sector; day-to-day management of the economy was in the hands of Ortiz Mena who did, indeed, have extensive relationships with the private sector. In any case, there was no repetition of the right-wing mobilisation of the early 1960s and no evidence at all that Mexican business tried to influence Díaz Ordaz in any direct way on explicitly political matters. Díaz Ordaz himself was a paternalist-corporatist of the Old Right, not an economic liberal of the New Right.

Although there is no serious evidence that the private sector in any sense controlled the Mexican political system, the hypothesis could perhaps be re-cast in a more 'structuralist' way. According to this view, it was not so much political pressure from the private sector as the logic of stabilising development itself which closed down the options facing the state. The problem was that the public policy measures which had in the past allowed Mexican presidents to win support from the left, and perhaps also from the people, were increasingly difficult to pursue. There were budgetary limits on public spending, imposed by the need to retain private sector confidence. Land redistribution was also ruled out because of fears of damaging private investment; the possibilities of further land distribution through public investment in irrigation had also largely exhausted themselves by the mid-1960s. Even an independent foreign policy risked losing private sector support.

This argument is discussed in more detail in the next chapter; there is something to be said for it. However the point needs to be made that critics of stabilising development were not concerned so much with direct private-sector input into government (for which there was little evidence) as with the logic of a development strategy. Nor is there evidence that the existing development strategy – which was, after all, producing significant levels of per-capita growth and genuine if limited increases in real wages – needed to be accompanied by so rigid a style of political management as that adopted by Díaz Ordaz. In this case, the role of the individual did matter.

One is left, then, with the personality of Díaz Ordaz himself. Díaz Ordaz, as we have seen, once described Duvalier as 'the son of a whore'. He did not say why, but one possible criterion for inclusion in this category is the mass murder of one's own people. There are also Solzhenitsyn's closing words in *Cancer Ward*; 'an evil man threw tobacco in the macaque-rhesus' eyes. Just like that....'[108]

Yet it would be unfair to classify Díaz Ordaz with Stalin or Duvalier; if the comparison were justifiable, no serious student protests would have been allowed to occur at all. Díaz Ordaz was provoked and over-reacted; his own soldiers may also have gone further than the president wanted. Díaz Ordaz was a complex figure and, on the whole, an unsatisfactory president – but he was not a monster. It may be that Octavio Paz' notion of *mestizaje*, in some ways misleading as a metaphor for Mexico as a whole, could nevertheless apply to Díaz Ordaz. He was an outsider – a provincial, of relatively lowly origins and mixed blood – who had made it to the top. Insecurity of status allied to personal ambition may have accentuated his interest in order and power, and his lack of sympathy with democracy or the 'values of 1968.' Certainly a more imaginative leader would have tried to find ways of mobilising the supporters of the system, or at any rate the opponents of the student radicals, as de Gaulle and Nixon (in their different ways) were able to do. A more popular figure might even have aspired to lead these new political forces – as Echeverría was to attempt after 1970. In contrast Díaz Ordaz appears to have considered the Mexican presidency mainly as an administrative post rather than as an opportunity to exert political leadership; on a variety of occasions, not just in 1968, he showed clearly that he was not a politician at all. Mexico paid a high price for this lack of political leadership.

# 3 From Counter-Insurgency to Economic Crisis: the Echeverría Presidency

'Echeverría was a better President than I; he knew how to choose his successor'. Díaz Ordaz, and many other Mexicans, saw the Echeverría administration as marking a complete departure from that of his predecessor. To some extent it was. Anybody listening to Díaz Ordaz cursing, Lear-like, his ungrateful putative son, might have believed that the two men were poles apart. However in some ways, notably in their belief in a fairly extreme form of presidentialism, they had more in common than either cared to admit.

Echeverría, even more than Díaz Ordaz, was a *Gobernista*. His political career began when he made contact with Sanchez Taboada, who was head of the PRI under Alemán. Echeverría worked on the 1952 presidential campaign and then moved into the federal bureaucracy. He worked in the education ministry for several years and became under-secretary of *Gobernación* in 1958. He was in *Gobernación* for twelve years, six as under-secretary and six as secretary. Like his successors, but unlike Díaz Ordaz, he had never stood for election until a candidate for the Presidency.

There is general agreement about the nature of Echeverría's character. Of his fussiness, or if one will, obsession with detail there can be little doubt. Díaz Ordaz once described him to Scherer: 'if he has nothing to do, he invents something. He is obsessed by work for the sake of work.' And on another occasion 'Every night he reads to me over the telephone the editorials of *Excelsior* as if anybody cared about such trivia.'[1] One of the central themes of Loret de Mola's *Confesiones* was that Echeverría involved himself obsessively in the minutiae of Yucateco politics; Loret believed this to have been a sign of Echeverría's malevolence but his evidence does not really bear out his contention. It appears rather as if Echeverría intervened merely because it was his habit to do so. He certainly gave state governors far less freedom of action than did Díaz Ordaz and intervened more openly in local politics; Echeverría removed five governors during his term of office, Díaz Ordaz had only removed one and López Portillo would only remove two.[2] There can also be no doubt that President Echeverría worked extraordinarily long hours and, on occasion, seems to have displayed more energy than balance. This picture of an interventionist and rather meddlesome figure is very much confirmed by various sources. Loret de Mola was not the only one of Echeverría's governors to have been driven nearly crazy by constant interference from the president. One source also recounts that Echeverría (as secretary of *Gobernación*) once invited him into his office for a long conversation; Echeverría said that he was going to reveal the true secrets of Mexican politics. What followed was a list of purely administrative details of such banality that the source wondered whether his leg was being pulled – but Echeverría was not joking.

Echeverría's alleged Machiavellianism is harder to document – but then such a quality usually is. Of the many instances that his critics have cited, at least three appear to substantiate the case. One of these was Echeverría's role, as Secretary of *Gobernación*, in the massacre of Tlatelolco. There can be little question that Díaz Ordaz ordered the action and that he used the army (which was not under Echeverría's control) more than the police (which was) in the repression. Echeverría was not, in any very direct sense, complicit. Yet Echeverría must either have agreed with the actions taken or not agreed. At the time he gave no indication whatever to Díaz Ordaz of any disagreement with his policy. He seemed the perfect loyalist.[3] Yet, once unveiled as the candidate, he moved swiftly to distance himself from Díaz Ordaz. On 1 September 1970 *Latin America* reported that Echeverría 'began jumping off the bandwagon much earlier than is usual for an incoming president'.

The interpretation most sympathetic to Echeverría is that he did have genuine reservations about what Díaz Ordaz was doing but that he kept these to himself in order not to damage his chances of the succession. What is quite remarkable is that he was able to hide his reservations in so convincing a manner.

Echeverría's deferential handling of Díaz Ordaz is also recorded by Loret de Mola in an amusing but telling minor incident.[4] In 1968 a Mexican Senator put forward the idea of lowering the voting age from 21 to 18. When the idea was put to Echeverría (as secretary of *Gobernación*), he replied that this was probably not the right moment to do this. Two days later, however, Echeverría told the senators that President Díaz Ordaz had the 'magnificent idea' of lowering the voting age to 18; this would be done and the senators were required to support the idea and to acknowledge presidential authorship.

A more important occasion in which Echeverría's behaviour appears to have been Machiavellian lay in his response to the Corpus Christi massacre of 10 June 1971. On this occasion an illegal student march – the first of Echeverría's presidency – was set upon by official thugs (*Los Halcones*) who even went as far as to pursue some of the injured students into the hospital and attack some of the doctors trying to treat them. All of this was done in full view of the press. The incident resulted in deaths, with estimates varying between 10 and 50.

Echeverría immediately dissociated himself from this violence and sacked Martínez Domínguez, *Regente* of Mexico City, and also Flores Curiel, head of the Mexico City police. He announced that a full investigation would be set up into what had happened. His public relations people explained, off the record, that these events were part of a right-wing attempt to discredit him and that they showed the intensity with which reactionary forces were trying to block him.

This version of events was widely believed at the time [5] but it is radically implausible. For one thing, if the story were true, then Martínez Domínguez would have had to be involved in some kind of conspiracy against Echeverría, then failed to have foreseen his own detection and dismissal and lacked any kind of follow-up strategy; he would, in other words, have had to have been politically naive or foolish and, in mounting some kind of challenge to Echeverría, something of a rebel also. Yet it is quite clear that Martínez Domínguez, whatever his faults, was no fool; he has also always been a loyalist who played the game by the rules. He thus remained silent throughout the whole Echeverría presidency despite his dismissal and subsequent ostracism. It just does not fit to portray him as an anti-Echeverrísta leader.

Moreover if one were to accept the conspiracy theory, then (as *Latin America* itself pointed out a year later [6]) instances of paramilitary thuggery directed against student demonstrations should have ceased with the dismissal of Martínez Domínguez. They did not do so: instances of such thuggery occurred in, among other places, Puebla, Culiacán (Sinaloa) and UNAM itself. Efforts by left-wing students to mount illegal marches and demonstrations were regularly countered by police or paramilitary repression. Could all of this have really happened *against* Echeverría?

Some years later, moreover,[7] Echeverría appears to have contradicted his own earlier version of events (or, at least, the semi-official one put out by the authorities and quoted above). He stated on this later occasion that he had never suspected either Martínez Domínguez or Curiel of 'criminal involvement' but only of a lack of vigilance. (In such a case why was Echeverría, so much the detailed interventionist, not more vigilant himself?) He also stated that the main reason why Martínez Domínguez and Curiel had been dismissed was to facilitate an investigation into the events of 10 June; Echeverría admitted in the same interview that this investigation was never completed, but did not explain why.

One possible reason for this non-completion is provided by the journalistic investigation of Julio Scherer. This provided clear evidence that the *Halcones* were a para-military force run by Colonel Díaz Escobar for counter-insurgency purposes.[8] Echeverría must have known of their existence and potential. (He told Luis Suárez that the *Halcones* existed 'to guard the metro'[9]; one is not sure that Mexico's metro travellers ought to have felt reassured). Had he taken the investigation into the incident seriously, he must have known of Díaz Escobar. It seems that Echeverría did indeed know of him, but not in quite the way his protestations might have led one to expect. In March 1973 Díaz Escobar was sent as military attaché to Chile; there, in complete conflict with official Mexican policy, he adopted an attitude of total hostility to the Allende government and strong support for the Pinochet coup. After relations between Chile and Mexico were broken Díaz Escobar was sent to the embassy in Peru, again as military attaché. In 1975 he was promoted Brigadier.

Under the circumstances, Echeverría's account lacks credibility. The most probable interpretation of events would surely start from the premise that the Tlotelolo massacre persuaded the authorities that the direct use of troops and live ammunition was not the best way to break up anti-government demonstrations. (As we have seen, the Mexican authorities told friendly embassies after October 1968 that the degree of force used at Tlatelolco had regrettably got somewhat out of hand.) Thus somebody (Díaz Ordaz? García Barragan?) had authorised the creation of a specialist para-military unit along the lines of the French riot police. Echeverría would have allowed the use of this unit in June 1971 against what was, after all, an illegal demonstration. Again, however, there was a loss of discipline. Instead of merely breaking up the demonstration, the *Halcones* killed a number of people and acted disgracefully; the fact that they were in radio communication with the local police also blew their cover and made it clear to the international press that they were by no means an autonomous or independent force.

As a result Echeverría's whole strategy of trying to co-opt the student movement and dissuade the radical left from violence was in jeopardy. Echeverría responded by doing the decent thing and firing a subordinate (or rather two of them). He also leaked a confusing and self-exculpatory story to the press in the hope of rallying support against a 'reactionary threat'. Like Díaz Ordaz, Echeverría evidently believed that the end justified the means. Like Díaz Ordaz also, he was officially believed.

A third occasion on which Echeverría was able, through some high profile grandstanding, to turn a difficult situation to his advantage occurred when he visited the UNAM in March 1975. A young student threw a stone at Echeverría which struck home and drew blood. Echeverría's immediate response was to shout a denunciation of 'young fascists' and 'groups manipulated by the CIA'. This line was taken up by government spokesmen and the official press: according to at least one press report [10] the result was public sympathy for Echeverría and a considerable political triumph. Later, however, his version was again somewhat different. [11] According to this later account the offending stone was thrown by a seventeen-year-old youth. Police arrested the youth but Echeverría ordered his release. Was this, asked Suárez, an incident connected with Díaz Ordaz, Martínez Domínguez, or an agency of the American Government? 'I don't believe this at all' Echeverría replied 'What mattered was how the event was presented politically'. The stone-throwing was 'objectively' pro-fascist; who was actually involved in the incident and why was beside the point.

Another factor, apart from fussiness and Machiavellianism, appears to have marked Echeverría's political life. He was generally successful in hierarchical relationships; he clearly handled Díaz Ordaz superbly well. His relationship with López Portillo, at least at the beginning, was also good. However Echeverría does seem to have had problems in dealing with strong figures within the system whose behaviour he was not fully able to control. We have already noted his treatment of Martínez Domínguez in 1971; in fact the latter had to wait until 1977 to make any kind of political comeback. Similarly Reyes Heroles was brought in to head the PRI in 1972; in September 1975 he was summarily dismissed, apparently for showing an excessive degree of personal independence.[12] Echeverría also sought during 1970–3 to undermine Fidel Velázquez, although later he had to admit defeat and make peace with him.[13] Again, in 1973, he replaced Hugo Margain, a finance minister who was apparently willing to stand up to him, with López Portillo who evidently was not. In 1974 it was the turn of a radical minister, Flores de la Pena, to be removed from office suddenly and without explanation. Then there is the question of why Echeverría passed over Moya Palencia for the presidency and gave it, instead, to López Portillo.[14] It may also be that Echeverría's rhetorical attacks on the private sector stemmed from his unwillingness to tolerate any group with the potential to act independently of Echeverría himself. Echeverría, then, was plainly a man who needed to be in control; his most hostile critics have accused him of megalomania.

A final feature of Echeverría's character stemmed from his marriage. The Echeverrías appear to have had a close-knit family life; they had nine children to show for it. (Echeverría originally declared himself opposed to birth control but later changed his mind.) When Echeverría, as secretary of *Gobernación*, needed to project a bland and boring public image the joke circulated that, in the Echeverría household, it was the father who got the children to sleep at night – he had such a talent for it. Ester Zuño de Echeverría, however, came from a noted political family in Guadalajara. Her father had been governor of Jalisco state; Maria Ester had noted left-wing sympathies and friends. While some other members of the Zuño family were more embarrassing than influential, there can be little doubt that Maria Ester sought to press her husband leftwards during his period in office.

Despite Echeverría's undoubted deviousness, therefore, there is reason to believe that his move to the left did reflect an underlying sincerity and consistency of view. He genuinely did seek reconciliation after the bloodshed of 1968 about which his own private feelings must have been extremely complex. He also hoped very much to avoid the kind of polarisation and near-civil war which was occurring in the southern cone of South America at this time.

Echeverría was not a violent man and he clearly believed that a degree of guile was necessary in order to hold Mexican political society together. In Machiavelli's terms, Echeverría was a fox rather than a lion – and Machiavelli believed that foxes generally defeat lions.

When considering Echeverría's strategy in more specific terms, a useful distinction can be drawn (following Loaeza) between the objectives of 'national unity' (which are essentially conservative) and 'revolutionary unity' (which are essentially socialist).[16] National unity presidents aim to reconcile the Church, the private sector and the middle classes while keeping lower-class organisations essentially subordinate. Revolutionary unity presidents seek the political exclusion of the private sector while offering (symbolic or material) rewards though not independence to lower-class organisations. Echeverría believed in revolutionary unity. He wanted to co-opt the left and bring it back into the system, although unlike Cárdenas (whom Echeverría in some ways took as his model), Echeverría's move to the left owed as much to a desire to channel mobilisation as to promote it. He also felt (rightly or wrongly) that the private sector had become too powerful and needed to be cut down to size. To understand why he essentially failed to achieve the latter objective we need to look more directly at the Mexican economy itself.

## ECONOMY AND SOCIETY IN 1970

The Mexican economy had enjoyed thirty years of unprecedented growth during the years 1940–70. In the second half of this period the currency had retained parity with the US dollar; at the end of the 1960s, Mexican inflation was actually lower than US inflation. There had certainly been an increase in inequality to match this growth, but real wages had increased steadily (after a sharp drop during the Second World War) and were at an all-time high in 1970.[17] The population, meanwhile, had grown rapidly – from 22 million in 1940 to over 50 million in 1970. During the 1960s, moreover, Mexico underwent the major change of moving from an essentially rural nation to one which was essentially urban.

It is now generally accepted that one of the keys to this performance was the rapid growth of agricultural production. Helped by previous agrarian reform and serious government help for the rural areas, agricultural growth reached 4.9 per cent per annum during 1935–46 and 7.6 per cent during 1946–56.[18] Agricultural growth continued to be rapid until the early 1960s and then it declined abruptly. This relative decline is generally attributed to several factors. Guaranteed prices for agricultural produce remained unchanged between 1963 and 1974, moving the internal terms of trade against agriculture. The direction of public investment also moved away from agriculture, possibly because the relatively 'easy' projects had been completed.[19] More complex kinds of change in the countryside may also have had their effect.[20] In any case, whatever reasons are adduced, it is clear that the contribution of agriculture to the Mexican 'miracle' (both in production and balance of payment terms) was in relative decline by 1970.[21]

The situation in manufacturing was more complex. Manufacturing production had increased rapidly during the period up until 1970[22] but there were strains and problems. For one thing Mexican manufacturing was heavily protected and internationally uncompetitive. The difficulties of import substituting industrialisation are well known; they include quality problems with output, the excessive rewards accruing to those who have access to the state and therefore to political connections as distinct from industrial competence, and continued dependency on imported inputs and technology. In the Mexican case these did not greatly matter for as long as agriculture generated a substantial balance of trade surplus, but by 1970 there was at least the prospect of future difficulty.

At a more political level there was also the problem of foreign ownership. Inevitably foreign companies looked either at the protected Mexican market or at the potential comparative advantage of some Mexican resource or resource-based product, and wished to invest in Mexico. Local capital, generally speaking, had no particular desire to resist the blandishments of foreign companies. The state had no particularly coherent policy towards foreign ownership but moved at times to limit or restrict it.[23] This was an item which Echeverría would put very firmly on the political agenda.

The same picture of progress tempered by fragility appears if one examines the savings/investment aspect of the economy. A key problem here is that the Mexican authorities believed firmly that exchange controls would not work in their country. (Short-lived efforts to impose them in 1982 would only reinforce this belief.) There were just too many points of contact with the US economy and too many limitations on the capacity of the Mexican financial

## The Echeverría Presidency

bureaucracy. Mexican wealth-holders, therefore, could not be forced to invest in their country. They had to be persuaded to do so. This meant at a minimum that the government authorities had to reassure private investors' fears of political trouble, no matter how exaggerated these might be (1960–61 as an example), or capital flight might begin. Capital flight would then interact with fear of devaluation in a vicious circle; this circle might also work as easily in its other aspect, with devaluation feeding through into inflation and political unrest. Ortíz Mena believed that the labour unrest of 1958–9 (referred to in the last chapter) had resulted from the devaluation of 1954. Even in non-crisis periods, the inherent preference of wealth-holders for the United States ensured that interest rates in Mexico generally had to be higher than their US counterparts and rates of profit also correspondingly higher.

Mexican industry obviously was profitable in 1970, thanks to import restrictions, low taxes and a low wage economy. However the high returns to capital available in Mexico were a key explanation for the high level of economic inequality in that country,[24] and it was to this inequality that many Mexican economists were, in 1970, increasingly objecting.[25]

Objectors to this pattern of growth admitted that development with stability had enjoyed some successes, but they stressed also some of its (real enough) shortcomings. Behind these technical arguments were political factors. Pressure for increased government spending was not just (or mainly) the result of economists' abstract appreciation of worsening income distribution; there was also the pressure of a growing urban population (and particularly urban middle class) and an increasingly young population. The student protests of 1968 were a telling indication of what might subsequently be expected if the system did not meet the demands of these emerging groups. Even Díaz Ordaz, who had a justified reputation for being an authoritarian hard-liner, significantly adjusted his spending priorities in order to respond to various kinds of political protest. Money was diverted into the Yucatán after the PAN won the municipality of Merida in 1967.[26] Even more important, there was a shift toward helping the urban and, above all, metropolitan middle class.[27] It was perhaps symbolic that the first line of the heavily-subsidised Mexico City metro opened in 1969.

A closely related problem was that of political control. The last president who had tried to carry out policies of nationalisation, land reform and limited income redistribution was López Mateos;

however he encountered such strong conservative resistance that during his last three years in office he returned to policies of almost pure orthodoxy; capital flight was a major factor in forcing this change of line. Now, as in 1958 though perhaps more so, the political system needed to find a new centre of balance some way to the left of Díaz Ordaz.[28] If the government sought to do this by moving away from a purely orthodox policy, would the necessary margin of financial manoeuvre still be present? Some of Echeverría's most influential advisers told him that this would not, in fact, be possible. In order to achieve his social and political objectives, they argued, a very different type of economic structure would have to be constructed. The state would have to move to the centre of the economy and the Mexican bourgeoisie would have to be financially, and politically, marginalised.

## ECHEVERRÍA'S POPULISM

The key element in Echeverría's economic strategy was to increase the government's intervention in order to facilitate a policy of social reform and political reconciliation with the left.[29] It is worth noting that the conventional wisdom of the period was supportive of this objective in principle, however much the intellectual climate might have changed in the twenty years since Echeverría's accession. Several West European governments had proved that it was possible to combine an efficient capitalism and rapid rates of growth with an interventionist ('welfare') state dedicated to providing health, education and the relief of extreme poverty. Indeed it was seriously argued that a welfare state was typical of, and even perhaps functional to, modern advanced capitalism.[30] Moreover in Britain and the United States even conservative governments (Heath in Britain, Nixon in the US) were willing to experiment with direct controls on wages and prices. By the standards of 1971 it was 'stabilising development' which was internationally unusual rather than the concept of 'shared development' which was adopted by Echeverría.

The same point also emerges when we consider the political climate in Latin America itself. In 1971 Allende was in power in Chile. Even more significant for non-Marxists was the Velasco regime in Peru which was already well on course with a radical programme of land and other property reform; these reforms had attracted a great deal of international attention and many scholars had concluded that General Velasco had adopted a promising strategy for achieving social peace and economic development. It was of course President Kennedy himself who had said, a decade earlier, that 'those who make peaceful revolution impossible make violent revolution inevitable'. There was a counter-insurgency rationale behind the Alliance for Progress, and the reforms of General Velasco. Echeverría was facing similar problems in 1971.

While there was certainly an international opinion willing to support any effort at social reform in Latin America, there were also unfortunately some rather difficult problems confronting any effort to move in this direction. These problems were not fully appreciated at the time, either in Mexico or elsewhere.[31] Some of them may be summarised here.

In Latin America, the worst poverty is generally rural.[32] The obvious measures to alleviate rural poverty – small scale public works and the provision of electricity, clean water, health care and schooling to remote rural areas – are likely to have a direct cost in terms of economic growth. It is certainly not an objection to such policies to say that they cannot easily be self-financing and will therefore have to be paid for by other sectors of society, but it does indicate a difficulty.

Moreover poor people living in remote areas rarely form a politically significant constituency. Mexico was no exception. We have already seen that local politics in Mexico was in decline by 1970; the real power had come to lie in the federal bureaucracy and not with local mayors or even state governors. The bureaucracy, obviously, was based in the capital, and senior appointments and promotions were made there. Given the fact that the subjective preference of most educated people in developing countries is to avoid living outside urban areas at almost any cost, there are obvious reasons why an increase in public spending on rural projects may actually end up benefiting mainly the metropolitan bureaucracy. In Mexico in 1989, for example, some three million people were employed in some form of public administration; of these no more than 150 000 worked outside the Federal District.

Those who demand reform the loudest, however, are not the rural poor but rather the urban middle sectors and, to some significant extent, the urban poor as well. In societies such as Argentina, in which around 90 per cent of the population is urban, this is not so serious a problem. In Mexico in 1970, however, attempting to improve urban services ran several risks. To the extent that it was successful, it encouraged migration into the cities – and particularly the Federal capital.[33] If the urban sectors were helped by subsidising food and gasoline, there would be economic consequences stemming from distortions in the price mechanism and overloading the budget. The costs of subsidising almost anything are commonly underestimated because of the additional demand that such subsidies engender.

If one looks at the records of other non-Marxist reformers in Latin America (Perón, Velasco, possibly also Carlos Andres Pérez in Venezuela), one sees that there is a kind of syndrome from which they all suffered, and to which Echeverría also was subject.[34] These cases are certainly not identical but they have enough in common to suggest that there was some flawed conception common to each. Each of these men took office at a time when the domestic economy was in a reasonable shape; they sought to capitalise on this situation by using the public sector in a very interventionist way in order to achieve social reform and popularity. Each, however, aimed at too many targets; they proposed to redistribute income in a progressive direction, to use the public sector to increase economic efficiency generally and to adopt measures which would increase their popularity.

One common failing in these approaches is that they led to an over-expansion of the size of government without a commensurate increase in either its effectiveness or in the means of financing its operations. This was certainly the case with Echeverría's Mexico. According to Zaid (whose figures, though somewhat speculative, are the best available) the total size of the public sector expanded from some 617 000 in 1970 to just over two million in 1975. As a proportion of the economically active population, this increase was from 4.8 per cent to 14.0 per cent.[35] Tello, quoting a different set of figures, gives a less sharp increase – from 826 000 government employees to 1 316 000, in increase of 59 per cent.[36] However Tello excludes local government from his reckoning, and staffing here also increased. The problem with the effectiveness of public spending is more complex; to discuss it fully would need a separate volume. Still, a few general observations are possible.

The first of these is that Mexico, again by no means alone, has a clientele system of public administration. If one excludes a relatively small number of technocrats at the top of the economics ministries, most people are given bureaucratic and political positions less because they have appropriate qualifications than because they have the right contacts. In fairness one should add that office holders who are manifestly incompetent may be dismissed or moved and that people without formal qualifications are rarely promoted into top positions. Nevertheless expertise, as such, is not always highly valued and the virtues of professionalism often overlooked.[37] Moreover job turnover is extremely high; it occurs not only with every new president, but with every cabinet reshuffle as well. Except in a few highly unionised companies and professions, there is very little job stability. (Unionisation, as in the case of Pemex for example, generates problems of its own.)

There is a considerable literature about clientelism, both in Mexico and elsewhere. There seem to be at least three points of consensus. The first is that clientelism has a powerful political logic behind it; it is bad for mobilisation and good for political stability.[38] Indeed the judicious use of clientelism played a major part in reducing conflict in Mexico after the revolution.[39] Under Echeverría also, there can be little doubt that the expansion of the bureaucracy influenced a significant part of the 'generation of 1968' away from insurgency and toward accommodation with the system.[40]

Secondly clientelism, by its nature, individualises public power; government is sub-contracted to particular interests and individuals. This is a classic recipe for minor (and sometimes not so minor) corruption and other forms of illegality. Thirdly clientelist bureaucracies are far more receptive to pressures from above than to demands from below because the link between either popularity or performance and success is highly uncertain. For all these reasons, clientelism seems to be good for control but bad for achievement.

Even without this general point, one would have expected serious problems to have arisen in Mexico from the sheer speed of the expansion of the public sector. The number of state companies increased under Echeverría from 86 to 740.[41] At the same time, however, there was lacking a proper co-ordinating or planning system.[42] State companies spent money but rarely published accounts; even where they did, these accounts were not properly scrutinised. Apart from state enterprise itself, there were set up under Echeverría (in the words of two researchers working in Yucatán) 'a bewildering array of credits, subsidies and investments'.[43] Here again there was no proper system of financial control. It is therefore not surprising that a lot of money was lost and that, as most observers agree, there was a considerable increase in corruption.

There is a general danger with all such populist strategies that hiring and spending will come to seem ends in themselves rather than means to ends. Indeed, to some extent the objective was to co-opt the post-1968 student interest by expanding the number of bureaucratic positions; in this sense hiring and spending perhaps was an end in itself. However Echeverría did aim to do more, and there were financial problems which were in any case likely to stem from what actually happened.

Yet another problem was that the main beneficiaries of state spending were to be found among the middle class. That this was true of Echeverría's Mexico comes out of any study of where the increased spending went. In education, for example, the student–teacher ratio improved between 1970 and 1976 at the level of tertiary education while worsening at the primary and secondary levels. Moreover even within the university sector 'the disproportionate increase in the numbers of those employed in federal educational services was to be found in the administrative areas'.[44] Moreover in the field of health provision, the Echeverría administration gave priority to 'large-scale high technology hospitals' [45] which were of little evident benefit to the majority of the population.

A great deal was also spent directly on consumer subsidies – notably on gasoline, public administration and food. Gasoline subsidies are of disproportionate benefit to the urban middle class [46] while subsidies on food and public transport are merely subsidies to the urban areas. Considered purely in accounting terms, more than half of the federal deficit in 1976 (more than the entire *increase* in the federal deficit under Echeverría) could be attributed to subsidies on official prices.[47] Meanwhile, although certain broad 'welfare' indicators – the numbers of people covered by social security; the number of homes provided with water and electricity; life expectancy and mortality rates – do show an improvement during the 1970s, there is no real evidence of further improvement over and above the general post-war trend.[48]

A further general problem with populism relates to the relationship between the state and private business. A populist policy depends on some degree of co-operation from a private sector which is likely to be in varying degrees disapproving of reform efforts but which the state is not in a position to control. Attempts to reinforce such control are likely to create additional problems; on the other hand, if the government gives too great a weight to private sector approval, it cannot hope to achieve its ambitions on other fronts. The whole point of populism, after all, is that it does involve a degree of financial unothodoxy and at least the promise of income redistribution.

Echeverría's relationship with the private sector started badly. Almost as soon as he took office he involved himself in a sharp clash with Coparmex, which was generally regarded as the most militant of the employers' organisations. Coparmex had complained that Echeverría, in one of his first acts as president, sent to congress a tax reform bill without having first consulted business associations. Echeverría sharply rebuked Coparmex, stating that the President had no constitutional duty to consult any private association on matters of this kind.

We have already seen that Mexican business regards the Mexican state with a particular degree of suspicion due to its formal exclusion from politics and the revolutionary history of the PRI. High level personal contacts between government and businessmen have been a partial substitute for formal representations. Echeverría does appear to have sought to maintain these contacts. One account suggests that informal communication helped defuse the conflict between Echeverría and Coparmex in 1971, but that channels were interrupted by the (presumably political) assassination of Eugenio Garza Sada by the left in 1973.[49] Echeverría made a point of trying to attend the funeral and found himself denounced by a member of the Garza Sada family for allegedly conniving with the guerrillas to destabilise Mexico. By 1975–6 the relationship between Echeverría and the private sector was one of undisguised and intense hostility. One suspects that there was an element of paranoia on both sides.

It is not clear how far economic trends in Mexico after 1970 can be explained by political factors. We do know that the underlying tendency under Echeverría was for private investment to fall as a proportion of GDP;[50] this decline was somewhat disguised by various investment incentives offered by the government during this period. Meanwhile Echeverría appears to have responded to private sector pressures (or at least anticipated private-sector reactions) when he decided to tone down proposed tax reforms in

1971, 1973 and 1974. As a result, the growth in tax revenue was far slower than the growth in public spending during 1970–6. The overall impression one receives is that Echeverría managed to get the worst of both worlds by postponing tax reform, in that he failed to allay business hostility but unbalanced his budget further in his attempt to do so.

## 1973 THE TURNING POINT

Whatever problems may have been latent in the Mexican economy, there were also some genuine strengths which might under other circumstances have told to greater effect. For one thing, inflation and inflationary expectations were very low. Although business confidence in Echeverría declined, it did so from a fairly high initial level. Another encouraging factor was the growth in manufactured exports. It had been a priority of the Díaz Ordaz administration to press manufacturers to develop export potential; the *maquiladora* programme had begun in the 1960s and efforts were made at the end of the decade to persuade car-makers to expand. Manufacturing exports were admittedly expanding from a low base, but the foreign exchange advantages were significant, particularly at a time when the contribution of agriculture to the balance of payments was moving from positive to negative.

What concerned Echeverría at the time, however, was the semi-recession which hit in 1971. It is usual for public spending to fall at the beginning of a *sexenio*, as the projects associated with the outgoing president have been completed and the new administration takes a little while to make its own plans. However the fall in spending in 1971 was unexpectedly sharp (there were apparently some technical errors involved here) and Echeverría became concerned. According to one source, 'the recession suffered in 1971–72 must have had a deep impact on the President and justified – at least politically – the shift towards an expansionary policy'.[51] Thus when public spending moved into gear, Echeverría became unwilling to listen to advice from orthodox economists who told him that the public sector deficit was becoming excessive.[52]

From the middle of 1972, Echeverría also began to tighten policy on foreign investment in Mexico. This tightening was only a matter of degree – foreign companies were not allowed a free rein even under Díaz Ordaz. As so often under Echeverría, however, the rhetoric rather outran the policy; attacks on (in the words of Cabinet minister Flores de la Pena) 'the chains of dependency and of useless colonialist economics' alarmed the private sector. According to a CIA study, there was in later 1972 'a temporary capital flight of some $300m'.[53] As an attempt to encourage and strengthen a national capitalism, these measures proved a signal failure; instead they brought the US embassy closer to the Mexican private sector, each of them concerned at rather different aspects of government policy.

Echeverría would, in all probability, have been constrained earlier and at lower cost had it not been for the opening up of two seeming sources of economic opportunity; one is tempted to call them different forms of fool's gold. It became much easier after around 1972 for Latin American governments to borrow heavily from abroad; a number of them did this, by no means only Echeverría's Mexico. Moreover in the light of the prevailing global inflation, real interest rates were negative, at least for a time. It was not only Echeverría who found it easier to borrow than tax or restrain the public sector. The second factor was that Pemex made a series of large-scale oil discoveries from 1972 onwards.[54] Echeverría did, however, treat the oil finds with some caution – far more than he showed to foreign lenders. The oil issue will be discussed in greater detail in the next chapter.

Some of Echeverría's supporters believe, however, that the most important reasons for Mexico's economic difficulties after 1974 were connected less with Echeverría's own strategy than with international factors beyond his control. It is certainly true that from 1973 onward some unexpected international events did add to his problems. The military coup in Chile, on 11 September 1973, triggered an emotional response in Echeverría and an equally emotional response, in this case supportive of the outcome, from the Mexican right. More serious, there was the first oil shock. When this occurred Mexico was still an oil importer, a situation which continued until the middle of 1975. Oil price increases also triggered a process of world-wide inflation. The United States began to record double-figure inflation, and some of this was also carried into Mexico. Perhaps even worse, the world economy went seriously into recession at the end of 1974 and did not start to recover until two years later.

These developments obviously posed problems for Mexican policymakers. One should remember that in the early 1970s it was the conventional Keynesian wisdom that economies should be run at a high level of capacity, and that the relationship between inflation and growth was essentially a trade-off. Few policymakers at that time gave full credence to the monetarist counter-argument that inflation and unemployment are not alternatives in the long run because inflation creates inflationary expectations which, after a period of time, become self-generating or even self-aggravating. It was therefore not especially eccentric for Echeverría's policymakers, at least at first, to adopt the principle that price stability was a lower priority than economic growth and to continue populist policies.[55]

In fact Echeverría's economic performance during 1974–6 has proved an intensely controversial topic.[56] There is no space to follow the discussion in detail. What can be said is that things turned out badly for the Mexican authorities. The current account deteriorated noticeably in 1974 and 1975 (despite the marked improvement in the oil balance in the latter year), and capital flight began to occur in a serious way in 1976. In mid-1976 it became clear that the government could no longer defend the *peso*–dollar parity; the *peso* was effectively devalued on 1 September 1976 and Mexico went to the IMF on 13 September.

The aim here is not so much to pass judgement on Echeverría's performance as an economic manager as to consider the implications of his economic policymaking for our understanding of the presidential institution. Several general points appear to stand out. The first is that Echeverría's decision to choose a broadly populist strategy made a great deal of political sense at the beginning, and was by no means out of line with various things that were then being attempted in other parts of the world. There is something in Laurence Whitehead's conclusion that Echeverría's

> economic strategy is best evaluated not as a mere product of arbitrary and irresponsible personal leadership but as a reasonably rational attempt to reinvigorate the political system, accepting a certain loss of short-term equilibrium as a regrettable consequence.[57]

The second point, however, is that this 'attempt to reinvigorate the political system' did not achieve serious progress in its ostensible aim of improving conditions for Mexico's poor. What it did do was attempt – by no means completely unsuccessfully – to co-opt the Mexican middle class. Moreover, given the economic inefficiency of this process, the strategy involved sacrificing some long-term growth (as well as price stability) in order to buy some short-term popularity for the system. It also entrenched a powerful new bureaucratic interest at the heart of the public sector. There is, therefore, some justification in the subsequent criticism that Echeverría's policy of expanding public spending was a costly and damaging substitute for real political reform.[58] It also reflected an attempt to centralise power rather than connecting the system more closely with civil society.

Third, despite Echeverría's renowned political cleverness and flexibility, he showed few of these skills in the field of economic management. As is often the case with Mexican presidents, he became less flexible as the *sexenio* wore on. Even his structuralist or Keynesian advisers would have been aware of the dangers of continuing with expansionary economic policies after the United States began moving into recession. It also did not help that in 1975 Mexico voted at the UN for a resolution equating Zionism with racism; the result was a Jewish – American tourist boycott of Mexico which cost much foreign currency. Nor did Echeverría's rhetorical attacks on the private sector during 1975–6 help very much either. In other words, while Echeverría did have an initial strategy, he seems to have lacked the capacity to rethink his approach as it became increasingly clear that his policies were encountering problems. Instead he complained about conspiracies and ploughed on – much as López Portillo was to do in 1982. Either he did not understand that economic constraints existed, or he did not care. In this sense he proved an even more authentically 'Presidential' figure than Díaz Ordaz.

In the end Echeverría's battle against the forces of Mexican capitalism ended in defeat and devaluation. It may have seemed reasonable in 1980 to argue that Echeverría, despite losing a battle over the devaluation issue, had in fact won the war. Hegemony had indeed been restored by a show of firm government, and devaluation was a mere blip in a long process of successful economic growth. A decade later, however, this argument looks strained. Inflation has been a serious problem in Mexico since 1973. Moreover, the crucial point is surely that an expanded public sector incapable of self-financing its own activities has the long-term effect of reducing the margin of governmental autonomy. This is because the government comes to need what it cannot control – namely private sector revenue. If it had not been for the oil boom and the continued surge in international lending to Mexico, the economic crisis of 1976 would have had more lasting effects than it actually did. As it turned out, it proved to be mostly a dress rehearsal for the far more definitive turning point reached in 1982.

CO-OPTATION AND CONTROL

Echeverría's economic policies were, as we have seen, to a great extent subordinated to his overall political strategy. His main political aim was to co-opt the left. One of the main reasons for this was that Mexico, like other parts of Latin America in the early 1970s, faced the threat – and to some extent the reality – of armed insurgency.

Those left-wingers who did resort to armed opposition were ruthlessly crushed. They were not sufficient in number to mount a serious military challenge to the state but they were quite enough to spread fear and add to dissensions within the political system. We do not have exact numbers. In an article for the *Financial Times* in May 1973 Riding suggested that 'from a military point of view the guerillas are unimportant. There are perhaps 300 who are active'. This seems to be too low (unless, which is not clear, Riding is referring only to the 'army of the poor' in Guerrero), if one considers that the same article refers to some 130 guerrillas in gaol at that time. In *Inside the Volcano* he estimates that there were some 200 in Guerrero and a further 1000 or so active in urban guerila movements.[59] If Riding got these figures from official sources, they might also be underestimates. According to one later account the army, on one occasion when operating in Guerrero, threw 180 captured but living guerrillas from helicopters into the ocean.[60] There must surely have been more than 20 guerrillas in Guerrero who met a different fate. Sánchez Rebollendo, obviously more sympathetic to the insurgents, refers to 'thousands'.[61] In any case organisations such as the IRA have been able to do considerable damage with an active membership of a few hundred people at most. The Mexican insurgencies between them probably involved, in total, numbers well into the thousands;

if the insurgents had been more successful in winning support from workers and peasants, they would obviously have numbered many more; on the whole, however, they failed to do this.[62] Echeverría responded to this threat with a degree of ruthlessness; in 1974, after Senator Ruben Figueroa (a man of 74) was kidnapped in Guerrero (possibly when trying to negotiate with the insurgents [63]), Echeverría mobilised the army. Although the army commander originally complained that the decision to send in the military had come too late, he seems to have been given a free hand to act with the force that the situation seemed to require. Echeverría in any case had informal links with many senior officers through the sub-secretary of *Gobernación*, Gutiérrez Barrios, who had trained as an officer and graduated from the military academy. It was, however, typical of Echeverría that his evident tolerance of military repression was balanced by some high-profile leftward moves a few months after the death of Cabañas in December 1974. Shortly afterwards the right-wing governor of Guerrero was forced to resign and placed under arrest for corruption; a little later the entire corps of 500 judicial police was arrested for the same alleged offence.[64]

An urban insurgency, undertaken by a number of different organisations including the *Liga Comunista 23 de Setembre*, was also violently repressed; there were disappearances and deaths under torture. Riding estimates that about 400 people were disappeared at this time;[65] the total is not likely to have been fewer. Insurgency was not finally defeated until the López Portillo presidency. A section of the left could not forgive Echeverría for playing his part in such actions.

Much of the left, however, found the insurgents profoundly threatening; its spokesmen tended to refer to them with either embarrassment or outright condemnation. Heberto Castillo cogently criticised the violent left[66] but also added that some activists in his own PMT (Mexican Workers Party) had been detained and interrogated by police; the question the police invariably asked, said Castillo, was whether the PMT was receiving any financial help (i.e. ransom money) from the insurgents. The imputation was vigorously denied. Moreover, after an apparent hesitation,[67] Cuba and the Soviet Union pointedly distanced themselves from the Mexican insurgency even though Cuba at any rate apparently supported insurgencies in other countries. Echeverría's attitude to non-violent opposition from the left was more complex but on the whole it seems to have been a mixture of public support and private manipulation. This is not an unusual combination in Mexican politics, or indeed politics anywhere. Echeverría wanted to attract the non-violent left but his ciritics are surely right to say that he did not want to open up the 'input' side of Mexican politics to any significant extent. He thought that changes of policy would substitute effectively for changes of political structure.

Echeverría did open the prisons and release those arrested after the Tlatelolco massacre. After the middle of 1971, following a short period in exile, spent mainly in Chile, they were allowed to live freely in Mexico. Then the fissiparous tendencies that seem to be so common on the left (not just in Mexico) reasserted themselves, although the publication of *Punto Critico* did form a rallying point of sorts.[68] The formal Communist Party remained unrecognised and subject to occasional repression. The left also found it difficult to embark effectively on party political activity. Heberto Castillo, with a small but impressive group of supporters (including Demetrio Vallejo, Carlos Fuentes and Octavio Paz) formed a kind of committee in 1971; however this suffered a number of splits before Vallejo and Castillo formed the Mexican Workers' Party (PMT) in 1974; Echeverría appeared to offer the party tacit support but Castillo found it impossible to secure official recognition. Castillo himself blamed bureaucratic obstacles.[69] The straightforwardly Trotskyist PST was also formed in 1973 but, again, failed to secure recognition. Also Trotskyist and stemming directly from the movement of 1968 was the PRT, the Revolutionary Party of the Workers, which in Oaxaca at least (as its name should indicate) was composed mostly of students.[70]

In fact until the political reform of 1977, party competition was not regarded on any side as a central political arena. Its apparent significance was further reduced by the fact that the PAN split in the early 1970s and could not agree on a presidential candidate to contest the 1976 elections. Much of the left remained abstentionist. Nevertheless, as under Díaz Ordaz, the system faced the occasional embarrassment – and its reaction was not very different from what it had been then. The PPS, for example, was widely believed to have won the vote in the elections for governor of Nayarit in 1975. According to one Rios Camarena, who claimed to have been directly involved in the rigging, the PRI 'won' only because of the fraudulent counting of false ballots. The PPS at the time protested strongly but privately at the rigging. Jorge

## The Echeverría Presidency

Cruikshank, leader of the PPS following the death of Lombardo, nevertheless accepted the official result and was given in return a seat in the Senate. The PPS split as a result of this transaction. Although this allegation of rigging was, not surprisingly, denied by the authorities, Cruikshank, in the words of *Latin America* 'made it clear that some pretty high level horse trading went on'.[71] The PPS was given control of a number of municipalities in Naryit as part of the compromise. Most observers now believe that Camarena was substantially telling the truth.

Party politics aside, there were two central areas of cooperation and conflict between Echeverría and the non-violent left during this period. One stemmed from the left's efforts to strengthen its position in the various 'mass organisations' and use them to radicalise conflict with conservative interests; the other stemmed from its attempts to expand the area of intellectual freedom and win the battle of ideas against the system. In both cases Echeverría's role was both ambivalent and controversial but his ultimate political objective was evident. He sought to use the left to attack his enemies on the right. On the other hand, he sought to curb the power of any genuinely independent left. He was, on the whole, unsuccessful in his efforts to curb intellectual independence on the left. His attempt (as it appears) to take over personally the corporate structures of Mexican politics led the country briefly, but interestingly, into uncharted waters.

It is the nature of 'mass organisations' in Mexican politics that their internal workings are Byzantine and it is seldom clear to outsiders whether they are more responsive to the wishes of those above or below. The interpretation that, in most cases, best fits the facts is that they respond mainly to direction and control but that their prestige owes everything to their ability to present the appearance of being genuinely 'of the people'. It may or may not be Mexico's good fortune to have three prominent organisations – the PRI itself, the Communist Party and the Catholic Church – all of which are highly skilled and experienced at 'front' politics. Certainly the Communist Party began the 1970s, as it had begun the 1960s, by organising a series of front organisations and supporting other left-wing organisations which it did not control directly. These latter included the 'democratic tendency' within the electricians' union.[72]

Echeverría began by encouraging the formation of 'independent' trade unions. These were not necessarily independent of the

Ministry of Labour (which had ample powers to put a stop to anything which it did not welcome), but they did break away from the CTM (and therefore the PRI). Conflicts within organised labour are not new in Mexico; Roxborough notes that 'insurgent movements have always been a feature of Mexican unionism'.[73] In this case, however, the new movement was a part of Echeverría's efforts to open safety valves on the left, but also reflected his distrust of Fidel Velázquez. Press attacks on Fidel Velázquez, and the surprising defeat of a number of labour leaders in the congressional elections of 1973, were also signs of official disfavour.[74]

The 'Democratic Tendency', within the electricians' union, was both independent of the CTM and militant. Velázquez responded to this apparent attempt to outflank him on the left by adopting a surprisingly militant position of his own. The result of this 'Dutch auction' was to worry employers and intensify private sector unease at government policy. Moreover, as the 1976 elections came closer, so the CTM's political leverage became increasingly important. By 1975 Echeverría was seeking to make peace with Velázquez, without totally abandoning his 'Democratic Tendency' allies. Fidel Velázquez was allowed the sought-after privilege of announcing the presidential candidacy of López Portillo in October 1975. Moreover, by a decree in March 1976, the extent of unionisation within Pemex was gretly extended.[75]

However peace was not achieved so easily. In 1976 a confrontation developed between Velázquez and Galvan (the leader of the 'Democratic Tendency') over control over the telephone workers. It seems that at first Echeverría adopted an attitude of semi-neutrality. However Velázquez accused 'elements within the PRI' of encouraging the dissidents and threatened his own general strike. When Galvan refused to back down, he met the combined opposition of Velázquez and the government and emerged a bad loser.[76] After 1976, the independent unions remained in place but there was no further challenge to Velázquez' predominant position as a leader of Mexican labour.

Echeverría's policy toward organised labour, therefore, was an at best partially-successful attempt to divide and rule. What is rather surprising in his approach is that the CTM posed no real threat to the Mexican presidency. It is perhaps true that Velázquez (who had supported the Tlatelolco massacre and been on good terms generally with Díaz Ordaz) was anathema to the young left-wingers whom Echeverría brought in as advisers, and that his continued prominence took away something from Echeverría's credibility as a radical reformer.

Another hypothesis is simply that Echeverría distrusted all independent sources of power. This theory is strengthened when one considers the relationship between Echeverría and the media. Echeverría publicly welcomed independent left-wing journalism but privately found it hard to take. An example can be found in August 1972 when the private sector announced a withdrawal of advertising from *Excelsior* in protest against its outspoken left-wing editorial policy. Juan Sánchez Navarro and some other business leaders complained to Echeverría about the line taken in *Excelsior*: Echeverría suggested that business try to pressure *Excelsior* directly rather than protest to government.[77] Echeverría then told Scherer that *Excelsior* should carefully because some business interests were threatening to mount a boycott against the newspaper. When they did so, the government waited some months before one minister denounced the boycott and called for it to be lifted; he stated that if the boycott was not broken the government would withdraw its own advertising from the pro-business Televisa company. This minister later recorded that he found strong opposition from within the cabinet to his proposed course of action.[78] However his intervention appeared effective and ended the dispute with all sides claiming victory.

Scherer's own account of this incident and strong suspicion of Echeverría gains credibility from the events at *Excelsior* in July 1976. The events themselves are complex but what they amounted to was that Echeverría either 'orchestrated' [79], or at any rate did nothing to prevent, a kind of mutiny at the newspaper which led to the expulsion of Julio Scherer's editorial team and the loss of its serious and independent evaluations of contemporary issues. Most observers, including this one, have found entirely unconvincing Echeverría's claim [80] that the events had nothing at all to do with him. The alternative suggestion is that Echeverría hoped to gain control of *Excelsior* in order to retain some influence over the incoming administration.

A final issue which brough Echeverría into complex interaction with the left and the Mexican private sector concerned agrarian reform. In order to discuss this issue, it is first necessary to provide a little background.

There are, broadly speaking, two diametrically opposed views about Mexican agriculture. According to one, which Echeverría held and can be described as radical, the promises of land redistribution entrenched in the Constitution and the actual progress of land reform were key factors in Mexico's political stability and economic progress. It is the case that peasant and *ejido* agriculture has often succeeded;[81] it is also undeniable that the PRI has drawn most of its political strength from the rural areas. The left wing of the PRI and many writers on 'the politics of modernisation' share the view that a critical factor in the ability of any system to remain stable during a process of rapid urbanisation and industrialisation is its ability to control the countryside politically.[82] In Mexico the efficient political machinery of the PRI, the legacy of Cardenista land reform and the fact (at least until the mid-1960s) of rapidly-rising agricultural production together offered an essentially happy prospect to all Mexican presidents up to, and to some extent including, Díaz Ordaz. However the increasing rural population, the growing difficulty of extending irrigation except at disproportionate cost, and the increasing power of conservative rural interests (including the interests of transnationals) appeared to threaten this progress. In order to revitalise the revolution, what was needed, or so the radicals believed, was a new assault on rural poverty and inequality.

The opposing view was that of Mexico's conservatives. They would have agreed that during the 1940–70 period a blind eye was generally turned to the technical illegalities perpetrated by a class of relatively efficient, capital-intensive farmers who found their way around government legislation designed to limit the extent of landholdings. The conservatives believed, however, that this growing rural differentiation was a good thing. Private investment, growing capital intensity and the use of more sophisticated chemicals offered better opportunities for increasing productivity than did a naive policy of land redistribution to small peasants or collective farmers.

Needless to say there were political as well as technical issues involved here. Because landowners could rely neither on the letter of the law nor upon any institutional input into the policymaking process, they tended to resort to various forms of corruption and illegality in order to protect their interests; the nature of Mexican politics, moreover, ensured that landowners with political connections could often get away with killing their opponents or those whom they found threatening. As a result there was in many parts of the Mexican countryside an extremely brutal contrast between the conditions which were formally said to exist and those which actually did exist. The result – additional to the tensions that land reform questions are liable to create in any country in which population is rapidly increasing – was to create additional insecurity. The potential for social conflict was extreme.

The PRI's peasant wing, the CNC, had a well-justified reputation for inactivity. This created a political space for the left which operated through broad-front organisations such as the UGOCM. When the government in Mexico City was clearly hostile to peasant radicalism, it could impose quiescence at the price of varying degrees of repression. However when the government in Mexico City was sympathetic, or at any rate unwilling to repress, there would be peasant invasions in various disputed localities.[83] Unfortunately as the population–land ratio worsened, the possibilities of a positive-sum outcome to these various conflicts declined.

Echeverría proved particularly responsive to peasant demands, partly as insurance against the threat from guerrillas and partly to try to increase the popularity of the government. An early indication was the appointment of Gómez Villaneuva, formerly head of the CNC, to be secretary of the Agrarian Reform ministry. Gómez Villanueva became a senior member of the cabinet and was spoken of in 1975 as a possible presidential successor. There were, in fact, a series of land invasions throughout the Echeverría presidency by peasants who believed the official response would be not entirely hostile. However what put the land issue on the national political agenda were the substantial land invasions in the northern states of Sonora and Sinaloa. In these cases peasants who had applied to be given land legally had become tired of waiting and started to take over the disputed land directly. It has been suggested [84] that Echeverría encouraged some of these invasions although there is no doubt that the left-wing UGOCM was also involved.[85]

The northern state of Sinaloa was an important site of these invasions. They seem to have begun in January 1975 and to have intensified in October 1975 following an announcement by Gómez Villanueva in September that the government was looking at all landholdings in the area and would expropriate those which did not correspond to the law. The government continued to be sympathetic to the peasants, refusing to consult representatives of the private sector and expropriating private land. A strike announced by local growers and supported by employers in other sectors did not change the situation.

In Sonora on 20 October 1975, a group of peasants (led by the local schoolteacher) also launched a major land invasion.[86] Rather than seeking to negotiate, the governor sent in police to remove the invaders; there were a number of violent deaths during the evictions. After a few crisis meetings, Echeverría removed the state governor (who had earlier been considered a particular loyalist of his) and replaced him with a veteran left-wing member of the PRI.

Under these circumstances land invasions in Sonora continued, and the government granted land titles to many of the invaders. Sonoran landowners also struck ineffectively against the expropriations. In April 1976 a new round of land invasions began. This time, however, Echeverría declared his firm opposition and the attempts failed. Tension continued to rise throughout 1976 as the agrarian reform ministry tried to head off actual or threatened invasions by decreeing fresh land reform and the expropriation of medium-sized holdings. At the very end of his term of office, Echeverría decreed a major expropriation and redistribution in Sonora while a series of land invasions also occurred almost simultaneously in Sinaloa and Durango.

## ECHEVERRÍA AND MEXICAN POLITICS

The Echeverría presidency yields a number of indications as to where the power lay in Mexico during the early 1970s. Least powerful of all the organised interests lay in the countryside. It was therefore possible for Echeverría and Gómez Villanueva to exercise effective leadership over peasant movements.[87] The alliance of peasant mobilisation and presidential support was far too strong for local landowners, even when these were able to win over the local governor; nor could the independent left really challenge the CNC, though it could hope to exercise a limited influence on the margin. The impression that the presidency was strong enough to control agrarian politics was verified further when López Portillo quietly and without serious difficulty ended the land reforms. But for what purpose could this control be exercised? The PRI was, and remains, overwhelmingly strong in rural areas. This matters electorally, although the increasing urbanisation of Mexico has greatly reduced the relative importance of the PRI's rural strongholds. However the system's ability to mobilise peasants, and expropriate and defeat a few landlords, fell far short of establishing countervailing societal power in the face of capital flight and economic crisis. If such was already true in 1940,[88] it was even more obviously the case in 1976. Echeverría in some sense 'won' his agrarian battles, but the victories were empty ones.

Echeverría's relations with the trade unions were more complex. The CTM was loyal, but not easily subjected to presidential domination. Fidel Velázquez was in the position of an old butler formally subordinated to a young and reforming master; while never challenging overtly, he was able to frustrate most of Echeverría's attempts to overturn existing structures. Moreover Echeverría had only six years to push for change; Velázquez had far more time to frustrate changes. What Echeverría did do was to create a new left-wing alternative to the CTM, but this was less subject to presidential control than he had hoped. Moreover conflict between the CTM and the 'Democratic Tendency' was damaging to the government's broader objectives, and Echeverría was finally forced to take the side of the CTM against his own creation. The conclusion might be that Mexico's urban corporate structures (principally the CTM and the Congreso de Trabajo) will support the presidency, but not as an individual president may wish.

With the intellectuals and universities Echeverría's relationship was also difficult. Although more tolerant than Díaz Ordaz on certain specific occasions,[89] his overall objective was co-optation and control – a policy sweetened by generous provision of symbolic resources and financial rewards. Given the dangers posed by left-wing insurgency at that time, Echeverría's policies were surely based on a plausible reading of what the system required at that time. Echeverría certainly did succeed in attracting more intellectual support than had Díaz Ordaz – not that this would have been difficult. However the emergence of some genuinely independent left-wing parties and also the conflict over *Excelsior* shows that not everybody on the left was willing to play in an orchestra conducted exclusively by Echeverría. The ghost of Tlatelolco was not exorcised so easily.

It was, however, Echeverría's relationship with the private sector which showed so clearly the limits of presidential power. Above all, there was the devaluation in 1976, which broke twenty-two years of parity with the dollar, and the combination of inflation and impending recession which suggested that a difficult time lay ahead for López Portillo. If it had not been for oil, and the fact that López Portillo and the private sector were in quiet contact during the later part of 1976, the situation might have been even more difficult. In the eyes of sympathetic critics, Echeverría challenged the private sector and lost.[90]

Left-wing observers at the time tended to see the Echeverría presidency as marking a conflict between reformists within the system and a conservative plutocracy; the outcome, in this view, showed that Mexico's dominant classes had become stronger than the country's revolutionary tradition. There is something to be said for this perspective. However there is an alternative view which is that the victory of the private sector – to the extent that it was a victory – was also a victory for Mexican pluralism. As noted at the beginning of this chaper, Echeverría had far more in common with Díaz Ordaz than either man would wish to admit. Both were extreme presidentialists with what might be called policemen's visions of national unity. Whereas Díaz Ordaz identified the main threat to political stability as coming from student radicals, Echeverría felt himself threatened by 'imperialism and the local bourgeoisie'.[91] Neither of these was necessarily a threat to Mexican stability, but both were threats to extreme presidentialism and both were resistant to antagonistic forms of social control.

Certainly there was something in the psychology of the two men that would help explain their attitude toward any kind of challenge or opposition. They were both power-maximisers in a way in which their immediate predecessors were not. Ruiz Cortines was old and had learned the value of restraint. López Mateos was ill. Alemán, it seems clear, was indeed an aggressive power-maximiser who plunged the system into a kind of crisis during 1951 and 1952.

It is, however, not just a matter of personalities. One must also take into account changes in the nature of Mexican political society. Most presidents would choose to be 'national unity' figures if they could; neither Díaz Ordaz nor Echeverría wanted to court independent opposition from civil society. They were both political insiders at the time of their accession to the presidency. Both staged confrontations because they saw danger to the system in what they confronted – 'subversives' in the one case; 'the oligarchy linked to imperialism' in the other. The perceptions were distorted but the phenomena they saw were not imaginary; the emergence of a radical middle class and an independently-powerful business sector are normal occurrences in any country at a certain stage of socio-economic development. It is also normal that a more traditional political system will find them hard to deal with.

The argument here, then, is that both Díaz Ordaz and Echeverría tried to rule Mexico in the 'old' way but found they could not; this realisation unbalanced them and made them desperate. As the differences within Mexican society widened, so a non-institutionalised conciliation from above became impossible. Echeverría did not want to institutionalise an independent left-wing politics – any more than Díaz Ordaz wanted to recognise an independent right. He wanted instead to defeat left-wing insurgency without unnecessary bloodshed (an objective with which many would sympathise) and (more controversially) to force business to terms with the existing political and presidential system.[92] He did have the means of controlling the right politically, but his efforts to develop the state as an instrument of economic control failed for lack of resources. Crucially the Mexican state did not have the economic punch it would have needed if Echeverría's attack on the bourgeoisie was to have had a chance of success. Yet Echeverría did not have an alternative policy. For all his political experience and ability to command the most minute detail, Echeverría misjudged his own country. It was no longer one in which independent interest groups would unquestioningly accept a presidential *fiat*.

# 4 López Portillo: From Boom to Bust

The López Portillo presidency reads like a story by Robert Louis Stevenson. López Portillo I ('Dr Jekyll') was an essentially conciliatory figure, concerned to repair fences with the private sector and other social groups after the damage done during 1976. This task accomplished, his main concern was with national unity which he understood in a far less narrow way than either of his predecessors. López Portillo II ('Mr Hyde') was a driven, almost maniacal, president who sought to make history; despite his grandstanding foreign policy, his main contribution to this was the bank nationalisation of 1 September 1982. López Portillo I was in evidence for most of the presidential term; López Portillo II emerged only fitfully during the second half of the *sexenio*. Nevertheless López Portillo II was remembered far more vividly and to far greater effect than his blander *alter ego*. He was largely in control as the *sexenio* ended.

Why should things have ended so dramatically? One explanation is that López Portillo was simply unsuited to the job and should never have been made president. Other observers put the blame on bad economic policies; López Portillo vacillated between a relatively orthodox and a radical-nationalist approach to policy, and thus had no chance of succeeding with either. It was, in this view, the effect of economic failure which turned Dr Jekyll into Mr Hyde. Certainly economic observers have had little difficulty pointing out the many mistakes that were made during 1976–82 and also their high cost.[1]

These assertions are (for the most part) undoubtedly true. However they are in some respects insufficient. For this analysis at any rate, economic statistics will be considered to belong more to the field of description than explanation. Explanation lies in knowing why López Portillo thought as he did, why he was advised as he was, and why so few people understood that something very serious was threatening until extremely late in the day; it is also worth asking why the bank nationalisation (of 1 September 1982) should have proved so popular.[2] It is suggested here that López Portillo was never, in any serious sense, a technocrat. He did not understand economics and his inability to comprehend what was happening explains much of his behaviour during the last few months in office.

## PERSONALITY AND CABINET

The word most used to describe López Portillo is 'frivolous'; the term is hard to define but encompasses the idea of a man who did not take his job seriously enough and could not bring himself to make hard decisions. 'He discussed the physical charms of his mistress at Cabinet meetings' was the dismissive comment of one well-placed observer. There was nepotism, far more corruption than is usual in Mexico and at the end a disturbing degree of incompetence. This perception owes something to hindsight; if López Portillo's term of office had ended in December 1980, or even 1981, things would have looked very different. López Portillo might then have been remembered for his statesmanship (the 1977 political reform), his activist foreign policy (particularly during the Nicaraguan revolution) and his good luck in presiding over the oil boom.

Even so the accusation of frivolity is well-founded. One source described López Portillo as 'a hedonist. Having to his own surprise reached the presidency, he reacted as if he had won first prize in the lottery'. Quite apart from anything else, he showed the most extraordinary lack of discretion in his personal affairs. By his own later admissions, he borrowed large amounts of money from a member of his cabinet and accepted a house as a gift from the notoriously-corrupt oilworkers' leader; this is almost certainly only a small part of a large story. López Portillo was surely not the first president of Mexico to have accepted gifts (or, in plainer language, bribes); nor was he the first to have taken a mistress or sought to promote the careers of members of his family. Where he was indeed unusual was that he made little attempt to conceal these things; he sometimes even gloated over them. It is nevertheless true that these private vices were only tangentially connected to his public failures, and they came to seem important precisely because of those failures. People are often willing to overlook a degree of private vice in a political leader who proves at least moderately successful in his public role. A failed political leader with a dissolute private life is, however, likely to maximise his own unpopularity. After he left office, López Portillo faced a period of public humiliation.

However things began very much better. López Portillo's background was unexceptionable. Like Echeverría he was identified with the Federal District rather than provincial Mexico. He had studied abroad, but in Chile rather than the United States; he received degrees from the University of Santiago in 1945 and from UNAM in 1946, both in law. López Portillo spent a number of years as an academic before joining the government in 1959. He did work in a number of economics-related ministries but (a fact rarely mentioned at the time) mainly as a lawyer. He rose in these positions until being taken on as a sub-secretary of the presidency in 1968–70; this is a senior political position and suggests that López Portillo was never just the creature of Echeverría. López Portillo's career then seemed vulnerable when he appeared to identify with Manatou rather than Echeverría in 1969. However Echeverría brought him into the cabinet as Treasury Secretary in 1973 (in which role he cannot be said to have excelled) before 'unveiling' him in 1975. It does say something about the *camarilla* system of Mexican bureaucracy that a man could rise high through economic organisations and acquire a reputation as a technocrat without having to prove himself in any very serious way.

López Portillo seems to have been *presidenciable* first and foremost because in his youth he had been a close personal friend of Echeverría; some authors have argued that he was chosen by Echeverría so that the latter could hope to maintain a degree of influence after 1976.[4] However while Echeverría obviously sought to choose a man who would be loyal to his own principles, there was very little evidence at the time that people thought López Portillo unfit to be president. At the time the comment was that, as the first president since 1958 not to come from *Gobernación*, he had not had the opportunity of putting together a personal team. Very few people remarked that his credentials as a technocrat were also somewhat suspect in that he had little or no formal training in economics or understanding of business; Echeverría, no economist himself, would surely neither have known nor cared about this.

López Portillo's first cabinet was quite revealing of the nature of the man himself and of his presidency. To begin with, there was the nepotism. One of his sisters took a senior position in the interior ministry (as director general of radio, television and cinema); he took another sub-secretary as his mistress; his eldest son, a nephew and two cousins were also given senior appointments in the government. His son Jose Ramón was admittedly a man of some ability (not helped by his father's description of him as 'the pride of my nepotism') but it was obvious that these appointments lacked discretion. Only a very arrogant man would have made them. Later on his mistress would become minister of tourism. His sister Margarita was evidently unsuitable for the position to which she was appointed and proved especially damaging both to the film industry and to the government's credibility.[5] According to Krause, moreover, López Portillo was only dissuaded by Reyes Heroles from appointing a close family member as minister of education.[6]

There were also some very independent-minded people in senior positions. These included Reyes Heroles who was given *Gobernación* and Díaz Serrano who was made director of Pemex. These were both outstanding although controversial figures. Díaz Serrano came from the private sector and quickly became identified with a market-orientated 'get rich quick' mentality which many Mexicans found distasteful. Under Díaz Serrano Pemex was more dynamically run, but also more corrupt, than it ever had been.

A great deal could be written about Reyes Heroles,[7] who was an intellectual and a liberal but also a political infighter with a taste for power. Because of his Spanish parentage, he was not *presidenciable*; for him, therefore, ministerial office was an end in itself and this gave him a freedom of action which other ministers did not have. He was always far more than just another creature of the president; as head of the PRI he had proved too independent for the liking of Echeverría and, in *Gobernación*, would eventually have the same effect on López Portillo. Meanwhile a part of his remit was to keep a check on any attempt by Echeverría to retain influence.

Other political appointments reflected the fact that López Portillo came into the presidency with only a limited degree of political experience. He did not, therefore, have a team as such with which to fill top political positions. In this respect, his first selection involved an uneasy mix of people including those who had worked in senior positions under Echeverría (Reyes Heroles, Sansores Pérez, Muñoz Ledo), those who had worked with Díaz Ordaz or were otherwise closely associated with him (Manatou,

García Paniagua), and the Foreign Minister Santiago Roel who was directly associated with the Monterrey group.[8] López Portillo's strongest field was believed to be economics. Here his first serious new departure was the creation of the planning ministry. Its original intention (apart from planning) was to rationalise and centralise the administration of the greatly-expanded public enterprise sector of the economy. According to one contemporary article 'private enterprise should be overjoyed at the creation of the SPP'.[9] because it was believed to be a mechanism that would keep the public sector as a whole under some kind of control. Later critics have argued, however, that the concept was seriously flawed because it separated those who were responsible for macroeconomic management from those responsible for controlling and budgeting the public sector. There would be a bias toward restrictiveness in one ministry, a bias toward expansion in the other, and the certainty of conflict between the two.

It is certainly true that bureaucratic rivalries between economic policymakers do not occur only in Mexico. However the creation of rival economy ministers had the effect of increasing presidential involvement in economic affairs; gone were the days when economic policy was organised in the finance ministry, and political affairs resolved in *Gobernación* while the president visited his mistress or retired early to bed. The tendency toward bureaucratic rivalry and policymaking insecurity was further increased by the fact that López Portillo tended to promote and listen to policymakers of very different views; he seemed to have difficulty making up his mind between them or pursuing any coherent strategy for any length of time. Thus his original economics appointments appear to have reflected a set of compromises rather than any coherent strategy. Carlo Tello (planning) and Oteyza (national patrimony) were identified with the 'structuralist' left while Moctezuma Cid (treasury) and Solana (commerce) were more orthodox economists. Before the López Portillo administration had completed a year, a clash between Tello and Moctezuma led to the resignation of the former and the dismissal of the latter. This was only a hint of what was to come.

It is a feature of the López Portillo administration that differences of opinion were allowed, indeed encouraged, within the government. The president often tried to balance them but at the price of compromise and indecision.[10] This is the style of a man who sought the virtues of consensus over those of consistent policymaking.

Nevertheless consensus-seeking itself marked a clear break between López Portillo's political style and that of Echeverría. As early as 10 December 1976, the government signed an agreement with 140 large companies who agreed to co-ordinate their investment intentions with state policy; this must surely have followed from discussions held, or contacts made, prior to López Portillo assuming the presidency on 1 December. López Portillo came under pressure from the old *Díaz Ordazistas* to distance himself from his predecessor; at the inaugural address Díaz Ordaz himself and Miguel Alemán conspicuously failed to applaud at the mention of Echeverría's name. (Since Alemán's term of office featured a devaluation, some massive corruption and an apparent attempt by Alemán to continue in power beyond his constitutional term, one might have felt that Alemán should have considered Echeverría more sympathetically.) In any case the arrest of Felix Barra, Echeverría's last minister of agriculture, on corruption charges in June 1977 was a sop to the *Alemanista* Right. Echeverría, meanwhile, was made Mexico's 'roving ambassador' to the Third World. The removal of Muñoz Ledo from the education ministry in November 1977 completed the process of easing out figures close to Echeverría whom the private sector and perhaps the President himself considered to be threatening.

The arrest of Felix Barra and a few others marked the first gaolings of senior figures on corruption charges for very many years. It subsequently became something of a tradition that the incoming president ordered the arrest of a few scandalous figures; this had the advantage of establishing the new president's authority and distancing him from the previous regime. However the arrests that took place in 1983 and 1989 did have a genuine connection with corruption; it is hard to attribute the same motive to López Portillo. The López Portillo government that in 1977 ordered the arrest of Felix Barra in the same year appointed Arturo Durazo as head of the police in the Federal District. This was after López Portillo had received a quiet warning from the United States government that Durazo had previously been involved in criminal offences.[11] As reported in *Latin America* however Durazo 'publicly promised to clean up corruption in the capital including the well-established *mordida* to traffic police for driving offences'.[12] Not many people were fooled.

## POLITICAL REFORM

López Portillo was concerned from the beginning of his presidency until near the end to achieve a rapport with the main interests within Mexico – the private sector, the intellectual left and the Church. To some extent, therefore, it can be claimed that he was an institutionaliser of power rather than just another autocratic president. This is certainly the strongest case that can be made on his behalf though the strategy was feasible only while the economy was strong.

There was an immediate problem which the political reform was designed to resolve. President López Portillo's election in 1976 was electorally opposed by the writing-in of the communist Valentín Campa; no recognised opponent appeared on the ballot paper. This state of affairs caused the authorities some concern; the PAN was undergoing internal problems and there was no 'tame' opponent on the left who could be relied upon to play the part of controlled opposition. Yet a Presidential election could only be a credible exercise if there was an opponent. This form of credibility was perhaps not of the very highest importance, but the costs to the system of a moderate political liberalisation did not seem excessive. Almost immediately after his inauguration, López Portillo began a dialogue with the left; what he had to offer was the early registration of the Mexican Communist Party. This was an offer which the communists themselves were keen to accept.

The reform of 1977 had two major features. The first was that it made it easier for opposition parties to obtain registration. Registration was not the same as legalisation (non-registered parties were not exactly illegal) but it conferred certain legal privileges including the right to present candidates for election and to enjoy the proportional representation provisions of the constitution. This opened the way for some of the parties of the left to enter the political process formally; the Mexican Communist Party soon secured recognition, as did some other Marxist parties. The second feature of the reform was that it increased the 'proportional representation' element of the Chamber of Deputies: of 400 seats, one hundred would be guaranteed to minority parties in proportion to their percentage of the vote.

For a time the results were not especially dramatic. A number of left-wing parties did achieve registration; seven new parties (six of them left-wing) contested the 1979 congressional elections. However rather to the surprise of observers the strongest opposition party in these elections was the re-constituted PAN. It was credited with 10.78 per cent of the popular vote, as against 4.99 per cent won by the Mexican Communist Party. Even so the combined left-wing parties took nearly 15 per cent of the vote. The 25 per cent opposition vote was enough to challenge the PRI's electoral monopoly although not its majority. Moreover the left found itself, for the first time for many years, in a position to provide serious independent criticism of the government; there was also some link between the left of the PRI and the formal left-wing opposition which could echo the arguments of the former without the constraints imposed by loyalty.[13] The fact of a stronger official opposition influenced in a number of different ways, the manner in which politics was conducted. This point will be considered in more detail later.

In the short-run the regime's intention, which was successful, (perhaps in the long-run beyond expectations) was to create the safety-valve on the left that had previously been lacking. Dissent was not intended to be a threat to the system, but rather a recognised social role and a necessary part of the mechanism for producing consensus. For the first time the system recognised formally that opposition was not subversion; indeed Reyes Heroles went so far as to say that a vote for the oppositon was a vote to strengthen the system. Meanwhile the reform of the PRI became far less of an issue. It is surely not coincidence that left-wing insurgency ended sometime in the late 1970s and has not reappeared.

Another important change came with the increased activity of the dissident press. Much has been written about the press in Mexico.[14] Government control over much of the press has been a fact for many years; during the Díaz Ordaz years an organised system of government payoffs to particular journalists (the *embute*) came into effect. Martínez Domínguez later stated that he had personally organised the rigging of the journalists ballot at *Excelsior* in August 1968 to make Julio Scherer the editor.[15] Echeverría, as we have seen, publicly welcomed the writings of the intellectual left in *Excelsior* but privately sought to undermine them. The scandal following the coup at *Excelsior* in 1976 (which became an international *cause célèbre*) made it more difficult for the government to control the press.

There was apparently a possibility that Scherer and his group of journalists would be invited to return to *Excelsior* in 1977, but for complicated reasons this did not happen. Scherer instead began producing a weekly, *Proceso*, which is now one of the most informative periodicals available. In the same year, a group of liberal intellectuals, around Octavio Paz and Enrique Krause, began to produce *Vuelta* and a more left-wing group began *Nexos*. In 1978 *Uno más Uno* started production. These were by no means mass publications. They did, however, have an influence beyond their circulation because of their official and political readership. Certainly López Portillo, who was in general a comparatively tolerant president, was on one occasion sufficiently annoyed by *Proceso* to withdraw government advertising from the journal. As he put it,

> Does a profit-making company, professionally organised, have the right to receive publicity from the state while opposing it systematically? This, gentlemen, is a perverse relationship, a morbid relationship, a sado-masochistic relationship which is close to many perversions which I shall not mention here out of respect for my audience. I pay you so that you beat me![16]

Never was one issue more clearly put. López Portillo, like his two predecessors and also like Louis XIV, really did think that the state was himself.

Nevertheless despite repeated conflicts with authority, the press and the opposition used their new-found freedom to expand the frontiers of political debate. An interesting example occurred in 1981 when *Proceso* published a document leaked from the Planning Ministry on the then very sensitive subject of Pemex. The issues involved will be discussed in more detail below. It is perhaps not very surprising that the Presidential press spokesman claimed that *Proceso* was wrong, in principle, to publish a confidential document in this way. Mrs Thatcher would have agreed with him. What is noteworthy is that at least one senior Mexican political figure (who leaked the document) sought to involve the press in intra-bureaucratic disputes.

A further step in the broadening of Mexican politics came with the papal visit to Mexico in January 1979. As we have seen, anti-clericalism ceased to be a serious factor in Mexican politics from around 1960; Díaz Ordaz moved slowly towards better official relations, but only in a very limited and cautious manner. [17] Echeverría went some way further: it was during his *sexenio* that the possibility of a papal visit to Mexico was first seriously discussed, and López Portillo continued with this policy of *rapprochement*. Most Mexicans are at least nominally Catholic[18] and in general profess themselves satisfied with the Church. Only a few are political Catholics in any strong sense, and there was little real tension in the post-war accommodation between Church and state. However by the late 1960s, 'radical' Catholicism began to have its impact in Mexico; the famous conference of bishops at Medellin took place in 1968; liberation theology formally came into existence in 1971.

In Mexico, Catholic radicals began forming organised groups such as 'Christians for Socialism' and some of them even participated in armed insurgency. The split between the social Catholic wing of the PAN and the more conservative northern business wing led to the failure of the PAN to put up a candidate in 1976. Meanwhile parties on the left began to explore the possibility of some kind of alliance with the left wing of the Church. The government was still continuing to seek further improvements in its own relationship with the Church. In 1976 the Church found itself in the position, at once happy and difficult, of having each of its wings courted by a different political interest. In 1977 it was the Mexican Communist Party which made the formal proposal that the constitution be amended to allow priests to become members of a political party.

Under these circumstances the papal visit of January 1979 was advantageous both to the Church hierarchy and the Mexican government.[19] The left failed to agree on its attitude; the Communist Party supported the visit while the PPS and some of the PRI opposed it. The right, however, was delighted; conservatives in the Mexican hierarchy hoped that the visit would enable the Pope to condemn completely the left wing of the Church. In fact he duly condemned liberation theology although he did not go as far as conservative Mexican Catholics had hoped. What his visit did do was to move the Mexican Church even further toward the mainstream of Mexican politics.

THE ELECTORAL DIMENSION

López Portillo made a number of changes to his cabinet in the first half of 1979. The removal of Sansores Pérez from the chairmanship of the PRI in January did not seem to be a matter of particular importance. Sansores Pérez was a political figure of the old school – a former governor of Campeche – who was certainly no innovator; when Sansores Pérez announced that, as part of the political reform, he would introduce 'transparent domocracy' into the PRI it was Fidel Velázquez who retorted that democracy in Sansores' PRI was indeed transparent – so much so that nobody could see it.

A more serious set of changes occurred in late May when Reyes Heroles, Santiago Roel (the foreign minister) and Ricardo García (the planning minister) left the government, to be replaced by Olivares Santana, Jorge Castañeda and Miguel de la Madrid. De la Madrid was the third planning minister in as many years (which suggests a certain lack of planning) while Jorge Castañeda was a far more 'Third-Worldist' figure than his predecessor. The most significant change, from a political standpoint, was in *Gobernación*; John Bailey interprets the removal of Reyes Heroles as implying 'a retreat from the political reform and the assertion of the President in political matters'.[20] It was surely a sign of growing presidential self-confidence. This leaves open the question of how far the actual character of the earlier political reform was something that López Portillo really wanted, and how far it was merely something that he was willing to tolerate.

Certainly the system was not seriously unhappy with the results of the 1979 congressional elections; the official result (which seems to have been reasonably genuine) gave the PRI and its allies nearly a three-to-one majority over the combined opposition. It was always the objective of the system to use its various political reforms to encourage pluralism within the opposition (though not necessarily pluralism within the system). The PRI was prepared to give up space to a multiplicity of small parties; this would not threaten its control over the major elected offices because these were filled on a 'first past the post' basis. The PRI would under these circumstances use party politics as a limited safety valve with the minimum threat to its own power.

The calculations were not upset at the national level until the Cuautéhmoc Cárdenas candidacy in 1988. At a local level, however, tensions began to rise almost immediately. Local grievances and problems could always generate, or threaten to generate, opposition victories in a way which would frustrate local PRI power arrangements. Some of these problems can be seen from two examples. In the case of Tamaulipas the result was, in a sense, paradoxical. Tamaulipas is perhaps the only state of Mexico in which the PARM has a base. The PARM was created during the presidency of Ruiz Cortines for a group of ageing and displaced revolutionary generals. Very few people voted for it, but the regime was anxious to keep it formally in existence; in Lajous' words, PARM was 'the putative son of *Gobernación*'.[21]

In Tamaulipas, however, the PARM attracted some serious candidates for local office; these were PRIistas who were dissatisfied with the candidates chosen by the official party and defected. *Gobernación* (under Reyes Heroles) sometimes approved these defections, which were often more apparent than real.[22] The PARM thus became the focal point of opposition to the PRI; in 1977 it won the town of Nuevo Laredo and in 1980 the town of Matamoros; it was beginning to look as though the PARM might threaten the PRI's control of the governorship.[23] However in the national elections of 1982 the PARM failed to reach 2.5 per cent of the vote and therefore had its registration cancelled, putting an end to its local challenge. A main reason for this failure was that opposition votes moved to the PSUM and other parties on the left. This is one clear example, at least, of the way in which the system was happy to use the existence of multiple opposition parties as a means of using its authority to 'divide and rule'. However it also gave the PARM a clear motive for seeking a more independent identiy.

in 1981 the left for the first time won control of a significant municipality. We have already seen that there was considerable left-wing mobilisation in Oaxaca during the early 1970s which was then repressed during the governorship of Zárate. A further political crisis broke out in 1977 following some student disturbances.[24] At this time the education ministry in Mexico City (under Muñoz Ledo) took a very different position to that of governor Zárate; Education Minister Muñoz Ledo was willing to accept a democratic vote of the students to choose between two different candidates for rector of the university while Zárate wished to impose the more conservative man. During the conflict a demonstration was fired on by the state authorities and a number of people died. As often happens in Mexico, high-profile killing of this kind, in addition to inflaming further an already tense situation, proved unacceptable to the president and *Gobernación*;

after further demonstrations and strikes (including an employer's lock-out), Zárate was dismissed from office a few days later. The new governor, despite his previous involvement in counter-insurgency, proved more moderate than Zárate. The more relaxed local climate and the political reform at the centre of the system provided an opportunity for the electoral opposition. The Mexican Communist Party combined with other left-wing organisations in a broad front to contest the 1980 elections in the municipality of Juchitán. These were won by the PRI but annulled by the authorities on the grounds of fraud – the annulment followed considerable national publicity given to the fraud allegations. New elections were held in 1981 and COCEI was declared the winner.

COCEI's victory, like those of PARM candidates in Tamaulipas, involved a combination of local and national factors. Locally the conflict between *caciques* and moderates had split the PRI; the PRI candidate was a moderate imposed by the pro-reform governor and resented by the local bosses. The PRI was thus weakened on both counts: hard-liners were reluctant to support the official candidate while the unpopularity of these hard lines still motivated many people to vote for the opposition.

The PRI authorities could find no effective way of responding to the COCEI victory in the short run. Local figures generally believed that Juchitán was being used by the Mexico City authorities as a kind of experiment. COCEI however refused to be co-opted and used its period in office to try to achieve radical social reform within the locality; the (short-term) effect of left-wingers in office was more mobilisation rather than, as Reyes Heroles had hoped, less. It was left to the de la Madrid government to decide how this challenge should be met.

## CAPITAL, LABOUR AND THE STATE

López Portillo also worked hard to win back the confidence of the business community, which Echeverría had alienated so comprehensively. During 1977 and 1978 a number of conflicts within the business sector were resolved mainly to the advantage of those who advocated accommodation with, or support for, the government. The 'radicals', who wanted business to follow up its opposition to Echeverría by adopting a more general opposition stance, lost ground to the accommodationists. López Portillo's courtship of the private sector enjoyed increasing success.[25] It obviously helped that a public sector fortified by oil income was in a happy position when it came to awarding contracts.

Another reason for the changing attitude of the business community was the López Portillo administration's attitude toward labour. In 1976 very real fears were expressed that the inflation and devaluation might spark off a wage-price spiral which would complicate policymaking under López Portillo. The incoming government successfully averted this danger (if it ever was a danger[26]) by supporting the CTM hierarchy and repressing illegal strikes mounted by independent left-led unions.[27] An early test of the government was resolved in July 1977 when a strike among the workers at UNAM, supported by the Communist Party, was suppressed by police without serious violence.[28] Existing independent unions were tolerated, but efforts to create new ones were discouraged. Meanwhile the advantages offered by the political reform discouraged the communists and other left-wing parties from pursuing their opposition to government labour policies. Conditions of at least semi-recession held back labour militancy during 1977 and 1978 although the number of strikes increased considerably after 1979. By 1979, however, the government felt sufficiently content with its oil income to respond to this increase in militancy by allowing real wage increases which were slightly above the rate of inflation.

One important issue decided (as it turned out temporarily) during the López Portillo *sexenio*, in a way which shows how his attitude of tolerance could become indecisiveness, was the question of Mexico's entry into GATT. Rather than making a firm decision as to whether or not to enter the agreement, he encouraged a debate on the subject within the government and the private sector. It is generally accepted that he himself supported the idea of GATT membership[29] but allowed the strongly-voiced opposition from supporters of protection to win the day. On 18 March 1980 he announced that Mexico would not enter GATT.

By late 1980 and early 1981 leading business spokesmen were almost 'euphoric'[30] in their support for López Portillo. They were even happier when, in November 1981, the government agreed to bail out the business group ALFA after some serious errors had led it into insolvency.[31] It appears, however, that López Portillo may have seen business support as an effective substitute for sound economic policy; in this respect he proved to be wrong.

Although the López Portillo government appeared until near the end to be situated some way to the right of its predecessor, it should not be forgotten that the left found some of his policies highly acceptable. This helps explain why an 'officialist' pro-CTM policy met with relative success. There is no doubt that the Mexican Communist Party was supportive and appreciative of López Portillo's policies toward Central America and his evident dislike of the US government. Moreover the continuing expansion of the state apparatus during the oil boom period, as earlier under Echeverría, helped left-wingers establish themselves within the public sector. There was also the legalisation of the Communist Party and other small parties of the left, and a reform which guaranteed them some congressional seats. Finally, at the end of the *sexenio*, there was the nationalisation of the banks. While the few remaining insurgent left groups found that they faced a state which still retained a capacity for violent repression, other left wingers found that they had never had things so good.

The real factor behind López Portillo's ability to reconcile the Mexican state to the interests of capital and – if slightly less completely – labour, was public spending. As we shall see below, the lack of accountability behind much public spending was a great economic problem; it was, however, a fact of considerable political value. This is because, broadly speaking, the political 'payoff' from a dollar of public spending is likely to be greater when this is a matter of discretion rather than of right. Security, like familiarity, can breed contempt. Thus under López Portillo, but on a greater scale than before (because more money was available), public money was used to reward loyalists, co-opt opponents, win political support and (almost incidentally to these main objectives) pursue various economic and social goals.

The essentially political objectives of state spending can be deduced from the spending decisions themselves. As occurred under Echeverría, the chief beneficiaries from state subsidies were the urban sectors and particularly the Mexico City middle class. Gasoline was cheap, metro fares were held down, the bureaucracy was expanding, the dollar was cheap (in the sense that the *peso* was seriously overvalued) and food prices were controlled. Almost all state companies made heavy losses – even on the (by no means wholly realistic) assumption that official figures are taken at face value.[32] Apart from Pemex (which will be dealt with in more detail below), the Federal Electricity Company was $10bn in debt by 1982; its income just covered sales and its ambitious investment strategy was almost entirely financed by foreign borrowing at commercial rates.[33] Even then, one quarter of the Mexican population still did not receive electricity. The picture in other parastatals is similar; investment was often heavy, financed by borrowing. Receipts from sales at best covered running costs and sometimes not even that.

This is not to deny that the economic growth of the period and the public spending undertaken did have a positive effect on the living standards of most Mexicans. Nor were all of the projects undertaken bad or all of the money wasted (though the quality of public spending was often very poor). However one problem was that the expansion of the public sector during 1970–82 created a set of expectations about the state which could not be met very easily, or indeed at all, in the following years. Money flowed into Mexico at an unprecedented rate during 1977–82 and created what was essentially the mirage of a public sector operating without financial constraints.

## PETROLEUM AND POLICYMAKING

A very great deal has been written about the Mexican oil industry.[34] To cover a long story briefly, Mexico enjoyed the dubious benefit of an oil boom between 1910 and 1920; production declined after 1920 and Mexico retreated further from the international oil market following the acrimonious nationalisation of its oil industry in 1938. Sometime in the early 1950s Mexico formally decided that it did not wish to continue to export oil, and instead Pemex (the state oil company) was required to do no more than assure Mexican self-sufficiency; Pemex turned its main attention to developing oil refineries and petrochemicals plants to meet growing local demand.

As Pemex tended to pay less attention to oil exploration, there came a time when its oil production increased less rapidly than local demand. During the later 1960s the director of Pemex, Reyes Heroles, became increasingly concerned about this problem. Once fears began to grow that Mexico would become dependent on oil imports, the priority put on exploration increased, and a long-term exploration programme was established in 1968.[35] In 1972 this new emphasis on exploration achieved results: the first of a series of major finds was made just at the time when existing reserves were beginning to decline. Oil production was stagnating, imports were increasing and Pemex – which suffered from price controls – was losing money.

Echeverría's response to these oil discoveries was (as so often) double-edged. On the one hand he did take steps to increase production; by the middle of 1975 Mexico had recovered oil self-sufficiency and shortly afterwards Mexico once more became an oil exporter. On the other hand, Echeverría became concerned to play down the extent of the oil discoveries in order not to over-attract US interest in Mexico. The United States, badly shocked by the world oil-price increases of 1973–4, was eagerly looking to Mexico as an alternative source of supply. Partly for tactical reasons, and partly because of the innate conservatism of some of the older Mexican geologists, the Mexican government issued estimates of oil reserves which were (to put it mildly) highly conservative.

López Portillo adopted a different tack altogether. During his campaign period he appointed Jorge Díaz Serrano to conduct a survey of Mexican oil reserves. Díaz Serrano reported that there was far more oil in existence than publicly admitted; armed with this information López Portillo doubled his estimate of the oil reserves almost immediately after taking office. Díaz Serrano was appointed director of Pemex.

Díaz Serrano was wholly committed to a strategy of maximising oil production. As was normal in Mexico, he brought a group of senior figures to work with him at senior levels in the organisation; he was successful in convincing the international community that his estimates of Pemex oil reserves were correct (this has not, in fact, been seriously disputed subsequently); and he convinced López Portillo (or at any rate the two convinced each other) that the 'oil card' held out great promise of permitting Mexico to overcome the economic crisis of 1976. During 1977 and 1978 a series of extremely bullish statements about Mexico's immediate and ultimate oil potential greatly improved the country's standing in the eyes of the international financial community. Economic growth resumed more rapidly, and strongly, than most people had expected when López Portillo took office.

Although things subsequently went wrong, the basic analysis of the expansionists had much to commend it. There were at least three powerful arguments in favour of a policy of rapidly developing oil for export. To begin with, the positive effect of oil revenue would be felt where it was most needed – in government finances and the balance of payments. The economic crisis of 1976 had stemmed from an excessive federal deficit leading to inflation, balance of payments crisis and devaluation. Oil exports held out the obvious prospect of short-term economic recovery. Secondly it was clear that the United States was increasingly concerned about its own oil supplies. By increasing its oil exports Mexico would both increase US respect for Mexico and increase Mexican leverage on the United States. Finally by controlling directly so important a resource as oil, the Mexican state (which López Portillo at any rate understood to mean the Mexican president) would increase its independence from the private sector. The balance of power would shift in the opposite direction as the private sector came to need the contracts which the government could provide. However López Portillo did not intend to use this revenue to confront anybody (except possibly the US government); rather, oil wealth appeared to hold out the prospect of a successful 'national unity' presidency, of exactly the kind that Díaz Ordaz and Echeverría had failed to achieve.

In 1977 Pemex published its sexennial plan. This provided for a doubling of oil production from 1.1m barrels per day scheduled for 1977 to 2.2m in 1982. Almost all of this increase would be in exports. Additionally major investments were programmed in refining and petrochemicals. Significant as these figures were, they were still relatively conservative in terms of both Mexico's resource potential and their expected budgetary effect. The expected outcome was a return to steady rates of growth, not an uncontrolled bonanza and the 'petrolisation' of the economy.

The more 'nationalist' wing within the government was, if only of necessity, prepared to accept this level of expansion of the oil industry. However, concerns were expressed on the left, both within the opposition and in the government, at some of the implications of relying on oil for economic growth. There was the fear that Pemex might become both over-mighty and over-corrupt. Nobody seriously doubted that there had always been some degree of corruption in Pemex and that this would increase as a result of the oil boom. There were fears that the oil wealth would distort the economy and possibly lead to the development of a 'Klondike' psychology; too much expansion might also generate inflation which would accentuate political conflict in a country where expectations had already been raised.[36] These were not so much arguments in favour of leaving oil in the ground, but rather in favour of a natural caution in respect of oil policymaking and, indeed, public policymaking as a whole.

At the end of 1978 these arguments seemed to be finely balanced. A dispute over the degree and timing of reflation in late 1977 was resolved by the resignations of both Carlos Tello and Rodolfo Moctezuma, who had championed opposing standpoints. For his part, López Portillo made it clear that he intended to steer a moderate line between the competing tendencies. As Bailey pointed out 'the underlying style involved creating an equilibrium between business and labour, conservatives and progressives'.[37] What threw everything out of balance was the Iranian revolution of 1978–79 and the second oil-price shock. When the price of oil hit $40 per barrel for a short period in 1979 López Portillo evidently came to believe that the Mexican economy had become invulnerable and that Mexico had become rich. 'Our problem', he said on at least one occasion, 'is how to manage abundance', and this Klondike attitude spread downwards through society.

This helps to explain why the public financial position in Mexico was allowed to deteriorate so sharply during 1980–1. In Paul Luke's words, 'what actually happened . . . was a startling nosedive of both public sector finances and the current account'.[38] In US-dollar terms, imports, having doubled between 1977 and 1979, then doubled again betwen 1979 and 1981. The operational government deficit (as a proportion of GDP) also nearly doubled, from 6.2 per cent in 1979 to 11.0 per cent in 1981. With no doubt whatever, this was at a time when a reasonably rapid rate of economic growth could have been sustained without the economic and fiscal imbalances that led to disaster in 1982.

## POLICY ISSUES AFTER 1979

This is not the place for technical discussion of economic trends under the López Portillo government. The underlying explanation for these deteriorating trends, far clearer than under Echeverría (where some key points remain genuinely controversial in a technical economic sense), was political. López Portillo became complacent and did not understand the potential dangers inherent in allowing an oil boom to run out of hand. He did not seek to follow coherent economic strategy of any kind.

As far as oil production policy was concerned, the 'expansionists', who continued to press for an increase in Mexican production over and above the previously agreed ceiling of 2.2m barrels per day, were allowed to go up to 2.5m and even 2.75m barrels. Their proposal for the ceiling to be lifted to four million in 1980 was rejected. On the other hand the 'nationalists' who objected to further growth of oil output still wanted the Mexican economy to enjoy a maximum growth rate. Oteyza, the patrimony minister and one of the most influential economic figures in the government, told *Business Week* 'The challenge we face is to raise our growth rate to 9 per cent or 10 per cent for a period of 10 years. Then there will be a reasonable chance of solving the unemployment problem by the 1990s.'[39] In retrospect Oteyza's ideas seem to have been overly optimistic, seriously flawed and dangerously influential with López Portillo. However they might have had more chance if oil production *had* been allowed to expand to 4m barrels per day – which proposal Oteyza strongly resisted.

There were also problems with other issues relating to the balance of payments. The 'nationalists' wanted to maintain a degree of trade protection and they did succeed in keeping Mexico out of the GATT; however imports were nevertheless liberalised significantly. If they had not been, part of the deterioration of the trade balance that occurred during 1980–2 need not have happened so quickly. What made matters still worse was that López Portillo (supported by the nationalists) sought to offset the inflationary effect of a hugely expansionist budgetary policy by holding down public-sector prices (notably gasoline) and overvaluing the exchange rate. It is on the public record that in 1980 Díaz Serrano publicly announced an increase in gasoline prices and that Oteyza publicly countermanded part of this increase. The thinking behind Oteyza's policy was that holding down official prices would enable the government to generate a Keynesian full employment boom while preventing cost-push pressures leading to rising inflation. Unfortunately when this policy ceased to be credible because of the widening trade gap, inflation increased as a result both of previous excess demand and the accelerated price increases that were needed to rectify the enormous fiscal deficit. The inflationary consequences were further aggravated by the devaluations which were largely forced by the widening trade gap itself.

It is a sobering thought that if the price of petrol had been allowed to increase in line with inflation after 1968, the federal budget would have been in surplus every year between 1968 and 1980 except for 1975 and 1976; when one allows that higher petrol prices would have had a slightly depressing effect on demand, the degree to which this single and simple policy instrument would have eased the pressures on the Mexican authorities during 1980–2 can hardly be exaggerated.[40]

A final example of policy inconsistency can be seen from the operation of the public sector. The nationalists put much emphasis on the value of public investment in bottleneck-breaking activities. For this to have been a viable strategy serious control would have had to be exerted over what the parastatal agencies actually did with their budgets. This control was lacking, most spectacularly in the case of Pemex (as we shall see, pp. 121–3) but also in the case of other government agencies. Moreover certain sectors of the economy, notably agriculture, suffered from deeper-rooted problems (relating to land tenure, intra-bureaucratic conflict, price control, lack of clarity over policy strategy and changing international circumstances) which an expanded budget could do little to resolve.[41]

It is difficult to avoid a harsh verdict on the quality of presidential decision-making after 1980. López Portillo seems to have chosen the easiest options from both the nationalist and the expansionist agenda without bothering to check for coherence. There has been no serious suggestion that Oteyza was personally corrupt or that he was in a position to check the corruption in Pemex; he did, moreover, have a serious economic strategy even if this was in some key respects flawed. The reality, which was that government spending and imports both increased rapidly, with neither priority nor control, was more than anything the result of (in Zaid's well-chosen phrase) 'the Presidential economy' rather than any specific economic doctrine.

One final point should be made about government thinking under López Portillo. The nationalists within the government believed that Echeverría's economic policies had been mostly right and had been undermined by problems from abroad.[42] There is something very deep in the Mexican culture which makes it temptingly easy to blame foreigners when something goes wrong at home. The problem was, however, that the real macroeconomic lessons of the Echeverría experience were not fully learned, except in that López Portillo, until the end, was careful not to antagonise the business community.

López Portillo believed, moreover, that the oil boom would continue to strengthen Mexico's economic position. According to Bailey, López Portillo sent to his cabinet copies of a book written by Servan Schreiber which stated:

> We know that the price of petroleum will not stop climbing. Having jumped in 10 years from 2 to 32 dollars a barrel, it is seen officially – and OPEC has announced it – that [the price] will be doubled from here to 1985. Or even before if, as is probable, another 'accident' of the Iranian type happens. This is something known.[43]

This was, perhaps, only a more extreme formulation of the idea – commonly held at the time – that the price of oil would rise throughout the 1980s. It is hard to know what to conclude from this in policymaking terms except that there is scarcely any position so absurd that a prestigious economist cannot be found to defend it, and that serious policymakers should generally be careful to avoid both gurus and wishful thinking. López Portillo embraced both passionately. Perhaps, as Zaid suggests, he was a gambler at heart.

In partial defence of López Portillo, it does seem to be surprisingly difficult for policymakers in raw material exporting countries to manage abundance effectively. Oil exporting countries with relatively large populations – Iran, Nigeria, Venezuela and Indonesia – did not as a group do particularly well either.[44] Distortions in the Mexican economy – an overvalued exchange rate, too many subsidies, too much public investment of doubtful quality (at worst a euphemism for corruption) – appear very much part of a syndrome common to most oil exporters at that time. Moreover Mexican oil production never amounted to more than 7 per cent of GDP; this was more than enough to provide a boost to the rest of the economy but not enough to compensate completely for problems elsewhere. Relatively speaking, oil had become as important to the Mexican economy as to the Ecuadorian – but not nearly so important as it was to the Venezuelan, let alone to the Saudi Arabian economies. López Portillo acquired a *rentier* mentality, but Mexico was in no position to live from oil alone.

## LÓPEZ PORTILLO'S INTERNATIONAL POLITICS

What seems to have happened was that López Portillo from May 1979 considered Mexico's economic problems to have been resolved, and turned his attention increasingly to trying to become an international statesman. It has typically been an aspiration of Mexican foreign policy to seek an international reputation for independence and radicalism in order to offset the close and perforce dependent relation Mexico has generally had with the United States.[45] López Portillo pursued this line much more actively than his predecessors. Moreover he evidently believed that the oil weapon had fundamentally altered the balance of power between Mexico and the United States; in this respect, as in others, he proved far too optimistic.

Early in the *sexenio* López Portillo was intensely irritated by a damaging misunderstanding that developed over the issue of supplying natural gas to the United States. Since Mexico had an abundance of natural gas and the United States a severe shortage it seemed logical for a pipeline to be constructed between Mexico and the US; the economics of the arrangement appeared excellent with the investment paying for itself within a year. In 1977 a group of US companies approached the Mexican government and offered to purchase 2m cu.ft daily of gas once the pipeline was built. The price offered was a generous one and the revenue implications excellent. However the gas pipeline was not in the original 1977–82 Plan and its proposed construction met strong opposition from the nationalist left. Díaz Serrano had to go to congress to defend the plan. Even so the López Portillo government showed every sign of disregarding this opposition and proceeding with the plan. It assumed that the US companies had secured the consent of the US government (which at that time operated a set of price controls on gas) on the terms of the proposed deal; unfortunately the companies had not done so. When the deal was sent to the energy ministry in Washington for approval, consent was withheld on the grounds that the proposed price would upset parallel arrangements with Canada. López Portillo was furious; he complained publicly that, while he had taken considerable risks to support the project against domestic opposition, he was left 'hanging by his paintbrush'. This was the last time he took any political risks with the nationalist lobby within Mexico. While it appears that much of the responsibility for the misunderstanding lay with the proposing companies, López Portillo blamed Washington in general and

President Carter in particular. In February 1979 Carter visited Mexico and was sternly lectured by López Portillo. Castro was far more warmly greeted when he visited the country in May of that year.

In the same month Santiago Roel was removed from the foreign ministry and replaced by Jorge Castañeda; Mexico's greater active involvement in Central America dates from this transition. Of particular importance was the active support which the Mexican government gave the Sandinistas. On 20 May 1979 Mexico broke diplomatic relations with the Somoza regime. When, in late June 1979, the United States proposed the creation of an OAS peacekeeping force for Nicaragua (to ensure that Somoza departed while the Sandinistas did not win) Mexico led opposition to these proposals. Mexico also offered some limited material support to the Sandinistas. After their victory in July 1979, they received financial and moral support from Mexico.[46] The Mexican government also progressively distanced itself from the government of El Salvador. In mid-1981 Mexico went further and, in agreement with France, called for a negotiated settlement to the civil war in El Salvador. During the years 1979–81 Mexican policy toward Central America was far closer to Cuba's than that of the United States. What is of note also is that Mexican foreign policy during this period was not merely extremely active but also extremely presidential although Castañeda himself very much encouraged this move toward foreign-policy activism. The CIA was only reflecting contemporary perception when it reported that:

> President López Portillo is the driving force behind the new initiatives: with two and a half years remaining in his term, the President is no longer so preoccupied with domestic problems and is intent on enhancing his own image in the foreign policy sphere. Mexico's growing oil wealth – and the leverage it provides – is facilitating his efforts.[47]

This assessment was in fact rather too sanguine. López Portillo was rather seeking a global role while neglecting to mind the shop at home. Once things had started to become difficult on the economic front, fear of losing face internationally was a further constraint on domestic policy.

## THE DENOUEMENT

By early 1981 the Mexican economy began to show the first signs of trouble. The rise in US interest rates at the end of 1979, and some signs of weakness in the oil market, combined to worsen the outlook for Mexican trade. Even so, most pundits (including the author) believed at that time that Mexico could ride out its troubles with comparatively little difficulty. More than anybody else it was López Portillo who proved them wrong.

The first sign that something was more seriously amiss came in June 1981 when Díaz Serrano resigned after a conflict over oil prices. Both he and López Portillo have subsequently written accounts of what happened then; despite some minor discrepancies, the general picture is clear.[48]

In the spring of 1981 international oil prices began to weaken. Díaz Serrano was persuaded by 'a small number of Pemex technocrats'[49] that Pemex needed to follow the international price downwards in order to maintain Mexico's market share. On 1 June Díaz Serrano spoke to López Portillo and asked permission to cut the price of oil; Díaz Serrano left the meeting believing that permission had been given while López Portillo later wrote that he had agreed in principle only and subject to the approval of the economics ministers in the cabinet. On 3 June Díaz Serrano did cut the export price of Mexican oil by four dollars a barrel. Other ministers, notably Oteyza, objected strenuously. López Portillo, who felt that the abrupt nature of the price cut had damaged his own 'Third-Worldist' credibility, did not try to protect Díaz Serrano from his critics. Shortly after an acrimonious cabinet meeting, López Portillo insisted on Díaz Serrano's resignation.

Following this resignation, the oil price was increased by $2 a barrel. In commercial terms this was a very poor decision; oil exports fell back and the Mexican trade balance and federal budget both deteriorated. In July prices were quietly reduced to the level which Díaz Serrano had originally set for them. For 1981 as a whole, final oil revenues were some $6bn below budget.

Naturally there was a good deal more at stake than these short-term commercial considerations. Díaz Serrano was an outsider in Mexican politics; he had come from the private sector to become one of the most powerful men in the Mexican government. It was clear to everybody that he was a possible candidate for the

Mexican presidency; López Portillo later stated that he had told him as much in December 1980.[50] On 18 March 1981, when the annual Pemex Directors' Report was presented, Díaz Serrano was eulogised by La Quina who, as head of the oilworkers' union, was then considered highly influential politically. Díaz Serrano was also believed by some figures within the Mexican government (probably wrongly) to be Washington's candidate for president on account of his earlier friendship with the then Vice-President Bush.

A certain amount of submerged conflict at the time of the succession is quite normal in Mexican politics. Political infighting, after all, goes on everywhere. However in the eyes of his considerable number of enemies, Díaz Serrano was not merely a political adversary but a radically unacceptable figure who must be kept out at all costs. These critics believed that Pemex was not merely corrupt but scandalously so. They also believed that Díaz Serrano had a potential for dividing the whole system due to his pro-US attitude and his lack of roots within Mexican public administration.

A very significant document in this context was leaked to *Proceso* and published in May 1981. The document was undated but appears to have been written around August 1980. It was written in the planning ministry. The document stated that insufficient controls existed within Pemex either from outside or within the organisation itself. As a result opportunities for corruption existed. Figures relating to fixed investment carried out by Pemex were slow in being compiled and in some cases untrue. (A common form of corruption, in Pemex as elsewhere, is for bribes to be offered or extorted in return for the offer of contracts; in accounting terms, therefore, their effect would be to increase the 'investment' figure.) There were also, in innumerable cases, anomalies which came to light when figures from various sources were cross-checked. By way of example, according to Pemex' official figures, petroleum exports in 1979 amounted to $4,075m. The Bank of Mexico gave the figure as $3,765m and the planning and budgeting ministry (SPP) gave it as $3,154m. These were not trivial differences. For 1980 the discrepancy between Pemex' and the Bank of Mexico figure amounted to nearly $800m. There were even discrepancies with respect to the actual amount of oil exported – and these were not trivial either.[51] While the report did not actually accuse the top directorate of corruption, it is difficult to see what other implication could possibly be drawn from what was being said.

The report also focused on some other points, such as the continuing subsidy on domestic oil prices, which were of greater economic importance. However the political impact obviously came from the allegations of corruption. In the words of Carlos Ramírez, the report indicated that Pemex had become 'a company without order, without control . . . administratively chaotic, financially insolvent, politically autonomous'.[52]

What the events of June 1981 indicate, therefore, was that Díaz Serrano had lost the moral credibility necessary to carry off an unpopular policy – that of cutting prices to maintain export volumes. For all of his faults, however, he did at least realise that a price cut was necessary if the momentum of public spending was to continue. López Portillo was prepared to turn a blind eye to the corruption within Pemex at that time (some suggest it was rather more than a blind eye), but he was not prepared to support his friend and collaborator when it came to taking an unpopular decision. His reaction was not based on principle, or even on rational long-term self-interest; it was rather a matter of wounded vanity and 'not wanting to know' when difficult decisions needed to be taken. This episode seems to bear out the judgement of a source quoted by Kraft:

> López Portillo had a very strong view of how life should be. He tried very hard to mould events in that direction and for a time he succeeded. But reality always mocks vision. It caught up with him and when the time for reckoning came, López Portillo grew irritable and blamed others and ran away.[53]

The rest of 1981 was marked by a similar lack of realism in respect of economic policy. Spending cuts were announced which did not take place. In July 1981 all the economics ministers together approached López Portillo and advocated some form of devaluation. He reacted emotionally and very angrily, and this was the last time that the economics ministers ever tried to influence him as a group.

There is little doubt that López Portillo believed at that time that his problems were more political than economic. There was by mid-1981 a good deal of jockeying for the succession (as is inevitable in Mexican politics). López Portillo gave two press conferences in July 1981 in which he denounced those who were speculating against the *peso*. He stated that he was facing concerted opposition from right-wingers worried by Mexico's left-wing foreign policy line and high international profile which was to be displayed at the international conference at Cancun in October 1981. He also appears to have believed that private-sector uncertainties over the succession (particularly after the fall of Díaz Serrano) were contributing to a difficult economic climate. For this reason he unveiled Miguel de la Madrid as his successor somewhat earlier than normal – on 25 August 1981.

De la Madrid was the most conservative of all the potential candidates and therefore the man (López Portillo believed) most likely to reassure the private sector. He was a genuine monetarist – of which there were very few in senior positions under López Portillo – and a man of innate caution on fiscal matters. There were also personal factors helping de la Madrid. He was a bitter enemy of Díaz Serrano – whose flamboyance, unconcealed ambition and political *parvenu* qualities represented everything which de la Madrid detested – and was happy to associate himself with the 'nationalist' ministers against him. De la Madrid was also close to López Portillo's son, who worked under de la Madrid in the planning ministry. According to one source, de la Madrid strongly supported the promotion of Jose Ramón from director to subsecretary and lost no opportunity to flatter and help him.

Even so, the final decision nearly went to David Ibarra who was the treasury minister. Ibarra was closer to López Portillo politically than was de la Madrid. He was essentially a structuralist economist, with a structuralist *camarilla* which could not help but regard de la Madrid as a threat. Ibarra's team was based on the UNAM university while de la Madrid's came mainly from the technological institute ITAM. There would be no vacancies under de la Madrid for structuralist economists in senior positions. However de la Madrid was evidently able to keep his conservative tendencies in check sufficiently not to alarm insiders such as Oteyza. His administrative experience, which was rather greater than Ibarra's, may also have counted in his favour.

These sexennial moves did succeed in buying a little time for López Portillo. However in November 1981 the government released estimates for the fiscal deficit for that year which were very much worse than anybody had expected. As we have seen in mid-1981 the government had decreed cuts in public spending, which did much to reassure at any rate some foreign observers about the future course of the Mexican economy. However in mid-November the government revealed that government spending in 1981 was running at 18 per cent above that originally budgeted and 55 per cent above 1980 levels. This extra spending was financed by short-term borrowing from abroad. Private sector concern at this turn of events was very much muted by the revelation that the largest private-sector company in Mexico, the ALFA group, had run into liquidity problems and needed to be rescued by a highly-subsidised loan from the government. Like the Mexican government, ALFA had invested not wisely but too well.

The main reason why public spending was not cut back during the second half of 1981 was that López Portillo did not want it to be. According to Teichman, during 1981:

> government officials were able to obtain increases in expenditure by taking their requests directly to the president, thereby increasing the budget allocation beyond that originally authorised. This occurred with increasing frequency in the last two years of the sexenio.[54]

Teichman points out that this practice was technically illegal, but there was nothing that could be done about it.

By February 1982 mounting problems could no longer be ignored. The CTM had received a 34 per cent wage increase in January 1982, which added to the concern of the private sector. Obviously this level of cost inflation could not be sustained without a devaluation. Anticipating such a course of action, the private sector intensified its export of capital; at this stage capital export was more of an exchange rate precaution than a sign of political opposition to the government. However the situation took a turn for the worse when López Portillo publicly declared that he would defend the *peso* 'like a dog'. A few days later he accepted the inevitable and devalued. For the next few months, between February and the end of August 1982, López Portillo vacillated. Typically he would attempt orthodox policies for a short time, abandon them as soon as the immediate pressure lifted; renewed crisis would threaten almost immediately and the whole cycle would be repeated. Thus the devaluation in February was not followed by serious austerity measures; instead there were price controls and attempts to protect the private sector from the costs of the devaluation.

López Portillo, despite having agreed to the devaluation, then dismissed the finance minister and the head of the central bank on

17 March. Their replacements, Silva Herzog as finance minister and Miguel Mancera as head of the central bank, had not been close to López Portillo. According to Kraft 'Silva learned about his appointment in Washington, Mancera was in Kuala Lumpur'.[55] Both later felt that they had been named as front men while real decisions were being made by a small circle of presidential advisers. Four days after the two men were appointed, a general wage increase was decreed despite their opposition. López Portillo's main objective appeared to be to avoid complete humiliation ahead of the presidential elections of July 1982, which were to be held under more open political conditions than usual so that any extreme popular reaction against the government would be hard to disguise. Moreover the selection of Miguel de la Madrid was not universally popular among the Mexican political élite – unusually García Paniagua, the head of the PRI, and Fidel Velázquez both made their unhappiness with the choice publicly known. This was an argument, which foreign observers also understood, for little to be done until after 6 July 1982.

The government did decree an austerity programme on 20 April 1982, but this was never properly implemented. However López Portillo did have some success on the political front. The presidential elections went reasonably well for the government. In congressional elections the PAN polled far more strongly than in 1979, gaining 17.46 per cent of the vote as against rather more than 15 per cent for the PAN's presidential candidate, and up from 11.4 per cent three years earlier. The tendency of the left-wing vote to fragment among a variety of competing parties was even more evident than it had been in 1979; the pro-system parties of the left also lost further ground. The presidential elections showed a similar pattern; Miguel de la Madrid won by a convincing but not an overwhelming majority while the PAN proved far stronger than any rival of the left. There is, however, some evidence of limited rigging of the results against the PAN in some northern districts of Mexico – but probably not on a sufficient scale to have materially altered the national picture.

However, rather than using the aftermath of the elections as an opportunity to carry out necessary measures, López Portillo apparently felt vindicated and chose to do nothing. Kraft states that 'just after the vote he told an American official that there was no longer an urgent need for the austerity program'.[56] It seems typical of his attitude generally that he appears to have believed that all economic problems had a political – even perhaps a personal – cause; good news was the result of the right political relationship with entrepreneurs while bad news was the result of conspiracy. By this time financial panic was settling in fast. The trigger seems to have been an announcement on 1 August that some administered prices (such as gasoline) would be increased. What was significant about this announcement was that the president did not announce it; the ministry of commerce did. This seems to have been the final straw; the private sector lost almost all confidence in López Portillo and money flooded out of the country. It was no longer just a matter of insurance against devaluation; political risk was now a major factor as well.

August was crisis month. Emergency discussions were held between government ministers (notably Silva Herzog and Mancera) and Washington. On 7 August Mexico made a formal application to the IMF with the acquiescence rather than support of López Portillo; the IMF mission arrived in Mexico in the middle of that month. By this time most economic policymakers – American as well as Mexican – were looking at their calendars or even their watches and counting the time until the change of government on 1 December. Kraft reports that, 'Silva regularly lunched with Volcker on visits to Washington. Silva kept assuring Volcker that Mexico was moving as rapidly toward the IMF as López Portillo would allow . . . Volcker adopted as his policy getting Mexico through to the next president.'[57] Washington, the US and also the European banks had virtually no choice but to look for a compromise with the Mexican authorities in view of the amount of loan capital tied up in Mexico; there was also obvious anxiety that a Mexican default would trigger action in Argentina and other Latin American countries.

The US Treasury had, according to Kraft, been privately concerned for some time about the deterioration of the Mexican economy:

> Staff aides had been keeping a wary eye on Mexico ever since . . . June 1981 . . . They had warned Secretary Regan of Mexican financial weakness . . . in October 1981. They had repeated the assessment for the Secretary in briefings prior to meetings he held with high Mexican financial officials on an almost monthly basis beginning in April 1982.[58]

However they proved slow to respond when crisis did hit, whether from error or from a deliberate policy of waiting until the situation became so bad that a serious deal was inevitable. Negotiations for 'the Mexican rescue' took place during mid-August. By this time these do appear to have had the support of López Portillo. On 17 August it was announced that Mexico would receive several billion dollars in official and private loans in return for various concessions by Mexico – notably increasing oil sales to the United States. Subsequent negotiations, this time with the commercial banks, took until the end of August.

On 1 September, to general astonishment, López Portillo natrionalised the banks and, with them, the substantial parts of Mexican industry which were owned by the bankers. This move had long been advocated by Jose Ramón, by Oteyza and by Carlos Tello. Indeed while the formal economics ministries were in the hands of orthodox economists, López Portillo continued to discuss economic matters with a small group of intimates; apparently it was this group which López Portillo in March 1982 asked for a series of policy options to deal with capital flight. One option was for the banks to be nationalised and exchange controls imposed. It was this option that the President ultimately preferred, while maintaining near-total secrecy in order to prevent wealth-holders taking further pre-emptive measures.[59]

In his speech of 1 September López Portillo sought to blame everything that had gone wrong on the private sector which had, he asserted, been involved in some kind of conspiracy against the Mexican government. He was himself in an emotional state and played dramatically on the nationalist prejudices of much of the audience. This was a new López Portillo, the populist orator and radical nationalist; the posture did not last long, but it was long remembered.

The nationalisation was widely applauded on the left[60] and appears to have been popular with many Mexicans, although opposed by the private sector and much of the middle class. The latter suffered from the fact that several billions of dollars held in dollar deposit accounts within Mexico (which were until then quite legal) were forcibly exchanged for pesos at a rate determined by the government.

This led to a further speculative attack on the Mexican banking system (particularly through demands for withdrawals from the foreign branches of Mexican banks), again covered by an emergency US bail-out. Meanwhile renewed efforts were made to get the López Portillo government to accept an IMF programme. According to Kraft, after 1 September López Portillo more or less allowed his economics ministers to handle things in their own way, but he did add Carlos Tello to the Mexican team negotiating with the IMF which also included Silva Herzog and Carlos Salinas. Tello was radically opposed to the orthodox agreement which was being prepared by the others but by late October he was isolated.[61] López Portillo also appears to have put feelers out to the governments of Brazil and Argentina, to consider the possibility of a combined declaration of moratorium; these, however, did not come to anything.[62] In early November the IMF letter of intent was finally agreed but the whole deal was made subject to the banks themselves putting up $5bn in additional lending. When López Portillo's term ended, final negotiations were still going on.

The bank nationalisation cannot easily be seen as a concerted effort to shift the direction of economic policy in the direction of 'structuralism'. It came too late and, even more important, it did not prevent continuing negotiations with the IMF and the US government. It has, rather, to be seen as a political move. It was partly an effort to save the face of a president who considered himself humiliated by the turn of events in 1982. It also fully fits the interpretation offered here which is that López Portillo never really understood the logic of economic behaviour; he considered all problems to be political problems. Just as his 'solution' to earlier difficulties was to re-accommodate the private sector (in 1977), nominate de la Madrid to the presidency (in 1981) and seek to ensure a successful election campaign (in early 1982), now the task, in his eyes, was to reassert presidential authority over an apparently rogue capital-exporting middle and upper class. The question in his mind was not 'how should the economy be run?' (the answer to which he did not really know, or indeed much care) but rather 'who rules Mexico?' – to which López Portillo believed he did know the answer and cared very much.

## POLITICS AND THE MEXICAN ECONOMY

López Portillo was a more benign authoritarian than either of his two predecessors; he did not deliberately seek enemies. His commitment to national unity was genuine and (with the help of

Reyes Heroles) relatively sophisticated. He proved that a high degree of presidential control could co-exist with a significant degree of civil and political liberty; he sought to base his power on the strength of his office and the PRI machine, rather than on the suppression of rivals.

What his period in office proved was that it is not enough for a president to secure a good working relationship with Mexico's main political interests; failure to secure such a relationship can be costly but there is another, more 'structuralist', logic that exists as well. The central fact here is that the Mexican state is not exempt from the laws of economics. The combination of oil wealth and expanded foreign borrowing hugely strengthened the financial resources of the Mexican state between 1977 and 1981; in 1981 the Mexican economy ingested $45bn of foreign exchange – which is around ten times the value of Mexico's exports in 1976 and far more than anybody could possibly have anticipated at the beginning of the López Portillo term. Most of this money went directly, in the first instance, to the government. Even making generous allowance for the fact that the money was used unusually badly from a developmental point of view (much of it being simply re-exported as flight capital), the Mexican state found itself in a far better fiscal position than it ever was before or is likely to be again. Even so, it was not exempt from constraints imposed by the market.

The point from the perspective of state–private sector relations is that in Mexico as elsewhere capitalists are driven by the logic of capital accumulation far more than the other way round; this is something which Marx understood but López Portillo did not. It is therefore almost useless for a state to try to co-opt private sector interest groups unless it can also control the markets within which the private sector has to operate. If pressed, Mexican capitalists (as well as foreign ones) will do what they think will protect their money and not what they think will please the government; political factors will play a part in their considerations, but the technicalities of of economic policymaking will matter at least as much and probably more. Successful governments in capitalist economies understand this point and seek to accommodate their policies to what markets will permit; López Portillo did not appear to understand that a politics of co-optation and control, applied to the private sector, could not work. The power of the Mexican bourgeoisie (like that of other countries) does not lie only or even mainly in its organisations; it lies in its access to, and ability to take advantage of, markets.

It is not clear that any Mexican government can fully, or even substantially, control one of the most important of these markets – that for US dollars. Most Mexican economists believe that exchange controls cannot work in their country – the experiences of late 1982 reinforced rather than shook this conviction. This apparent inability is obviously a major constraint on the ability of any Mexican government to make economic policy autonomously – a point which is instinctively understood by almost every Mexican. Another factor, which has perhaps not received sufficient attention, is that the Mexican public sector during 1970–82 was not surplus-generating; it was surplus-absorbing. López Portillo even more than Echeverría borrowed internationally to finance subsidies on food and petrol and to 'invest' in bureaucrats and offices. If a government is seeking to use the public sector to control private investment, then it must be able to find the necessary resources. It is not possible to do this if it is pursuing an expansive pro-consumer policy at the same time – a fact which Perón, Velasco, Allende and many other Latin American political leaders have also failed to understand.

The reason why most elected left-wing governments in Latin America do not in fact pursue an austere investment-led type of socialism is that such a strategy is obviously unpopular; in the world as a whole it is more commonly associated with dictatorships than with democracies. Even here it has tended more to failure than to success. It is in any case hard to imagine how an essentially clientelist and political bureaucracy (on the Mexican pattern) can be expected to operate a dynamic and developmentalist public sector. It is even harder to see how such a thing could happen in a climate of oil-intoxicated euphoria.

In sum, López Portillo made his most serious economic misjudgements because he believed he had a set of policy options that he did not in fact have. Not even the unusually favourable international circumstances of 1978–81 provided sufficient resources to insulate the Mexican economy from the normal operation of world and domestic markets; nor is it easy to see how the Mexican state could have acted decisively so as to increase its autonomy. It is because of this lack of autonomy that the Mexican government needs the co-operation of the private sector (including the international private sector) and for this reason the power of the Mexican presidency is inherently limited. Co-optative political strategies can change this situation only on the margin while confrontational strategies are likely to aggravate it.

Meanwhile what of López Portillo himself? He was surely not the kind of man who could 'look on triumph and disaster and treat the two imposters just the same'. When he looked upon triumph it went to his head. When he looked upon disaster he made a bad situation far worse. He had neither the intellectual preparation nor the psychological resources to cope with the economic downturn after 1981. The situation unbalanced him and made him desperate. Perhaps he was never quite balanced enough to be a good president.

# 5 De la Madrid: The Limits of Orthodoxy

Miguel de la Madrid Hurtado, unlike his three predecessors, was not a man who imposd his personality upon the presidential office. He accepted the system, and generally sought to play by its rules. He was more restrained in his use of power and willing to accept personal criticism than Díaz Ordaz had been, and less activist than either Echeverría or López Portillo. The significant changes which took place in Mexican politics during 1982–8 cannot easily be attributed to the personal defects or idiosyncrasies of de la Madrid. It was rather that his caution and lack of personal assertiveness showed more clearly than before the way in which more impersonal forces were transforming the nature of Mexican politics.

Certainly the de la Madrid presidency reinforces the argument that possession of nearly absolute despotic power does not guarantee the ability to shape the course of events. In July 1988 de la Madrid's chosen successor was badly embarrassed by his lack of popular support; the opposition was accepted as the victor in the elections in the Federal District and several other states – and there is reason to believe that it may have polled more strongly than officially acknowledged. Even apart from the electoral dimension, the de la Madrid government was one of unexpected transformation. At the end of his term Mexico was far less presidential and far more overtly pluralist than at any time since 1940.

In fact Miguel de la Madrid came to power with the reputation of being competent as an economist, inexperienced as a politician and in background some way removed from the mainstream of Mexican political society. In Kouyoumdjian's words 'he was U.S.–educated, a fluent English speaker and an openly practising Catholic, all attributes which were, to say the least, unusual among recent presidential incumbents'.[1]

De la Madrid was born in Colima in 1934 into an upper-middle-class background of Spanish descent; as some of his critics pointed out, his was exactly the kind of family that the revolution was directed against. Two of de la Madrid's ancestors were in fact governors of Colima under the Porfiriato. However de la Madrid's father died when his son was very young; the family then moved to Mexico City where Miguel grew up. De la Madrid gained his first degree from UNAM, but then studied at Harvard. He joined the Mexican government as a lawyer and economist and moved through a variety of administrative positions before becoming Planning Minister in 1979.

As we saw in the last chapter, de la Madrid was 'unveiled' before the true magnitude of the 1981–2 crisis manifested itself. His selection, though not a total surprise, was greeted by a lack of enthusiasm on the part of the traditionalist wing of both the PRI and the left. It was no great surprise that he identified himself, in the context of Mexican politics, as a moderate conservative. This orientation is clear from his first government.[2] Almost all commentators agree that this was selected from a very narrow group of people; it was of high technical calibre and, for the most part, economically liberal. It contained two essentially independent figures. These were Jesús Silva Herzog and Manuel Mancera, who had played major roles in negotiating with the United States government and the IMF during 1982, and were made Finance Minister and governor of the Central Bank respectively. Apart from these, however, most of the top economics positions went to members of de la Madrid's inner *camarilla*. As a result the cabinet was far more narrowly based than López Portillo's first cabinet had been or than Salinas de Gortari's first cabinet was to be.[3] De la Madrid's critics believed that he listened to an excessively narrow group of advisers. The Planning Ministry was given to Carlos Salinas de Gortari – a young man with a brilliant academic background but in other ways an unknown quantity. Other figures close to de la Madrid appointed to senior but second-line technocratic positions included Ramón Beteta who became head of Pemex, Hector Hernández who became Commerce Minister, and Gustavo Petricioli who became head of the state-owned development bank NAFINSA. The only Keynesian or structuralist figure put near the centre of economic management was Labastida Ochoa. He was also an old confidant of the President and was given the new secretaryship of Energy and Mines – which involved keeping an eye on Pemex, which was an organisation de la Madrid distrusted deeply. Labastida, however, was the exception; the days of 'structuralist' economic influence were over.

De la Madrid's economic knowledge and experience was genuine; it was, therefore, a defensible choice to 'presidentialise' the administration in a way which was historically unusual for Mexico. However the political positions were almost equally presidentialised; given de la Madrid's almost complete lack of electoral experience, this was potentially a more serious problem. Admittedly Reyes Heroles, who among other things had once taught de la Madrid, returned as Secretary for Education; he was undeniably a political heavyweight and one of very few ministers with genuine political experience. Many of the other positions were again filled by members of de la Madrid's own *camarilla*; few of them had any genuine independent weight.

Thus the underlying pattern of the de la Madrid presidency, that of relatively decisive economic policymaking and caution amounting to indecision on political matters, stemmed from the presidential personality itself. De la Madrid believed that presidential power should be exercised with restraint; he was not, by temperament, an innovator and did not surround himself with people likely to take a different view.

## 'MORALISATION' AND ITS LIMITS

An early indication of caution on the political front came when the government announced an anti-corruption policy which was then confined to extremely narrow limits. In fact 1983 was a good year for an anti-corruption initiative. López Portillo had led most Mexicans to believe that oil-led abundance had radically changed their economic prospect. By the end of 1982 it had become clear that this was not so and that severe economic crisis had struck. 'Corruption' was an easy explanation for this turn of events; it was made more plausible by the fact that it contained a degree of truth. Even though corruption was not a sufficient explanation for the economic crisis, there can be no doubt that it was extensive. Furthermore López Portillo's extraordinary tactlessness ensured that it was not even especially concealed.

De la Madrid began with the belief that it should be possible to reduce drastically the incidence of corruption in Mexican political life. There was much talk of 'moralisation' at the beginning of his term of office but, sadly, very much less by the end. It is true that de la Madrid went much further with his anti-corruption measures than any Mexican president before him; it is also generally accepted that he observed appropriate standards of ethical conduct during his own period in office. Thus while his 'moralisation' targets were inevitably selective, it would be wrong to see them simply as an exercise in political expediency. Yet, to the extent that they aimed at reassuring the public and also key interest groups (including Washington) that corruption in Mexico was no longer a serious problem, it must be said that they failed. De la Madrid did not even succeed – as López Portillo's own somewhat inauthentic anti-corruption policy had done – in helping to establish presidential authority.

Anti-corruption policy took two forms; there was the trial and punishment of those believed to have behaved corruptly during the previous *sexenio*, and there were procedural measures designed to make corruption more difficult in the future. As far as the first issue was concerned, the main target of investigation was Pemex. A number of senior figures within Pemex were accused of corruption but the most important charges were brought against Díaz Serrano himself. In mid-1983 he was accused of irregularities and eventually sentenced to ten years in prison; in fact he served a little more than five. Another important figure to 'fall' was the police chief Arturo Durazo who was eventually extradited to Mexico from Los Angeles. Durazo was without any doubt an exceptionally scandalous and violent individual and also a man who showed little or no discretion in his financial affairs. He built for himself a huge pseudo-Greek mansion which could not possibly have been afforded on the salary of a police chief; the residence came to be popularly known as 'the Parthenon' and Mexicans joked that Melina Mercouri was about to ask for its restitution to Greece.

While these cases were certainly flagrant, those singled out for punishment were (as Meyer has pointed out [4]) outsiders who had come into the system; they were not really men of the system with a long tradition of service to the PRI or the government. It would not have been difficult to make corruption charges stick against other senior figures but the system closed ranks to protect its own. Perhaps the key issue was what to do with leading members of the oilworkers' union – some of whom had become internationally notorious for their flagrant illegalities. At least one senior presidential adviser recommended arresting the top union leadership of the oilworkers but de la Madrid decided against this.[5] The oilworkers were subsequently to make life very difficult both for the head of Pemex, Ramón Beteta, and for de la Madrid himself whose authority was not strengthened when in 1986 he allowed himself to be publicly insulted by a relatively junior figure in the oilworkers' union.[6]

A further problem facing de la Madrid was what to do with López Portillo himself. During 1983 and early 1984 there were some pressures for him to be tried formally on corruption charges.[7] De la Madrid obviously enjoyed his own political position due to the support of López Portillo and presumably felt a debt of gratitude towards him. However López Portillo was (to put it mildly) under suspicion for possible acts of corruption. He was bitterly unpopular in 1983–4 because many Mexicans saw him as the man who had almost single-handedly squandered the oil boom. The arrest and trial of López Portillo would have cleared the air; letting him alone would permit a closing of ranks at a price in terms of credibility. De la Madrid chose to let him alone.

One source suggests that de la Madrid did genuinely believe that the problem of corruption could largely be solved through appropriate bureaucratic procedures. According to this source, de la Madrid was discussing the question of corruption with his aides during his campaign in 1982, when one aide incautiously remarked that it would be impossible to stamp out corruption in Mexico. De la Madrid disagreed strongly; he outlined his plans for ending corruption. These amounted to a set of procedures intended to have the effect of making it far easier to detect. De la Madrid did, for example, set up the *Controlería* with the role of examining the accounts of state enterprises.

Some of these steps probably did a modest amount of good. It is, however, quite obvious that they fell drastically short of what a serious law enforcement policy would have warranted. Corruption in local and regional government was scarcely checked. What was worse, when it was clear that firm presidential action would not be forthcoming, political power in many localities and regimes shifted back from relatively honest figures who had the potential for retaining popular confidence within the system to local *caciques* whom de la Madrid could neither influence nor control. These *caciques* treated those figures within the system who took the 'moralisation' argument seriously not merely as opponents but as enemies; in a number of cases de la Madrid proved unable or unwilling to provide physical protection, let alone political support, for reformers within the system whom he had originally seemed to support.[8]

Also serious was de la Madrid's failure to deal with the growing narcotics problem and the violence which it engendered. To take only two examples, the murder of an undercover US official by the narcotics mafia in 1985 put serious strains on Mexico–US relations; it did not help that one key suspect was first arrested and then allowed to escape into exile. The murder of the popular Mexican journalist Manuel Buendía in 1984 was greeted with shock in Mexico itself; de la Madrid went to the funeral. However in 1989 the head of de la Madrid's federal security police, Zorrillo, was arrested and charged with the murder; it was alleged that he had ordered the killing because Buendía was on the point of discovering Zorrillo's own role in the narcotics trade. A hostile critic would consider de la Madrid's advocacy of anti-corruption policies which he essentially failed to follow up as amounting to abdication of presidential authority.

## THE MEXICAN ECONOMY IN 1982

In de la Madrid's eyes, the most important task of his presidency was restoring the domestic economy to a reasonably firm footing. Allowing for the relatively technical vision of a former planning minister, serious arguments were being put – within the administration as well as outside – that a fundamental change of direction would be needed if Mexico was to recover fully from the crisis of 1982. While demands for 'radical change' can come from a variety of points on the political spectrum, the most influential voices in de la Madrid's Mexico were coming from the economic liberals.

These liberals, as well as critics from the private sector, believed that the role of the public sector was the crucial problem facing Mexico. As we have seen, the expansion in the role of the state during 1970–82 had a number of objectives – most of them political. The expansion in the public sector, while it lasted, provided opportunities of maintaining social control through clientelist politics. By 1983, according to one estimate, some 20 per cent of all employed Mexicans worked in the public sector.[9] It provided employment for the graduates which the national universities were turning out in increasing quantities. There was some progress in meeting social objectives although probably not much more than might have been predicted from the process of economic growth itself.[10] The left supported an expanding state – enthusiastically applauding the bank nationalisation – because they believed that this provided a check upon rampant capitalism. As the bank nationalisation in fact showed, there was indeed some short-run popularity to be won by a government attacking the private sector in the name of national unity.[11]

Until 1982 the average Mexican did not have to pay toward the cost of running this kind of public sector. It had been met by expanding oil production and by borrowing internationally. After 1982, however, there was no way of insulating the Mexican public from these costs. There were several possible ways of meeting the obligation – all of them unpleasant. Options included sharply-higher public-sector prices, cutbacks in public investment, a sharply-rising internal debt, an increase in taxation or – in the absence of a clear decision to accept one or more of these choices – that invisible form of taxation known as inflation. The option of sharply reducing the size of the public sector was difficult enough even in the long-term, and in the short-term virtually impossible.

If the touchstone of economic liberalism (in Mexico in 1983) was the belief that the role of the public sector had expanded, was expanding and ought to be diminished, then there were many economic liberals in the de la Madrid government. Moreover the private sector, shocked by the bank nationalisation, was pushing far more aggressively for liberal economic measures than it had in the past. An increasing number of voices from the private sector began pressing for political change as well.

Some of de la Madrid's advisers and a number of leading figures in the Bank of Mexico (notably Mancera) wanted a rapid move in the direction of radical economic reform. Radical reformers, moreover, wanted to go well beyond merely checking public spending and so returning to the orthodoxies of 'stabilising development'. They wanted an end to Mexico's essentially protected and subsidised urban economy and society; instead they wanted local manufacturers to be made to compete on world markets and foreign investment to be allowed in, more or less as the market decided.

De la Madrid himself was a cautious man, though somewhat bolder on economic than political matters. However the 'political' ministers inevitably tended to prefer caution; the CTM trade union confederation was opposed to the whole new direction of economic policy and the government believed that it could not afford to alienate Fidel Velázquez entirely. In any case, in 1982 very few Latin American governments with any pretensions to popular support were willing to carry out a thoroughgoing liberalisation of their domestic economies.

De la Madrid took power just after an agreement had been finalised with the IMF. He enforced an orthodox stabilisation plan with some vigour. Real GDP fell by 5.3 per cent in 1983 and imports fell by more than half. The government deficit fell from 16.1 per cent of GDP in 1982 to 8.9 per cent in 1983. Public sector prices were increased and public investment reduced. There was a considerable fall in real wages. Economic restructuring (as opposed to deflation) was more limited but there was a decontrol of interest rates. There was the first of many attempts to renegotiate the foreign debt to commercial banks.

The political costs of this economic stabilisation were seen as considerable. However some economists believed in 1984 that the measures taken in 1983 had achieved most of what needed to be done. It was certainly true that the public sector deficit, the rate of inflation and the balance of trade were all moving in a favourable direction in early 1984. De la Madrid evidently believed that it was possible to undertake a limited reflation without prejudicing the longer-term objective of liberalisation. In the event, this proved to be a serious miscalculation, possibly the result of over-optimism induced by the normal 'honeymoon' period enjoyed by most incoming presidents.

## THE ABORTIVE POLITICAL OPENING 1982–84

Local and regional politics became increasingly important during the presidency of de la Madrid. This was not really because of any inherent change in the very limited powers and financial resources of local governments but rather because national and international observers tended increasingly to see the handling of local conflicts as a test of credibility for the system as a whole. Moreover, as Mexico became more urban and the size of the middle class increased, so the number and strength of challenges to local *caciques* intensified.

We have already seen that the political reform of 1977, while leaving the opposition parties well short of the capacity to mount a serious challenge at presidential level, did give them a chance of

## De la Madrid: The Limits of Orthodoxy

success in particular localities. Moreover the economic crisis which hit Mexico in 1982 further increased the vulnerability of the PRI. Over the longer term, the prospects for electoral opposition were also increasing as a result of socio-economic change. Urban voters, and particularly the urban middle class, have proved far more likely than peasants to exercise an electoral option against the system.[12] In many, perhaps most, cases this was less likely to be exercised on ideological grounds than in support of a particular figure or as a protest against the government or government candidate.

De la Madrid appeared to take an early decision that unfavourable election results would be accepted. One important test came on 5 December 1982 when the town of San Luis Potosí voted for an opposition candidate; this was the same Dr Nava as had defeated the official candidate in 1958. An even more important test came on 3 July 1983 in the northern state of Chihuahua and also in neighboring Durango. In Chihuahua the PAN won virtually all the main municipalities including Chihuahua itself and Cuidad Juárez.[13] The PAN also captured the municipal capital in Durango.

It is important that these defeats suffered by the PRI are not exaggerated. The PRI still won most local elections and was far stronger nationally than any of its rivals. Where the PAN did win, there was an important protest element in the vote. The events of 1982 – particularly the bank nationalisation and the brief experiment with exchange control – were particularly resented in northern Mexico. A lot of provincial business interests turned to the PAN as a way of expressing their rejection of the 'socialism' of López Portillo.

Why should the system have found this electoral opposition so threatening? It is natural that local political interests should have been concerned. As already noted, local political office was often seen as a reward for loyal co-operation and as a recognition (rather than a direct source) of political power. Patronage could only work easily when elections themselves were essentially non-competitive; this was particularly the case when the machine itself worked far less well, and was in consequence far less able to mobilise genuine support, than had been the case in the past.[14]

Regional loyalties also needed to be considered. There had always been some kind of regionalist spirit in some parts of provincial Mexico which was at best sceptical of political authority in the capital. The north, in particular, was more rootless, more capitalist and far less collectivist than the centre and south of Mexico. There can be little doubt that some of these anti-system feelings were exploited by the PAN in Chihuahua and other northern states. If the PAN had been allowed to perform well in Baja California Norte and Sinaloa, where local elections were to be held later in 1983, the results might perhaps have threatened to give the PAN 'a power base from which it could start seriously to challenge the PRI's national hegemony'.[15]

Finally there were fears, to some extent genuine but also deliberately exaggerated, that a resurgent and threatening right-wing would emerge from electoral liberalisation. The right certainly had become noisier and more overtly hostile to the system. The Church was notably more outspoken after 1982 then it had been earlier. It is hard to say how many businessmen committed themselves after 1982 to a full-scale rejection of the dominant party and presidential system in Mexico but the number had surely increased significantly over pre-crisis levels.[16] Meanwhile there were voices in Washington predicting, perhaps hoping for, the destabilisation of the Mexican political system. Apparently William Casey, the head of the CIA, pressed his agency to produce alarmist reports on Mexico in order to justify his arguments that there was a 'domino effect' from Nicaragua.[17]

We do not know exactly how these pressures combined to persuade de la Madrid to reverse his policy of respecting opposition election victories. What seems to have happened is that some forces within the system became alarmed and then persuaded de la Madrid that policy should be reversed. A particularly important role seems to have been played here by Fidel Velázquez, whose relations with de la Madrid were not good. Velázquez had publicised his unhappiness with the unveiling of de la Madrid in 1981; in 1983 he found himself in the intensely difficult position of needing to act with some conviction as labour leader at a time of sharply-falling real wages without going too far. De la Madrid, however, demanded public loyalty on all occasions and criticised Velázquez in public for some fairly harmless grumbling about the economic situation; the Labour ministry also attempted to build up the CROM and the CROC, pro-system labour organisations which in some ways rivalled the CTM, in order to put a check on Velázquez. However de la Madrid may well have come to believe that he could not afford to alienate Velázquez decisively for fear of splitting the PRI. In late 1983 both Velázquez

## De la Madrid: The Limits of Orthodoxy

and Gamboa Pascoe – another veteran *PRIista* labour leader – made particularly aggressive statements directed against the PAN[18]

Under these circumstances de la Madrid evidently decided that the risks attached to allowing an electoral opening were too great. Starting in late 1983 the PRI and *Gobernación* simply received instructions, or possibly just permission, to do whatever was necessary (up to and including wholesale ballot-rigging) in order to secure results acceptable to the system. A few opposition victories were allowed, but in general the tide was simply rolled back. While there was a price in terms of credibility and international respectability, the internal opposition had no immediate answer to the regime's policy of simply declaring the election results which it wanted (in some cases declaring it had won even before the votes were counted).

Much the same fate overtook the plan to reform the PRI from within. The PRI was in 1983, as it had always been, a party of affiliates. Individuals could not join the PRI directly but only the CNOP, which had a limited though admittedly influential role within the system. This permitted the peasant association and, far more important, the labour unions affiliated to the PRI to nominate individuals for particular elected offices. These individuals were therefore loyal to those organisations that affiliated them but not necessarily popular either with other members of the PRI or with the electorate as a whole. The system was a good way of maintaining control but a poor way of meeting the needs either of ordinary voters or of individual party members. Labour did relatively well out of the system, and labour leaders feared that a more open procedure would enable articulate middle-class activists to dominate and thus crowd out workers' nominees. At the end of 1982 the Congreso de Trabajo had nominated to elected positions a total of 93 members of the Chamber of Deputies, 16 Senators, and two state governorships; in addition, there would have been very many nominees to elected office at lower levels.[19]

Voices had been heard, at various times, calling for reforms which would strengthen the link between individual membership of the PRI and candidate selection. We have already seen that Madrazo had attempted to reform the PRI to turn it into more of a membership party in the 1960s and that his efforts were repudiated by Díaz Ordaz. In 1983–4 a rather similar set of proposals was considered. These would have introduced some kind of primary system for the selection of PRI candidates, with voting taking place under the joint supervision of the national executive of the PRI and *Gobernación*. An experiment was attempted in Nayarit in 1984 but, despite the strong advocacy of such reform by the national Secretary of the PRI, de la Madrid quietly aborted the experiment. Again it is likely that he was influenced by Velázquez' complaints to the effect that there were, as it was, too few workers' representatives in elected positions; Velázquez was obviously opposed to a reform which would have ensured that there were fewer still. In Norman Cox's understated conclusion 'the reconciliation of sectoral quotas with local preferences may not always be easy'.[20] In the end, it was the effort to reform which lost out.

Thus de la Madrid began with a policy of allowing party competition, which he then reversed. He replaced it with a commitment to reform within the system, which he then also reversed. While it is true that both reforms were controversial and faced strong opposition, it is far from clear that his best strategy was in fact quietism. It rather appears that de la Madrid wished to make changes but did not have the necessary confidence to stick to his guns when faced with opposition. His (for the most part) politically inexperienced cabinet cannot have helped him very much. In 1984 he told an American academic that he did not believe Mexico was ready for democracy as such. He preferred to maintain Mexico's essentially corporatist structure, ignore critics of right and left but avoid intolerance or over-reaction. It is true that he responded to criticism more calmly than did any of his predecessors,[21] but he failed to use his political authority to much effect.

There are several points to be made about this style of politics. One of the main themes of this book is that Mexican politics cannot afford a 'non-political' style of presidential leadership because its other political institutions are seriously flawed. (Readers will note that this argument has nothing at all to do with that type of approach which bases itself on Mexico's allegedly-authoritarian political culture.)[22] The de la Madrid presidency provides a good test for the hypothesis that presidential good behaviour is an adequate substitute for effective leadership. In my view, the hypothesis fails.

It was certainly possible in 1984 to find independent-minded and well-informed Mexicans who were largely sympathetic to the abandonment (or at any rate postponement) of further political reform. The PAN had at times acted very aggressively. In December 1984 an attempt to rig the ballot in a number of municipalities in the northern state of Coahuila led to major violence incited by PAN militants, the sending in of the army, and an international incident which was widely reported in the United States. Yet the PAN evidently did not have a distinctive policy orientation which was seriously different to that of de la Madrid – except for a kind of political Catholicism which few Mexicans supported.[23] Moreover the government did seek to reconcile the system with local business interests, whose tendency to switch their support to the PAN largely accounted for its renewed strength. Many state governors were appointed who were notably sympathetic to business, and a number of prominent businessmen were encouraged to stand for local political office. There was, in any case, little or no political discrimination against ex-PANistas;[24] often former opponents of the system were welcomed into the PRI, sometimes with nearly farcical results. On 1 April 1984 (appropriately enough) in local elections in Nueva Casas Grandes (in Chihuahua) the PRI and the left-wing PSUM fielded former PANistas, while the PAN fielded a former member of the PRI. On elections held on that same day at Madera (also Chihuahua) the PRI put forward the same man as had fought the 1983 elections for PAN.[25]

Meanwhile some gestures continued to be made to the left; two new left-wing parties were recognised in 1983–4, and a new left-wing daily (*La Jornada*) was allowed to come into existence in 1984. Although the government did use some force to end the Marxist experiment in Juchitán, it tended in practice to be fairly tolerant of criticism and unwilling to repress heavily. Even in Juchitán, no deaths were reported.

However while the short-term tactical situation did facilitate a policy of 'political closing' during 1984, the government was building up problems for itself in the longer-run. One problem comes from the nature of Mexico's political institutions. The PRI does face a legally-recognised opposition which has certain privileges stemming from the fact of recognition. It also has to face regular elections; Congress is re-elected after three years, and there are state governorship and municipal elections somewhere in Mexico every year. Consequently there can be no question of rigging one set of elections and waiting for the next *sexenio*.

Elections have to be managed, one way or another, every year – sometimes every few months. However while the rigging of an occasional election in a remote part of Mexico may once have passed with little challenge, a continued policy of rigging everything created a cumulative effect in the eyes of the opposition and the media. It also enabled fraud itself to become a powerful election issue on which all opposition to the system could unite.

A second problem stemmed from what we have already seen to be the very poor quality of many local candidates. The central authorities sought, in some cases at least, to appoint more competent (if not necessarily more popular) figures to local office. However they were labouring under the self-imposed limitation that, as we have seen, de la Madrid stopped his 'moralisation' campaign well short of attacking established figures within the system. Notorious *caciques* such as La Quina of the oilworkers and Jonguitud Barrios of the teachers' union continued to prosper and to dominate politics in particular areas. An example of the kind of situation to which this gave rise occurred in Nuevo Laredo in 1984. The politics of this town were dominated, for many years, by the corrupt local boss of the CTM. However in 1983 a new reforming mayor was imposed by the PRI. One of his first steps was to reduce the budget deficit by cancelling the contracts of 13 non-existent gardeners, allegedly employed by the city, whose pay in fact went straight to the CTM boss. Outraged by this attack on his privileges, the CTM boss declared a general strike. This was brought to an end when an angry populace burnt the house of the CTM boss and forced him to flee to the USA. In most cases, however, it was the corrupt local powerbroker rather than the imposed reforming administrator who won the day.

A third factor was that the policy of paternalism and rigging, however faithful to the traditions of the past, increasingly came under attack during the de la Madrid *sexenio* from intellectuals committed to democracy as an end in itself. An important step in this process was publication of Enrique Krause's seminal *Por una Democracia Sin Adjectivos* in *Vuelta* in 1983.[26] What was involved here was the coming together of two very different political traditions. The right had, after the experiences of 1976 and 1982, increasingly lost faith in the value of a strong president guaranteeing the processes of capital accumulation by dividing, ruling and where necessary repressing workers, peasants and students. The authoritarian state was seen in a very different light when it started to expropriate property, introduce exchange control and ally itself diplomatically with Cuba against the USA.

While it is natural that many on the left should have interpreted this change of heart with some scepticism, it also followed a change of emphasis in both Washington and the Vatican. The Catholic Church in the 1980s was far less willing to support dictatorships than it had been in the 1950s and 1960s; in responding to liberation theology the Vatican was careful to reject Marxism – but it did not reject democracy or social reform. The Church had travelled a long way from its anti-communist crusading of the early 1960s. Washington's journey had been more recent. It is demonstrably true that, with the significant exception of the 1961–3 period, post-war US governments did not put a very high premium on the importance of democracy in Latin America *per se*; indeed they often sought to undermine democratic reform movements due to (usually exaggerated) fears of 'Communist infiltration'. However Washington's need to develop a coherent anti-Sandinista propaganda line, and its disappointing experience in cultivating the Galtieri regime in Argentina, do seem to have convinced the Reagan administration of the advantage of appearing to support democracies. This general change in policy line, as well as undoubted irritation in Washington at López Portillo's foreign policy, combined to produce a certain distancing between Washington and the PRI. Although Díaz Ordaz and Lyndon Johnson had been close in the 1960s, the mere fact that de la Madrid was something of a conservative was not sufficient to re-establish a close relationship between Reagan and de la Madrid. Moreover the US media, and some notable figures in Congress, were on the whole even more sceptical than Washington of the Mexican system. This scepticism came to focus directly on allegations of ballot-rigging within Mexico; suddenly what might have appeared a relatively unimportant event in international terms (such as the rigging of a ballot in Sonora or Chihuahua) became a highly publicised issue.

The main problem with avoiding political reform, however, was a much more simple one. Until the early 1980s the Mexican system was reasonably popular; dissent was generally restricted to places where the shoe pinched particularly hard. Recession and stagflation do however tend to reduce the popularity of any government. As time went on and the de la Madrid government's economic problems mounted so the government's party-political position weakened. The policy adopted during 1984–6, of refusing to accept any significant opposition victories, simply disguised an increasingly difficult situation and thus made it more difficult to deal with over the longer term.

## MID-TERM PROBLEMS

What remained centre stage during 1984–7 was the continuing difficulty of managing the Mexican economy. After all, whatever other problems there may have been, the Mexican economy did achieve sustained growth over the whole period from 1940 to 1982; between 1982 and 1988, however, there was a sustained fall in living standards. Since most, though by no means all, contemporary observers were disagreeably surprised by the partial failure of the 1983 stabilisation policy, it is worth asking why economic management should suddenly have become so difficult.

One of the most negative factors was that some $70bn had fled Mexico during the speculative panic of 1981–2. There had been periods in the past when capital had fled Mexico, but it had generally returned once policy had restored confidence. This time, however, it was different. The difference lay partly in the cumulative effect of two sexennial crises, partly in the condition of the Mexican economy itself and partly in far less favourable international conditions. After previous economic crises (1961 and 1977) recovery came largely from taking advantage of new international opportunities. In 1961 the United States had directed official aid towards Mexico, and other parts of Latin America, as part of the Alliance for Progress. In 1977 there had been the oil discoveries. In 1983 the situation was very different; international factors were strongly negative. They included the crippling cost of debt service and the problem of real oil prices which declined slowly during 1981–5 and very sharply indeed during 1986.

With the benefit of hindsight it is clear that the problems which de la Madrid faced during 1982–3 were not susceptible to quick or easy solution. De la Madrid seems to have underestimated his difficulties; he had given several press conferences early in his administration which predicted that Mexico would enjoy a sustained economic recovery by 1985. If he had believed differently, what might he have done? There is an argument that a truly major programme of political and economic reform would have changed expectations; this might have reassured those Mexicans who had successfully exported their capital and induced some capital repatriation. There is, moreover, the Machiavellian precept that a ruler who has to take unpopular measures should take them all at once; there is nothing worse than having to continue to disappoint people.

However it was in 1984 still a minority view that something had gone quite radically wrong with the whole economic process; most economists believed that Mexico faced nothing more serious than a period of adjustment after which is would be possible to return to the kind of growth rates prevailing in the 1960s. The international financial community also tended to believe this. Some Mexicans in quite senior positions did not appear to realise that the economic situation was serious at all. Early in 1984 the energy ministry was talking seriously about the possibility of contracting another nuclear power station and the British embassy was approached about possible bidders. De la Madrid had himself served in senior governmental positions prior to 1982; he would have shared the opinions of figures such as Silva Herzog that a total economic 'shock' policy was not necessary. Such a policy would in any case have been especially risky given the lack of overt crisis conditions or of any sense within the policymaking élite that drastic change was inevitable.

In 1984, therefore, the government began to ease up and allowed the economy to expand, with little further effort at re-structuring. Positive economic growth was recorded during 1984 and the first half of 1985. However signs began to mount early in 1985 that severe problems were developing. One of these problems was external and largely beyond the control of the Mexican authorities. The real price of oil had been in slow decline since 1981 but a degree of producer solidarity(which de la Madrid shared even if López Portillo had not [27]) had kept this decline within bounds. In early 1985 there was a further period of oil-price weakness. Mexico sought to maintain prices but suffered a severe fall in output levels in the first half of the year; prices were eventually cut in both May and July but Mexico suffered the worst of both worlds. The slowness of the price cut had cost custom while the price cut that had eventually to be made cost revenue. (The policy of producer solidarity was eventually abandoned, but not until 1986.) Moreover the policy adopted in 1984 of allowing the real value of the peso to rise as a counter-inflationary move led to sharp rise in imports and, later, a reduction in non-oil exports. By mid-1985 Mexico was facing a balance of payments crisis. Matters were made much worse by a devastating earthquake which hit Mexico City on 19 September, killing over 10,000 people. The economic consequences were also very damaging; the earthquake did attract some international sympathy for Mexico but obviously damaged the tourist trade and also destroyed a number of economic installations. Finally all calculations about the Mexican economy were upset at the beginning of 1986 when the world oil price collapsed with very serious implications for the future of Mexican exports. At some point between the middle of 1985 and the beginning of 1986 de la Madrid had to face the fact that his economic strategy had gone badly wrong and that serious difficulties would continue for the rest of his *sexenio*.

Why had this happened? The hard-line economic liberals within the government had few doubts. The Bank of Mexico, for example, published an exceptionally clear and outspoken report in early 1986 which began by asserting that genuine economic progress had been made during 1983. However from late 1984

> worrying changes [could] be seen in some fundamental variables. The declining trend of inflation and the build-up of international reserves went into reverse and the current account of the balance of payments worsened. The most important causes of this deterioration include the financial requirements of the public sector; 1.5 billion *pesos* had been budgeted for this and the outcome was a requirement of 2.8 billion *pesos* (9.6 per cent of GDP).[28]

The motives for this overshoot in public spending were, to some extent, political. The government had become concerned about the danger of political attack from the right and had responded by making public funds available to loyalists on a selective basis. Companies which remained loyal to the public sector enjoyed what were effectively subsidised loans from the nationally-owned banks. State governors were allowed supplementary budgetary allocations, particularly in regions where the opposition posed a threat.

Even if such a process had not been allowed to get out of control in a short-term budgetary sense, there was something inherently self-defeating about a tactic which involved extending precisely those aspects of state power to which its critics most objected. One presidential adviser, whose preference for lower spending and more open elections had been overruled, wrote bitterly to de la Madrid that 'the bureaucratic and union controls over the population are increasingly ineffective in quelling the growing opposition to the regime, and they also have effects which are counter-productive'.[29]

Within the Mexican government the Banco de México report was seen as an attack on the public sector as a whole and on Planning Minister Salinas de Gortari who was in theory responsible for managing it. Although the report undoubtedly reflected the views of Mancera, the report could not have been published without the support of de la Madrid who thus indicated his unhappiness with the whole 'consolidationist' attitude to economic policy. De la Madrid had by then come around to the view that consolidationism had not been enough and that a deepening of market liberalism was necessary. The earthquake and the oil price collapse thus brought about a climate where radical economic reform was once again on the agenda.

Nevertheless, the government had undoubtedly enjoyed some political rewards from the recovery in living standards which occurred during 1984 and early 1985. Mid-term elections were held in July 1985, at the height of the boom. It is difficult to put very much trust in the official results, due to the fact that there was transparent ballot-rigging in a number of areas. Cornelius describes Sonora in 1985 as 'one of the dirtiest elections in recent Mexican history. Both the PRI and the PAN had used every possible means, legal and illegal, to try to control the electoral process'.[30] The figures for the congressional elections, in which fraud is likely to have been less, show a decline in the share of the vote for the PRI from the 69–70 per cent achieved in both 1979 and 1982 to 64.8 per cent. Most of these losses corresponded to gains made by the smaller parties, mainly to be found on the left. The PSUM and the PAN also lost electoral share compared to 1982.

Even if one makes due allowance for an element of ballot-rigging, there was no real evidence that the electorate was yet moving from the dissatisfaction undoubtedly felt at government policy to large-scale support for any of the main alternatives. While there were continuing signs that the PRI was losing ground in urban areas, its ability to maintain tight control over rural localities was not yet seriously threatened.[31] There was also evidence that the government, while unwilling to allow the opposition to break new ground, was willing to make some concessions in order to maintain the appearance of democratic competition. The PAN was ultimately declared the winner in eleven Congressional seats – an all-time high.

Yet the 1985 elections continued a trend which had started the year before, according to which opposition politicians began to unite in a demand for clean elections. Given a 'first past the post' electoral system, the PRI could technically continue to govern even with a relatively small share of the vote, provided that the rest was scattered among a range of opposition parties. In 1985 the PRI with just under 65 per cent of the official vote, still led its nearest rival by a four-to-one margin. Even allowing for the element of exaggeration induced by ballot-rigging, the PRI was still far stronger than any other party. Even if the PAN had won the Sonora governorship, the PRI's hold over the political system as a whole would scarcely have been threatened. On the other hand opposition unity did pose some kind of threat, at least in principle, by threatening to undermine the 'divide and rule' techniques with which the PRI had become so familiar. Fraud itself was becoming an issue on which the government was becoming increasingly vulnerable to attack.

## THE FALL OF SILVA HERZOG

The collapse in international oil prices in January 1986 changed the outlook for the Mexican economy from troubled to potentially catastrophic. It also made clear to most informed Mexicans that 'national unity' policies were no solution to the economic crisis. Left-wingers within the system began meeting in early 1986 in order to look for ways of pressuring the government to move in a more populist-nationalist direction.

This was one direction in which de la Madrid clearly had no intention of going. Instead he chose to move toward a deepening of the market-orientated reforms which had been cautiously attempted during 1983. De la Madrid believed that Mexico's international creditors had little option but to accept gradual economic reform, since they themselves had a great deal to lose from the collapse of Mexican creditworthiness – and, still more, from any threat to Mexican political stability as a whole. However the stakes were now very high and, partly for this reason, a tighter discipline came to be imposed within the cabinet. Carlos Salinas, temporarily out of favour with de la Madrid because of his failure to control public spending during 1984–5, came back into line. He took Pedro Aspe as his sub-secretary and successfully re-formed an alliance with Mancera. In May 1986 de la Madrid reshuffled his cabinet and brought a prominent 'political' figure, Alfredo del Mazo, into it as Secretary for Energy. As we shall see (p.154) this left Silva Herzog in a difficult position; he, like Salinas, had originally been a consolidationist but from the spring of 1986 he began switching his rhetoric into a much more nationalist line. He was then asked to resign, and did so in June 1986.

The fall of Silva Herzog illustrates further the nature of presidential power and is worth considering in some detail. The first point to make is that a cabinet minister with presidential aspirations (which Silva Herzog clearly had) has to strike a difficult balance if he is to catch the eye of the existing president. If he does too little he may be dismissed as ineffectual. If he does too much, he risks being rejected for being more royal than the king. The fate of Uruchurtu, dismissed as *Regente* of the Federal District by Díaz Ordaz allegedly for being too popular, is quoted by students of Mexican politics as a case in point, neatly encapsulated by Fidel Velázquez' dictum that *el que mueve, no sale*. (He who moves when the photograph is taken will not come out in the picture.)

There is a further complication which relates specifically to the cabinet of de la Madrid and, perhaps by extension, to the nature of a system dominated by technocrats. It is generally accepted that in Mexico a candidate for president must have served in one of a small number of key ministries. With the exception of López Mateos (ex-Labour minister), all Mexican presidents since the war came either from *Gobernación*, the planning ministry, or the finance ministry. Most (though not all) of the pre-candidates for president also came from these ministries, and the last three presidents have come from planning or finance. Holders of these offices are therefore seen, and are likely to see themselves, as potential presidents. What this means, though, is that any economics minister has to cope with political rivalry of a kind which may make it more difficult for him to do his job. The problem will become worse at the time before the official unveiling becomes shorter.

Under de la Madrid two economics ministers were considered from the outset to be possible presidents. One of these was Silva, and the other was the Planning Minister Salinas. These two were policy allies (in the sense that they were both orthodox economists), but inevitably also political rivals; it is also clear that they were not fond of each other. As a consequence the making of economic policy under de la Madrid was weakened from the beginning by a degree of bureaucratic infighting. Policy was constrained not just by the political needs of the government as a whole, or those of the president, but by the rivalries and political needs of various Secretaries. Silva had certainly sought to recruit personal allies in his search for advancement and to distance himself from some aspects of the government – correspondents of some key foreign newspapers clearly understood that Silva did not like the policy of ballot-rigging and preferred a more liberal approach to domestic critics.

Silva also appears to have felt particularly threatened in early 1986 when Alfredo del Mazo was brought into the government as Energy Minister. Del Mazo, who had been governor of the State of Mexico, was an accomplished politician with good contacts with the CTM. He was also seen as a close personal friend of de la Madrid who once described him as 'the younger brother I never had'. As a former state governor, and the son of a senior politician, del Mazo had the political experience of which de la Madrid evidently felt the lack. Del Mazo was believed to be sympathetic to a more traditionally nationalist line of policy than the one being pursued at that time but he had links with business and was very far from being an ideological left-winger. He was good-looking, a good speaker and evidently at least moderately popular with the general public. His promotion to the cabinet immediately signalled that he was to be considered a potential president. A number of informed sources in fact believed him to be the front-runner. According to one source, Silva was quite rude to del Mazo at one of his first cabinet meetings, describing him as a child prodigy; de la Madrid was said to have been unamused. In any case, it seems likely that Silva was afraid of being isolated as 'the minister from the IMF' at a time when a potentially more popular figure was emerging into the limelight. He seems also to have underestimated de la Madrid's own commitment to orthodox economics.

The removal of Silva as Finance Minister therefore proved to be a successful exercise of presidential power in that it simplified both economic decision-making and the presidential succession. Silva's replacement, Petricioli, was a relatively bureaucratic figure rather than a man who carried serious political weight. Salinas de Gortari however emerged as super-minister and presidential front-runner; economic policy became considerably more coherent. At the same time, the presidential succession appeared to remain open due to the fact that Bartlett (the *Gobernación* secretary) and del Mazo remained in the running.

The fall of Silva Herzog was, therefore, more important for what it indicated than for what it produced. At the beginning of 1986 de la Madrid was generally perceived as an economic liberal and political conservative. He was perceived similarly, only more so, at the end of his term in 1988. Only those observers who expected to see a policy move toward the centre as the end of his term drew nearer were proved wrong. In a sense the surprise, at least in policy terms, was that there were no surprises.

Even so, there was a more pronounced move in the direction of economic liberalism after 1985. In 1983 De la Madrid had, on the whole, been concerned to stabilise rather than reform. Above all, the size, behaviour and assumptions of the public sector did not significantly change.[32] Thus when policy was partially relaxed during 1984, government spending again overshot targets and the bureaucracy again sought to offset the costs of an inflationary domestic policy by controlling and restricting imports. The *peso* therefore became overvalued. Senior bureaucracy meanwhile insulated itself from economic pressures by awarding itself substantial wage increases – which were naturally denied to lower-level bureaucrats and public sector workers. In 1983 the number of public-sector employees actually rose.

Moreover, there was little or no progress with the task of privatising state enterprises. De la Madrid had made it clear that he did not intend to return the banks to the private sector after 1982. One influential private sector analysis complained in early 1985 that 'the list of companies on sale was never published in full and no sales have been subsequently announced; on the contrary, certain bids for companies are known to have faced enormous bureaucratic barriers'.[33] Even where grudging and piecemeal changes were made – to the regulations on foreign investment and on the relaxation of imports – they did not have a great deal of impact on private sector confidence because of the general mistrust that indecisive government policy had engendered.

In the second half of the de la Madrid *sexenio*, however, many of these problems were at any rate partly addressed. Instead of imposing any kind of economic shock, it was de la Madrid's style to allow the thrust of his policies to develop gradually although at an increasing pace from the beginning of 1986. In that year Mexico joined GATT – a move which López Portillo had earlier apparently ruled out – and embarked on a concerted policy of tariff reduction. Renewed efforts were made to sell state enterprises to the private sector and some serious (though still limited) privatisation did take place in 1987 and 1988. Meanwhile debt renegotiations with the commercial banks (under the auspices of the United States government) continued; they had not really ceased at any point after August 1982. Debt-for-equity swaps came to be permitted, and there were the first serious signs of a pick-up in private investment.

On the international front it appears that Carlos Salinas quickly filled the vacuum left by the departure of Silva Herzog and began establishing relations with Washington, particularly with James Baker who was then Secretary of the Treasury. Salinas seems to have promised Baker that many of the changes for which the United States had been pressing would be carried through, albeit at a more deliberate pace than the United States had wanted. Despite some scepticism, Washington, the IMF, and the banks had little choice but to agree to give Mexico the benefit of the doubt.[34] Meanwhile Salinas was able to convince de la Madrid that Washington would cooperate in offering further finance to Mexico: this would prevent the need for truly drastic deflation in 1986 and allow needed adjustments to be spread over a longer period.

Until shortly before de la Madrid's visit to Washington in July 1986 it was not clear whether a deal would be possible or not. In the end, US voices favouring good relations with Mexico (notably Paul Volcker and James Baker) won out over the sceptics and de la Madrid was able to satisfy his US allies of his seriousness in continuing with a market-orientated reform programme. The Baker package for Mexico was essentially agreed by September 1986 although final approval from the banks did not come until November. A year later, Mexico's international financial position was looking more healthy.

## POLITICAL DEVELOPMENTS 1986–88

Political change in Mexico during 1986–88 was extremely rapid and complex. However three major dimensions of change can be identified. One had to do with changes in the relationship between the state and private capital. De la Madrid seems finally to have become convinced during 1987 that his policies of economic restructuring required formal negotiations with the private sector; this did not involve merely the formal recognition of the official business organisations but extended to serious bargaining with independent employers' associations. De la Madrid, earlier in his term, had publicly denounced the independent employers' organisation Coparmex and called for Mexican businessmen to operate purely through the official business organisations; in 1987 de la Madrid did not merely negotiate with Coparmex (and the equally independent employers' coordinating commission, CCE), but actually accepted its representations in preference to the more protectionist policies advocated by the officially-recognised confederation, Canacintra.[35]

Evidently de la Madrid came to accept that a market-orientated and export strategy required a shift in economic power, both from smaller and more traditional business to the larger companies, and also from the state to the private sector as a whole. Big business in Mexico had survived Díaz Ordaz' paternalism and Echeverría's hostility to become a direct negotiator with government.

What seems to have forced the issue was that the economy, although somewhat helped by the Baker agreement, continued to suffer a number of problems of which one of the most serious was a high and accelerating rate of domestic inflation. De la Madrid obviously feared that additional uncertainty over the *destape* process would prove a further aggravating factor, a fear which the stock market crash of October (similar to, but more severe than, the crash which took place in other parts of the world) clearly accentuated. Thus from around this time de la Madrid began serious negotiations with the private sector and rather more cosmetic negotiations with the CTM before announcing an Economic Solidarity Pact in December 1987. While this was in some senses a heterodox stabilisation plan, it was far more free-market oriented than similar plans announced in Argentina in 1985 and Brazil in 1986 and it contained a number of measures (such as further privatisation of state assets) which the larger and more independent business organisations were demanding. However one of its key elements was the hope (in the event partly justified) that lower nominal interest rates would improve the government's fiscal position while lower inflation would reduce its unpopularity.

The second major area of change was the electoral reform of October 1986 which offered a commitment to some kind of electoral pluralism. Proportional representation was introduced into state legislatures, and further encouragement was given to national opposition parties. The third major change was also electoral. However this was not a matter of institution-building by negotiation but rather related to a major split within the official party itself. Each of these changes had major implications for the pattern of presidential politics in Mexico.

While some Mexican presidents have become increasingly autocratic as the end of their term of office approached, de la Madrid seems if anything to have become more conciliatory. This is possibly because he really did have no desire to continue to hold power after the end of his term, or even to write his place in the history books by making some dramatic gesture. After leaving office he told one interviewer (who believed him) that toward the end he was positively counting the days until he could step down. Consequently de la Madrid did what rule-observing Mexican presidents 'should' do, which was to try to make life as easy as possible for his chosen successor.

One target for conciliation was the party political opposition. Conciliation followed exceptionally blatant rigging during elections in the state of Chihuahua in July 1986; here the PRI declared itself the winner in practically every contest despite total and undisguised incredulity. This uncompromising attitude led to major acts of disaffection within Chihuahua itself, the formation of a united front among the opposition parties to protest at continuing electoral fraud and a circular letter signed by a number of leading Mexican intellectuals calling for the elections to be annulled. One PANista went further and took his complaint to US Senator Jesse Helms; as a result congressional and media criticism of Mexico intensified within the USA. This development was hardly welcome to a government which badly needed support from Washington if it was to turn around the difficult economic situation. Beyond this, there was a real danger that the opposition would boycott or possibly disrupt the 1988 presidential elections unless there was some reversal of policy.

## De la Madrid: The Limits of Orthodoxy

The response to the rigging in Chihuahua does seem to have persuaded de la Madrid that the PRI had gone too far in insisting on its electoral monopoly. The president of the PRI was quickly sent away to govern the state of Hidalgo (one well-connected source indicated that he clearly did not wish to go) and *Gobernación* produced a new electoral reform. The most important feature of this reform was that proportional representation would be introduced into local and state elections. The form this took was that a number of seats would be allocated automatically to parties which failed to win. Additionally a further element of proportional representation would be introduced into the Chamber of Deputies to add to that which it already had.

This, as the opposition parties quickly realised, was an important change. It gave opposition parties a guarantee of representation in the legislature in every state in Mexico. Opposition party leaderships now had some real patronage to offer, thus helping them to build nationwide machines, while local PRI leaders realised that their every act could be scrutinised and possibly denounced in public. While fraud might still take place, this guarantee of representation across the whole of the country promised to increase the status of opposition parties in their *national* role. It also had the effect, which was not immediately foreseen, of giving the PRI's hitherto-satellite parties (the PPS and the PARM) a potentially independent base if they were to break away from the system. It is likely that the reform gave away considerably more than it intended.

Lugo Verduzco was replaced as head of the PRI by Jorge de la Vega Domínguez. De la Vega was an old political professional who, during an extensive career, had served under every president since Díaz Ordaz. However de la Vega, despite his political experience, was not an especially impressive figure; some well-informed Mexicans tended to consider him a source of amusement.[36] Even so, he had few actual enemies and a wealth of contacts. To improve further the image of the system, the unpopular governor of San Luis Potosí was removed soon afterwards and replaced by a more acceptable figure.

Meanwhile there were, during 1986, increasing signs of disaffection within the left wing of the PRI itself. On the left, the diagnosis of the situation appeared reasonably simple. The PRI was, in this view, potentially a mass popular party. Its ideological objectives – nationalism, some form of social democracy within an inclusionary political system – were those which the majority of Mexicans could be expected to share. Yet the PRI was losing popularity because the government was committing itself to an economic policy which manifestly was not working. What was needed, in this view, was pressure from the rank and file of the system (that is, from local political activists) to change economic policy in a populist direction.

The Democratic Current within the PRI came to public attention in August 1986. This was at a time when there was already increasing speculation about the question of who would get the nomination as de la Madrid's successor. There is no evidence of any particularly close connection between this Current and del Mazo, who was the most traditional of the main contenders; however it is clear that the Current was clearly hostile to the candidacy of Carlos Salinas and to the cause of economic liberalism generally. What was also clear was that the Current was no more than the small tip of a very large iceberg. Its leaders, Cuauhtémoc Cárdenas and Porfirio Muñoz Ledo, were men of considerable political stature whose chances of further advancement were effectively blocked. Muñoz Ledo had been close to Echeverría (whom he served as Labour Minister and head of the PRI) and had served in López Portillo's cabinet. However he had lost his job as Mexico's ambassador to the UN under de la Madrid after some undiplomatic behaviour over a parking space, following this up with a personal confrontation with Mexico's foreign minister. Cuauhtémoc had served as governor of Michoacán but lacked the credentials as an economist which were becoming necessary for a move into the Cabinet; his views, in any case, were far too left-wing to be acceptable to de la Madrid.

Another development was the growing competition for the succession itself. This offered an unusually clear choice between the political styles of the potential candidates. One of these was Alfredo del Mazo. Del Mazo was (as far as the imprecise term fits anyone) a populist. He was, of all the potential candidates, probably the most hostile to any idea of opening the political system to genuine opposition victories. A relative of one foreign correspondent in Mexico City was engaged in overseeing local elections in a district of the State of Mexico when she was surprised by a telephone call from del Mazo himself; del Mazo ordered that the election results show a complete victory for the

PRI (the *caro completo*) – and so they did. Del Mazo was known to be close to Fidel Velázquez and believed also to be close to Lugo Verduzco, head of the PRI at the time of the Chihuahua fraud. Del Mazo was known to be the choice of many, if not most, PRI activists.

At the other pole in terms of political style was Carlos Salinas de Gortari. Salinas had earned no less than three postgraduate degrees from Harvard – two Master's and one Doctorate – by the age of twenty-eight. He was undoubtedly the best-educated potential president in the whole of Mexican history. After completing his education, Salinas worked in the planning ministry; he began working with de la Madrid in 1979 and rose with him. After the resignation of Silva Herzog, Salinas was the man most responsible for economic policy. Salinas had (and has) a certain natural puritanism which contrasted sharply with Silva's flamboyance but his political and economic outlook seems to have been almost classically 'technocratic'. He was, in other words, committed to market-orientated economic policies and to alliance with the United States; conversely he was unremittingly hostile to mass mobilisation and 'populism' but relatively tolerant of formal political oppositon. His refusal, while a member of de la Madrid's government, to look for a political base of his own was striking. Salinas knew that the real power lay with the president and he worked hard to catch the eye of the one man, not the multitude. Salinas was opposed by the Democratic Current, Fidel Velázquez and the leaders of the PRI.

The third potential president (assuming that a further three figures, although officially described as pre-candidates, are not taken seriously in this context) was Manuel Bartlett, the Secretary of *Gobernación*. Despite his hard-line reputation, no less than three differently-placed sources in 1985–6 told me that he was not especially intolerant of opposition. On several occasions he apparently wished to negotiate with the PAN, but found himself overruled or pre-empted by less tolerant figures heading the PRI. Before being made Secretary of *Gobernación* by de la Madrid, Bartlett was a fairly junior figure whose career had not particularly prospered. Even when Secretary of *Gobernación* he seems not to have been able to impose his personality. It would not, perhaps, be unfair to see him as an agreeable and decent mediocrity – a servant of power rather than a leader of men. However he might have been considered a compromise candidate if del Mazo and Salinas had ever succeeded in blocking each other and he did have the political backing of a number of insiders.

By choosing Salinas, de la Madrid evidently selected the man whom he himself believed would make the best president. If he had chosen the man most likely to be popular, either among the electorate or among the PRI activists, he would have chosen differently. If he had chosen his closest friend, he might again have chosen differently. Yet Salinas stood for many of the same things as de la Madrid; de la Madrid, who was always more of a true believer than an opportunist, therefore chose him.

The Salinas candidacy was radically unacceptable to the Democratic Current. Almost immediately afterwards, Cuauhtémoc Cárdenas announced that he would run for the presidency. In November 1987 the PARM officially nominated him as its candidate and other parties of the left swung over to support him in the subsequent months. Cuauhtémoc's candidacy did not lead to wholesale defections from the PRI, although he could count on some very significant covert allies including La Quina of the oilworkers' union.

This is not the place for a detailed discussion of the 1988 election campaign. What is clear is that for the first time since the early 1950s the official party faced a major electoral challenge. Moreover, unlike its reaction during 1940–52, it did not respond with a policy of wholesale ballot-rigging. In some places there surely was dishonesty; in others the local *cacique* simply delivered the vote to the official party.[37] However in the large urban centres the strength of the opposition vote could not be denied. In the Federal District, Cuauhtémoc Cárdenas was declared the winner; his supporters were also elected to the Senate where the PRI candidates narrowly avoided coming third behind both opposition parties.

The PRI did hold the Estado de México and the state of Jalisco, though not by impressive majorities, but the PAN won seven of the eight congressional districts in the city of Guadalajara. The opposition also won several other states, especially those where the government was particularly unpopular.

For the system as a whole, this was evidently a bad result. Why should it have occurred? It is reasonable to suppose that a more politically-attuned figure than de la Madrid or a more competent party manager than de la Vega could have produced a stronger performance by the PRI; de la Madrid appears to have blamed shortcomings in the organisation of the official party.[38] There is also the obvious fact that falling living standards during 1982–8 produced a loss of popularity for the government. Against this, the suddenness with which serious opposition emerged may have somewhat limited the challenge. Since competitive party politics was quite a new concept in Mexico (and even now is an incomplete one), many disaffected Mexicans abstained rather than voting for an opposition party. However, enough did vote for Cárdenas to produce a close election. Whatever the future may hold, it is unlikely that any Mexican president will again be able to ignore public opinion, or indeed political organisation of any kind, and forge ahead with an economic restructuring with little concern for his own popularity or the political organisation of his own society. This is by no means clearly a bad thing.

It would also be interesting to have a fuller analysis of the role which the minor pro-system parties played in 1987. It was the PARM which, by supporting Cárdenas' presidential candidacy, actually made it possible for him to run; it did so even though there were opposing voices raised within the party.[39] Supporters of the decision believed that it would finally end the PARM's reputation as being a weak pro-system party which nobody would support. This logic was, of course, electoral and related to the tendency both in 1982 and 1985 for independent left-wing parties to attract support away from the PPS and the PARM. Thus as electoral politics became more open, the position of the pro-system parties became increasingly uncomfortable and they eventually decided to make a clean break with the PRI.

This specific illustration makes a more general point. The Cárdenas candidacy may well have been the catalyst which decisively moved Mexico toward an era of mass politics. However, this occurred in a political system which was already changing, rather gradually it is true, in the direction of greater emphasis on electoral competition. The institutional bases of electoral competition increasingly existed. There were (perhaps too many) opposition parties. The opposition had a number of seats in Congress and also in local assemblies. It had some experience of local government. It operated, moreover, in an environment in which an increasing proportion of educated public opinion wanted a more competitive electoral system and in which Mexico's handling of internal political questions was increasingly a matter of international scrutiny. All of these factors had reinforced the increasing pluralisation of Mexican politics during the previous generation.

## BY WAY OF CONCLUSION: MEXICAN POLITICS IN DECEMBER 1988

De la Madrid and his close allies appear to have diagnosed the crisis of 1982 as the consequence of bad presidential style and wrong economic policymaking. They did not see it as being mainly caused by societal change or inadequacies within Mexico's political structure; there were Mexicans who did believe this to be the case, but their criticisms were – in general – brushed aside by de la Madrid. De la Madrid sought to be a more ethical, and more technically qualified, version of a traditional Mexican president. He believed that the system's Golden Age was to be found during the presidency of Ruiz Cortines. It was in keeping with this idea that, after a brief experiment with competitive elections in 1983, de la Madrid put the clock back to a traditional style of *alquimía electoral*.

These beliefs were almost certainly sincere but almost certainly misguided. De la Madrid's conception might have been a reasonable one if the crisis of 1982 were taken in isolation, but the conflicts of 1968 and 1976 surely related far more to changes within Mexican society and the inability of the system to cope with them than to mere individual error. For one thing the state was far larger and more important than it had been in the early 1950s. The question of 'who is to guard the guardians?' was therefore even more acute. Moreover Ruiz Cortines, unlike de la Madrid, did intervene in local fiefdoms to a great extent; he removed more governors than any subsequent president. Although an appeal to the president against the local corrupt bureaucrat or office-holder may not be the ideal safety-valve, it is a great deal better than nothing at all. De la Madrid appeared to believe that, if he demonstrated a high standard of personal conduct, he could lead by example alone; the evidence, however, did not support him. A medieval chronicler wrote of the twelfth-century English king Stephen that he 'was a mild and Christian man, and under him no justice was done'.

Moreover the system, below presidential level, has not yet found a satisfactory way of dealing with criticism from the articulate or the wealthy. As we saw in the Introduction, the system has tended to afford marginality to the poor, corporatism to the middle sectors and neopluralism to the intellectuals and the bourgeoisie. While the system has always fallen far short of its 'revolutionary' pretentions in its treatment of the poor,[40] it nevertheless seems clear that the poor cannot on their own mount a serious challenge to the system. On the other hand, the 'corporate' sector of Mexican politics seems to have served the system well; whether or not it has served the members of this sector well is, of course, a different question. Controlled support from organised labour played a major role in anti-inflation policy in 1977 and again in 1987; moreover while de la Madrid was certainly inconvenienced by La Quina, the system has on the whole proved highly capable at dealing with difficult *caciques* – as La Quina himself found to his cost in January 1989. Until the system itself split, in 1987–8, it also proved highly capable of containing threats from below.

The real problem that the system faced, and still faces, has been its inability to deal with alternative élites. The instinct of any revolutionary élite is, no doubt, to destroy or at least drastically tame all independent sources of power. Mexican Jacobinism was never as thoroughgoing as that of some other revolutionary societies, but Mexican politics nevertheless remained anti-pluralist for many years after it had ceased to be anti-capitalist and supportive of political mobilisation. Moreover the PRI was not designed to represent the views of an articulate membership, but to reward conformity and control elections; all efforts to reform the PRI by turning it into a members' party have been successfully resisted. The strongest argument against this kind of reform was that it might undermine the 'conforming' part of the Mexican system.

Thus the system responded to demands from the intellectual left, first by closing up and repressing, and later by expanding the role of the state so as to accommodate graduates into the bureaucracy. It is obvious that both solutions were badly flawed. The one led to the spectre of 'bureaucratic authoritarianism', the other to the fact of economic failure. De la Madrid sought to avoid both of these responses, but he could offer no real solution – except the negative one of using power with a certain amount of restraint. If there is to be a solution it must surely lie in extending the effect of the political reforms of 1977 and 1986 and allowing Mexico to develop into a genuine multiparty system. There are many European examples which suggest that a competitive party system can co-exist with some form of societal corporatism.

The system has also suffered from difficulties in its relationship with the private sector. Conflicts have occurred from which both sides have emerged as losers. What seems to be clear is that the private sector, and Washington, after 1982 wanted a combination of economic and political reform. They were not content, as the private sector generally was under Díaz Ordaz, to defer contentedly to a neo-Hobbesian despot. It may well be that de la Madrid's reluctance to carry through institutional reform postponed somewhat Mexico's economic recovery and so increased the popularity of the left-wing opposition in the 1988 elections. There was a strong feeling among at least some of de la Madrid's top economic advisers that poor communication with the private sector was partly responsible for the slowness with which bourgeois confidence was restored. Hence, no doubt, the change to a strategy of negotiation during 1987.

It is nevertheless possible to see the final outcome of the de la Madrid presidency as relatively benign. Mexico has, willy-nilly, acquired some kind of competitive party system without losing its corporatist structure altogether. The over-deferential quality of public debate and political analysis is far less in evidence than was once the case, but there is no serious sign of a descent into anarchy or total irresponsibility. The Mexican economy suffered some serious setbacks, but avoided hyper-inflation. It is far less dependent on oil exports than it was in 1982 and there is reason to hope that renewed growth will be based on far firmer foundations than was the case during 1970–82. De la Madrid may have succeeded in doing what he should have done, if not in what he wanted to do.

# 6 Conclusion: The Presidency and Political Change

Daniel Cosío Villegas characterised the Mexican presidency as 'an absolute monarch for six years'.[1] There is an obvious sense in which this statement is true; there is virtually no constitutional check on the power of the Mexican president.[2] We have seen that each of the last four presidents of Mexico carried out a number of wholly arbitrary acts (fewer perhaps in the case of de la Madrid) for which they did not in the least expect to be held personally responsible.

But how much do the presidential personality and presidential politics actually matter? One rule-of-thumb way of testing this is to see whether one could provide an adequate account of Mexican socio-political development since 1965 leaving the presidency out of account altogether. A Marxist or economic structuralist would say that the most important changes during this period were determined by governmental effects to rebalance the economy.[3] Economic growth until 1970 was based on the exploitation (in both senses) of the surplus provided by reformed agriculture and by a narrowly pro-private sector industrial policy which gave the state little margin to operate independently. This 'model' was becoming impossible to develop much further because agriculture was already in relative decline and because the familiar 'import-substituting industrialisation' bottlenecks were beginning to occur. From 1970 to 1982, therefore, the Mexican state sought to intervene far more in the industrial development process but faced financial difficulties which neither foreign borrowing nor oil exports could ultimately alleviate. (An economic structuralist would also give due weight to the inherent problems associated with managing an oil boom.) After 1982 the state had little option but to seek a resumption of growth through a renewed opening to the world economy, with policies of trade liberalisation, fiscal orthodoxy and cuts in public programmes. It would not surprise a Marxist that such a reorganisation would have implications for a range of activities such as industrial relations [4] and that it would be bitterly contested within Mexico. A Marxist would fear that a deeper authoritarianism might now develop behind a facade of liberalism and 'selective democracy'.[5]

A pluralist or modernisation theorist, engaged in debate on these lines, might feel free to express more optimism. He would stress that Mexico has in the past twenty-five years (notwithstanding the 1980s recession) become more urban, educated and middle class. He might admit that the traditional PRI and presidential authoritarianism, for all of its faults, was a good and effective method of ruling rural and first-generation urban Mexico. It was not as rigid or repressive as a military dictatorship, but not as capable of 'massification' or subversion as full-scale democracy. The argument would be that rapidly developing and urbanising societies are particularly prone to the kinds of upheaval which Mexico has since 1920 successfully avoided. The pluralist would add that Mexico has gone through the whole post-war period without encountering the political crises or breakdowns which occurred in Chile, Argentina and Uruguay (and also Greece and Turkey) between 1966 and 1982 – or the even more severe crises which afflicted a number of European countries between 1919 and 1945. Moreover the contrast between the political stability of present-day Mexico and the violent upheavals of the 1810–1940 period is striking. However the pluralist would say that now, given the fact that socio-economic development has eroded the former bases of system legitimacy, it is entirely appropriate that Mexico should be moving toward a system which gives far greater weight to elections and party competition.

Both of these views, the structuralist-pessimist and the voluntarist-optimist, direct themselves to important realities. How much would these views need to be influenced by a taking-into-account of the presidency in Mexican politics?

One immediate consideration is that the power of the presidential institution itself makes it quite possible for one observer's authoritarianism to be another observer's democracy. Even if the formal requirements of democracy were met (free elections – their outcome honestly recorded – between competitive parties with no kind of 'vanguard' relationship with state power), the Mexican system would still have a strong system of central authority. These 'strong government' aspects of the Mexican system can be explained in terms of the fact that it did not emerge, as the US system did, from a reaction against an arbitrary despotism; rather it emerged from experiences of chaos and anarchy as severe as any in the American hemisphere this century. The fact that Mexican writers are increasingly arguing for a less powerful presidency[6] is in some sense a tribute to the contribution which the system has already made in 'taming the bronco' in Mexican society.

Liberal critics have certainly been concerned at the authoritarian nature of the system and the absence of redress in the face of bad and arbitrary government. Granted, they would say, that the presidential institution has protected Mexico against some of the evils that might otherwise have befallen it; but has it not introduced many evils of its own? Is it not an illusion, as Locke asked three centuries ago, for a people to expect safety by entrusting themselves to a despot? Is a despotism not precisely that form of government most dangerous to any people? And does not power itself corrupt more dangerously than anything else?

Foreign observers have often seen this danger. Just over thirty years ago there was a discussion within the British Foreign Office about the nature of the Mexican political system. It was Sir Henry Hankey who commented:

> It seems to me that this system is workable only so long as the condidates successively selected by the retiring President are people of restraint and sound common sense. The opportunities for abuse of power and the apparent lack of any of the normal 'checks and balances' usually associated with democratic regimes do not offer any guarantee of permanent political stability.[7]

Some may recognise here the voice of Cassandra. If we take presidential decision-making in 1968, 1976, 1981–2 and 1986 we are likely to find events which seem to strengthen the arguments of writers like Locke and Madison – men suspicious of power – rather than Hobbes or the latter-day apologists for 'moderate despotism'.

One effect of presidential power, then, which both Marxists and pluralists need to take fully into account, is the ability of presidents to deliver shocks to groups which they see as constituting a threat, thereby shaking the system as a whole. I think the word 'shock' is better than crisis in that it takes more fully into account the arbitrary and short-term factors behind presidential responses to threat. So far, the effect of these presidential shocks has been to speed up the alienation of powerful interests from the state and also from something which might more broadly be called the 'revolutionary system'. The effect of all these shocks taken together has been to leave a considerable number of people dead, to damage Mexico's international reputation and significantly to reduce Mexican living standards.

It would, however, be misleading to compare the Mexican presidential system with the hypothetical alternative of perfection. It is clear that the Mexican political system is in many ways already and unavoidably undergoing rapid change. It would be moderately, though not absurdly, optimistic to see these changes as heralding a move in the direction of greater pluralism. If presidential power were as destructive an influence as is sometimes asserted, this move could not now be taking place. Instead the Mexican system would be responding to threats either by disintegrating or by closing up, repressing dissent and refusing to recognise the need for any reform.

This leads on to a second point about presidential power. The Mexican president has the ability, when he wishes, to clamp down on petty tyrannies and local abuses of authority. Many Mexicans would vastly prefer the relative impersonality of presidential government to the far more despotic kind of rule often preferred by the local *cacique*. Moreover the promise of an evolution toward greater pluralism is, for the moment, threatened far more by vested interests within the system than by any presidential excess. Successful political reform cannot be introduced in Mexico only from above, but pluralism under law cannot possibly be achieved without presidential support. In a non-pluralist and often non-legal environment the practical alternative to presidential power is too often gangster power and even narco-power; de la Madrid's caution led to the ascendancy, not of the PAN or independent unions, but of Jonguitud, Felix Gallardo and La Quina.

## THE LIMITS OF PRESIDENTIALISM

Another line of criticism of the Presidential system is more empirical. Mexico (like any other country in the world) needs high quality political leadership. Does the evidence show that the system can provide it? A sceptic would point to what, at least until 1982, looked like a consistently deteriorating trend in presidential performance. The last Mexican president who is generally considered a success was Ruiz Cortines. López Mateos also defended the system successfully at some apparent cost to his personal values. After that, the picture worsens. Díaz Ordaz' efforts to use the Olympic Games to enhance Mexico's international reputation failed disastrously; he also found himself openly repudiated by his own choice of successor. Echeverría failed to reorganise or even control the economy; his term ended in devaluation and policy reversal. At least Díaz Ordaz and Echeverría, controversial though each of them was, did have their supporters. López Portillo was not controversial. He was a failure; despite the fact that he was in some ways more benign than either Díaz Ordaz or Echeverría he failed to control either his own behaviour or the Mexican economy. He ended up not merely unsuccessful, but positively ridiculous; when López Portillo was recognised in Europe by a group of Mexican tourists they barked at him in an ironic reference to his earlier promise to defend the peso like a dog. De la Madrid was certainly a better president than López Portillo; he had a seriousness and consistency of purpose which commanded respect. It is quite possible that his economic reforms will prove to have been far-sighted. However, it would be hard to consider as fully successful a presidency which ended on so unpopular a note. A few months before the 1988 elections, de la Madrid predicted that the PRI would win twenty million votes; in the end it won nine million.

If Mexican presidents are so powerful, then why have they not been more successful? Personal factors aside, I believe that the answer comes out of a distinction, first drawn by Michael Mann, between despotic power and infrastructural power.[8] Despotic power (I adapt Mann's distinction slightly) means, quite simply, the power to command and be obeyed. 'I say to a man come, and he cometh; go and he goeth, do and he doeth'. The despotic power of a state, then, consists of its ability to command – and where appropriate monopolise – force. There may need to be a degree of legitimation (depending on which definition of legitimacy one chooses to adopt), but a distressingly large number of unpopular and incompetent despots have ruled for long periods in a variety of countries. In any case what is definitionally central is the fact of rule rather than the fact of legitimacy.

Infrastructural power relates to the ability to succeed in pursuing defined policy objectives through mobilising resources. Except in pure totalitarian regimes, infrastructural power is diffused within a society. To bring it to bear therefore requires a degree of societal cooperation. To achieve it, the state must enter into (implicit or explicit) relationships with various groups and perhaps with civil society as a whole. These relationships are often complex. It is however fundamental that infrastructural policy objectives cannot be met by a mere process of command; they demand a degree of consensus or at least coalition-building.

There has, between 1952 and 1988, been no major challenge to the despotic power of the Mexican system. In other words there was not any serious likelihood that the PRI would be overthrown by force, that it would split so badly as to be unable to continue in power, or that it would allow itself to be defeated in presidential elections. Despotic power in Mexico was in the hands of the president; the only real limitation on his power was the 'no re-election' rule which seems to have been introduced and sustained by political insiders as a means of regulating intra-élite conflict; the right of an outgoing president to nominate his successor appears to have been something of a quid pro quo.[9] No Mexican president since 1952 has ever willingly accepted a challenge either to his despotic power or to his ability to nominate a successor of his choosing.

While the system has maintained its control of despotic power, it has been unable to control or entirely cope with the fact that the amount of 'infrastructural' power in the hands of civil society has been increasing. This helps to explain why the Mexican system, authoritarian as it is in many ways, does not wholly have the 'feel' of an authoritarian society; there is, rather, a great deal of competition and conflict but so far almost entirely at the infrastructural level. The question which has been debated (most often) then, is not 'who should rule?' but rather 'what should appropriate policies be?'

The extension and consolidation of despotic power is one of the main themes of Mexican history in the years after the revolution. The largest step was the elimination of extreme *caudillismo* and the centralisation and civilianisation of power. We have noted the further extension of central government once this initial process was complete and the assertion of national over regional and state power; this was a process which continued well after 1952 and is in some ways continuing still. Until 1940, however, the Mexican government did have to contend with the possibility of its own armed overthrow from a combination of internal disunity and societal rebellion.

The group activities and social movements of the past thirty years, which we have considered here were however not for the most part threats to the despotic power of the state. It is perhaps just possible to argue that the left-wing insurgencies which occurred sporadically between 1960 and 1976 could be considered as such. Yet the story of the student movement of 1968 was not mainly about threatened violence from below (though Díaz Ordaz, like General de Gaulle, apparently believed for a time that it was), but about the opening of channels for political expression; it is similarly hard to see how the workers' movements of 1958–9 were direct threats to state security. It is also quite obvious that the 'bourgeois' opposition after 1982 did not have a state–threatening character. Cárdenas' election campaign of 1988 possibly was a threat to the system, but in the short run it had a chance of wresting power from the PRI only if the latter could be prevailed upon to yield gracefully. In 1988 there was no suggestion that it would do so.

We have already seen that the performance of the Mexican system after 1940 has some features of a Hobbesian bargain. According to the terms of the bargain, the state tolerates no challenge to its authority; in return it affords physical protection and some basic rights to its subjects. In other words, the state must be secure in its control of despotic power if it is to offer anything to its subjects by way of return. It is clearly part of the thinking and also in the interest of a Hobbesian state to identify any demand for freedom or autonomy, and any attempt to change public policy except by the most deferential of means, as a direct threat to state security. However by relentlessly closing safety valves and denying the validity of plural interests, it may succeed in turning some dissent precisely into a direct challenge to security.

During 1964–88 the Hobbesian bargain remained partially in place in Mexico. Yet when it reasserted, or attempted to reassert, its despotic power the Mexican state set back its pursuit of a number of 'infrastructural' objectives. It then chose to resume its pursuit of these objectives, by making some real political concessions. These have now accumulated to the point where the inner structures of the Mexican state are under pressure as never before. Development of genuinely competitive democracy in Mexico is, now, a real option.

Let us consider this argument in detail. The repression of the student movement in 1968 seriously damaged the state in the eyes of the Mexican intelligentsia. It is true that the Mexican intelligentsia, for many years before 1988, generally failed to connect with 'the masses'. Attempts to reconstruct the *Cardenista* coalition of the 1930s failed, both in the aftermath of the Cuban revolution and subsequently. This does not mean, however, that intellectual opposition to the system could simply be written off. Intellectuals have established important contacts within their own political system and also with intellectuals in other societies, with the international press and therefore foreign decision-makers. It is noteworthy that, at the beginning of 1989, Cuauhtémoc Cárdenas's first serious foreign tour as unofficial leader of the Mexican opposition was to the United States. Personal contacts and friendships exist between Mexican intellectuals and journalists, on the one hand, and foreign correspondents of the international press on the other. There is some direct exchange of information – sometimes of a non-attributable kind. Newspapers such as the *Financial Times* now regularly report on clashes between the state and dissident peasants in Tabasco, Michoacán and other places which readers of that newspaper a generation ago would scarcely have known existed.[10] *Time* and *Newsweek* regularly quote certain prominent Mexican intellectuals about developments within their own society.

There is, of course, no direct or immediate trade-off between the Mexican government's record on human rights or its respect for election results and its ability to win relief on a proportion of its debts. Nevertheless the international community is not always willing (as perhaps it was a decade ago) to consider the economic prospects of a society in isolation from the nature of its political system or the willingness of its rulers to respect human rights. Rulers who suffer a poor image in the international press and find themselves denounced in the US Congress may well suffer no loss of despotic power; however their (infrastructural) policy options may well be circumscribed. For Mexico, with its inevitable dependence on US capitalism, the costs of a poor image may be considerable.

Beyond this observation, which is to some extent a generalisation, we have the historical record since 1968. Echeverría was sufficiently respectful of many policy recommendations from the intellectual left to have accepted them, and co-opted a number of left-wingers into his administration. It is partly because the system found it necessary to co-opt the left after the shock of 1968 that it now finds itself with a scarcely manageable and highly expensive state bureaucracy.[11] The system has certainly been criticised for responding inappropriately to the shock of 1968; in the eyes of some of its critics, it should have reformed its politics rather than altering its policies.[12] What is on the record is that it did respond, and on a considerable scale.

Mexican intellectuals, moreover, do influence the thinking of people within the system.[13] At a time when the system is less sure of itself than formerly, intellectual dissent or the promotion of new ideas, forcefully articulated in local periodicals which have a guaranteed élite readership, can influence policies. It can also encourage divisions within the system and also reveal – thereby undermining – various manipulative ploys to which the system has resorted. In sum, then, the Mexican intelligentsia matters.

This is still more evidently true of the private sector. We have also seen, on several occasions since 1959, that the bourgeoisie has been able to exert considerable pressure on the Mexican state. It was in the 1950s and again in the 1960s pressing for a direct role in public policy making. Díaz Ordaz (through Martínez Domínguez) publicly announced in 1968 that he was not prepared to accede to this demand. Echeverría went even further; he directly criticised COPARMEX for requesting a direct input into policy. Both presidents asserted their belief that it was wrong for the Mexican private sector to have independent economic power. By 1976, however, it had been made clear that the private sector did have economic power and was prepared, if necessary, to use it. The Mexican state, as such, was not threatened but its economic performance was.

The same drama was played out, more erratically, under López Portillo, who originally made a show of allowing the private sector a direct policymaking voice; the GATT debate was to be the key example of this. However once his economic plans had failed, López Portillo – like his predecessors – interpreted policy setbacks as a direct bourgeois attack on his own credibility. He responded by nationalising the banks, though stopping short of a full-scale attack on those responsible for exporting capital. The long-term damage done to the Mexican political system was limited – but that done to the economy was very considerable.

It is now quite obvious that the government needs the private sector to invest in Mexico; the private sector does not need to do so, however, and evidently cannot be forced. The government is not therefore wholly free to make economic policy. Efforts by Mexican presidents to assert state power over the bourgeoisie essentially failed; it is highly unlikely that any Mexican president will in the foreseeable future take measures which the private sector seriously resents. Instead Mexican presidents must seek to govern within this constraint.

The story of Mexico's opposition parties is similar. The authorities until recently tended to take the view that these should be encouraged to exist but not permitted to compete or exert real influence. López Portillo (following on from López Mateos and Echeverría) encouraged opposition parties because he did not believe that they could be a threat. However these parties acquired a strength which the system found surprising, first in the north during 1983–6 and then again with the emergence of the Cuauhtémoc candidacy in 1988. As with other challenges, there was no direct threat to state power (notwithstanding some rather wild rhetoric by the PAN in 1983–4) and the system could (and presumably can) continue to rig election results without any real fear of precipitating violent revolution. However the system eventually found that the (infrastructural) cost to its reputation was becoming excessive; reputational damage compromised its other objectives such as the ability to attract investor confidence. The PRI's resort to shameless ballot-rigging also exacerbated conflicts within the system.

It is too early to say whether the PRI is likely to face, or would accept, electoral defeat in 1994 – but the question is by no means an absurd one; to have asked a similar question in 1983 about the 1988 elections would have seemed so. We do know that in 1988–9 President Salinas preferred to accept an opposition-controlled governorship in Baja California Norte and a substantial opposition presence in the Mexican Congress rather than face the costs of continuing to rig ballots. As a consequence there is now a genuine (even if imperfect) electoral dimension which is a constraint on the policymaking autonomy of the Mexican president and a possible indicator of a fundamental future change in the nature of the political system.

What seems to have happened since 1964 – perhaps since 1958 – is that each presidential term has seen the emergence of a newly confident and increasingly independent sector of civil society. The president has sought to repress or inhibit this emergence; this attempt has led to some form of crisis. The successor president has always gone at least some way to win over and reconcile the alienated group. In doing so, he has not just restored a balance but permitted the further evolution of the system itself. We shall return to this point below. The key argument here is that a central feature of the past generation has been the diffusion of infrastructural power through more sectors of Mexican society. This is precisely what 'modernisation theory' would have predicted.

One of the charateristics of infrastructural power is that groups who possess it tend, on the whole, to be relatively privileged in other ways as well. It has always been a criticism of liberalism that (according to its critics) it does little or nothing for the poor and disadvantaged in any society. Can it be argued that the greater political openness that undoubtedly exists in Mexico has occurred at the expense of those collective values which were most justly considered revolutionary? Is the gain to pluralism balanced by a loss in equality? Fidel Velázquez would answer in the affirmative. The rewards available to discipline and solidarity are less in Mexico than they were; the rewards to technocratic education and, indeed, many forms of educated articulateness are very much greater. The rewards to capital are, perhaps, greater still.

We do not know, but are likely at some point to discover, whether a less loyal and disciplined labour movement can develop its own form of (countervailing?) infrastructural power. The labour vote, and the labour presence within the PRI, are considerable. It is open to the President to disregard labour organisations as they are presently constituted (a fact made quite obvious since 1983) but is there a potential for influence of which a more independent labour sector could make greater use? And can the rural poor take advantage of the more competitive electoral situation to force the state to take more note of them? What is certainly true is that the Mexican state had few scruples in suppressing challenges from groups which had no real independent source of power. The 'old left', based on the Cárdenas coalition of the 1930s, lost out badly during the post-war years. Because it had no independent control over resources, this left was powerful only while it enjoyed a sympathetic hearing from government. Sanderson finds that left *agrarismo* failed in post-war Sonora because it was 'totally excluded from the system of rewards available to the regime, while [its] leaders were being offered lucrative and prestigious inducements to prostrate themselves before the government'.[14] The 'mass organisations', in which the left vested such hopes, in practice existed almost entirely on state sufferance.

## PENDULUMS AND PLURALISM

It is not especially new or startling to claim that the Mexican president is less powerful than he sometimes seems. What is more difficult is to trace out the dynamics of the relationship between the Mexican presidency and developments within civil society.

Needler's 'pendulum theory' is a good place to start.[15] According to this, left and right-wing social forces are not powerful enough to constrain every Mexican president but they do count for enough to influence the system over the longer term. It therefore suits both individual Mexican presidents and the system as a whole if a long-term balance is created between left and right-wing Presidents. A right-wing president will often be followed by a left-winger; sometimes the adjustment will be more gradual but there will in any event be a long-term movement toward – and across –the political centre.

Empirically this theory has worked quite well. The trajectory has gone from Cárdenas (left) to Avila Camacho (centre), Alemán (right), Ruiz Cortines (centre), López Mateos (left and centre), Díaz Ordaz (right), Echeverría (left), López Portillo (centre until 1982, then violently left) and de la Madrid (right). It must of course be accepted that these designations (left, centre or right) correspond to popular perceptions of how presidents act and are therefore to some extent arbitrary.

This theory, while in some ways helpful, lacks the dimension which we have already discussed. The power of the Mexican state is gradually reducing and that of certain sections of society increasing. Mexican presidents have therefore tried to balance things, but not always successfully. Each of the last four presidents confronted an important source of infrastructural power and, in some sense, lost. The effect of these defeats has been cumulative. As a consequence the policymaking autonomy of the Mexican government has rarely been so limited. It has to deal with foreign bankers and investors (and with Washington which influences them), local capitalists (with their foreign bank accounts), an electoral opposition which captured Mexico City in 1988 and elected a governor in 1989, and an intellectual élite which is increasingly influential in shaping media and international images of Mexico. The state does not face any of these interests completely without cards, but it is in a position of relative weakness which is unprecedented at least since 1940. The process by which groups and sectors of Mexican society became increasingly autonomous and demanding will continue. The best way for the authorities to respond is probably through some explicit commitment to pluralism under the rule of law, but system change is an unpredictable matter at the best of times.

To see some form of pluralist evolution as a positive development is to adopt the view that the state and civil society are in some sense potential adversaries. This is not a position that every Mexican would recognise. Conservative supporters of the system tend to see it as seeking to protect society from renewed upheaval and violence. Left-wing supporters see it as the only protection against US-style capitalism. In this case at least one of the social forces mentioned above ought to consider a diminution of state power as seriously threatening. My own view is that these pro-state interpretations were plausible in the early 1960s but are far less so now. Again, the point is worth arguing out.

In 1960 Mexican political society, like that in many other parts of the non-communist world, could be understood broadly in terms of a few rather simple concepts. There was a left, a right and a centre. The left supported policies of state socialism involving some degree of expropriation of private assets. The Latin American left was supportive of the Soviet Union, enthusiastic about the Cuban revolution and deeply suspicious of the USA. The left sought, with varying degrees of success, the support of the organised working class and sectors of the peasantry. The Latin American right was religious and deeply antipathetic towards communism. It was broadly supportive of the United States although still somewhat suspicious (less so than in the 1930s) of the more materialistic and 'liberal' aspects of North American society. Right-wingers tended to be middle class or wealthy; they grudgingly accepted the need for governments to adopt some kind of social welfare policies, but stressed property rights and rejected the notion of equality.

Mexico was distinctive in that the PRI continued to rule from a broadly centrist position. However in the early 1960s responses to the Cuban revolution led – in Mexico as in several other countries of the region – to a greater degree of polarisation between left and right. The slogan of the Mexican right *cristianismo si! comunismo no!* really said it all. This polarisation was potentially very dangerous particularly because of the strength of the Catholic Church. The incompatibility of Catholicism and Marxism led to civil war in Spain in 1936. The Cuban revolution led to a cycle of mobilisation and counter-mobilisation in South America culminating in military coups and 'dirty wars' in several different countries.

What the Mexican system sought to do, then, was to head off what it saw (rightly) as a genuinely threatening situation. López Mateos manoeuvred to hold the system together; the fact that he manoeuvred more to the right than the left indicated more the balance of force within Mexican society than López Mateos' own preferences. The occasional acts of state violence and repression, which did happen under López Mateos, could plausibly be justified in terms of this greater good.

What has changed since 1960? In a word, virtually everything. Internationally, and in Mexico, state socialism is in intellectual retreat. In 1960 there was every chance that an armed Castroist left would seek to spread revolution to the rest of Latin America. After 1979 there was, it is true, a serious suggestion that revolution might spread throughout Central America; some imaginative spirits were even asserting that there might be a domino effect upon Mexico.[16] However by early 1989 Cuauhtémoc Cárdenas was telling journalists that Mexico should honour its foreign debt pending renegotiation (which was exactly the position of the government), and visiting the United States. By this time exceedingly few Mexicans believed that there was much to emulate in revolutionary Cuba or Sandinista Nicaragua.

There is now, in other words, neither hope nor fear that revolutionary communism will spread to Mexico from Cuba. At the same time, while international communism has become less threatening, international Catholicism has become less reactionary and rigid. Catholics are now told that they must favour social justice. Many Catholic activists now align themselves with the left of the political spectrum; many voted for Cárdenas in 1988. Michoacán, once the stronghold of the *cristeros* and *sinarquistas*, has radically changed its position on the political spectrum. Thus, as pro-communism (at any rate pro-Castroism) lost much of its force in Mexico, the same came to be true of anti-communism. In 1961 the PAN had been urging López Mateos to take even more drastic and repressive measures against the left than those already in place. In 1986 opposition parties of the Marxist left and the Catholic right formed an alliance against the ballot-rigging practised by the Mexican state. Nor is this kind of convergence purely a Mexican phenomenen: in 1989 a coalition was formed in Greece between the conservatives and the communists against the social democrats, and something similar also happened in Bolivia.

In 1960, therefore, it was realistic for commentators supportive of López Mateos to see the state as keeping the peace between two potentially antagonistic sections of Mexican society. In 1990 the peacemaking role of the state is far less apparent and the 'divide and rule' aspect more obvious than ever.

Another important contributor to this change of climate (as both cause and effect) has been the United States. Between 1963 and 1976 Washington showed itself quite happy to support military governments or other forms of authoritarian regime in Latin America. It also seemed for a time as though Jeane Kirkpatrick's line – that authoritarian systems were acceptable allies – would influence the Reagan administration decisively. By around 1982, however, it became clear that this was no longer the case; Washington began to distance itself from the military regimes of South America.

Washington has never seen Mexico in exactly the same light as other Latin American countries. Even so, we have seen that during the 1960s US governments had no problems with the more illegal and authoritarian aspects of Díaz Ordaz' security policies. Yet US support for Mexican authoritarianism was always more fragile because the perceived opposition came from the right rather than the left; more than one US ambassador to Mexico is reputed to have had a soft spot for the PAN.

What seems to have happened in the period after 1982 is that US attention focused on abuses of power within Mexico to a far greater extent than the US administration had intended. This attention came more from the media and Congress than from the administration, which for its part had to respond in some degree to the pressures arising. Some US conservatives, moreover, felt that López Portillo had humiliated their country and were eager to take advantage of Mexico's renewed weakness to highlight what they saw as the shortcomings of Mexican political society. What is clear is that de la Madrid, who was as pro-US as Díaz Ordaz and far more respectful of human rights, did not enjoy as much immunity from serious scrutiny north of the border. Instead there were real pressures to open up the Mexican political system alongside the opening which was gradually being introduced into the Mexican economy. Thus when Cárdenas emerged as a major political figure during the course of the 1988 elections, efforts to whip up an 'anti-communist' response in the United States failed totally.

Socialism versus anti-communism, then, was the key conflict in Mexico in 1960; it was a societal conflict which the state tried, to the best of its ability, to mediate. This issue became slowly less salient from around 1976, and rapidly less salient after around 1986. Other issues have replaced it. I would argue that there are two key issues presently in dispute. One is that of economic management; Mexican economic growth, seen as relatively unproblematic until late 1960s, continued but with problems until 1982. The de la Madrid *sexenio*, however, was one of severe setback. The question of how growth is to be resumed, how it is to be financed and what the distributional implications of growth-producing policies are likely to be, are obviously at the forefront of debate. The second question is that of democratic pluralism itself; how far should it be encouraged to develop in Mexico?

Questions of economic growth and management are likely to focus increasingly on the role of the public sector. Echeverría and López Portillo constructed a greatly expanded state sector for reasons which seemed good at the time. Echeverría's belief, which if it had proved well-founded would have changed everything, was that state investment could efficiently finance continued economic expansion. In fact, however, the expansion of the state did not generate resources; rather, it consumed them. The effect of this was to a considerable extent disguised by the oil boom and by the expansion of foreign borrowing from 1970–82. Disguise is now no longer possible. If Mexico is to have a large state sector, then Mexicans will have to pay for one. The incentive for those outside the public sector to seek to tame it could hardly be greater. One question then concerns the political strategy which economic liberals will use to pursue their objectives; will their strategy be supportive of pluralism or hostile towards it? And where will the losers from this re-orientation go, politically speaking?

A crucial issue relating to democratic pluralism is the role of the PRI. While it is possible to imagine that a Salinas government could be popular if things go well, public confidence in the ruling party itself has surely descended below the danger level and possibly below the point of no return. The PRI was spectacularly rejected in Mexico City, both at the time of the earthquake in 1985 and the election in 1988. Many Mexicans evidently believe that much of their political establishment is made up of vested interests which represent nobody but themselves; the fact tht the term 'dinosaur' has been coined and applied to some figures within the system rather makes the point. Nor are provincial party figures exempt from this general discontent as we have seen in Michoacán and Baja California Norte in 1989. Much the same point can be made about the CTM. It would be rash to speculate too much about this before Fidel Velázquez' final retirement or demise, but what is clear is that not all of the CTM's power and influence is likely to survive Fidel. And will its loyalty to the system survive him?

In sum, then, the system is far less 'above the battle' than it was in 1960 and far more directly in the firing line. In the eyes of many Mexicans it is less the referee than the opponent. At the same time many of the old institutional supports of the system – notably the PRI and the CTM – are weakening, just when autonomous group pressures are strengthening. It seems clear that the resulting situation may be an unstable one.

However any approach which focuses on group process only will always bias analysis in the direction of exaggerating instability. My core argument, the main theme of this book, is that the Mexican system is a set of arrangements constantly being redefined (not necessarily in the direction of equilibrium) around its only fixed element – which is the presidency. A strong presidency can survive a weakening of such élite institutions as the PRI and the CTM, just as previous presidents survived the weakening of the revolutionary army, the revolutionary family and the mass base which the system had enjoyed in the 1930s and 1940s. What any president will need is to create new political institutions to replace the old declining ones, and a new kind of political appeal which can win over a large enough proportion of the population (and, it must be said, middle-class population) to be electorally convincing. This may seem a tall order, but it is by no means an impossible one.

# Notes

## 1 INTRODUCTION: THE MEXICAN POLITICAL SYSTEM

1. For a short but amusing discussion of this point see M. Needler 'The Significance of Recent Events for the Mexican Political System', pp. 201–17. J. Gentleman, ed., *Mexican Politics In Transition* (Westview, 1987).
2. A good example is Judith Hellman, *Mexico in Crisis* (Holmes & Meier, 1983).
3. The most articulate critique of this kind is G. Newell and L. Rubio *Mexico's Dilemma: The Political Origins of the Economic Crisis* (Westview, 1984).
4. Sol Sanders Mexico, *Chaos on Our Doorstep* (Madison, 1986).
5. H. Aguilar Camín, *Despues del Milagro* (Cal y Arena, 1988).
6. D. Cosío Villegas, *El Sistema Politica Mexicana* (Joaquin Mortiz, 1975) is the most effective exponent of the 'extreme presidentialism' thesis; from a very different viewpoint see S.K. Purcell and J.F.H.Purcell, 'State and Society in Mexico: must a stable polity be institutionalised?' in *World Politics*, vol. 32, no. 2 (January 1980).
7. J.G. March and J.P. Olsen 'The New Institutionalism' *American Political Science Review*, no. 78 (1986) pp. 734–49.
8. FCO 371 AN 1015/12. 2 June 1958.
9. This discussion is the subject of an extensive commentary in Cosío Villegas, *La Sucesión Presidencial* (Joaquin Mortiz, Mexico DF, 1975).
10. P.H. Smith, *Labyrinths of Power*. (Princeton, 1979).
11. M. Basáñez, *La Lucha por la Hegemonia en México*. (Siglo XXI, 1983).
12. FCO 371 AN 1015/1. 21 January 1958. Memo from Sir Anthony Noble.
13. See, for example, R.A. Camp 'The Political Technocrat in Mexico and the Survival of the Political System', *Latin American Research Review* 20, no. 1 (1985).
14. Ibid.
15. For example Ian Roxborough, *Unions and Politics in Mexico: The case of the automobile industry*. (Cambridge University Press, 1984) and A. Alonso, *El Conflicto Ferrocarrilero en Mexico* (Era, 1972).
16. On this see Ilán Bizberg 'La Crisis del Corporativismo Mexicano' (Mimeo, 1989).
17. Report to the President, 24 January 1951.
18. John Gledhill 'Agrarian Social Movements and Forms of Consciousness', *Bulletin of Latin American Research*, vol. 7, no. 2 (1988).
19. Gilbert Joseph '*Caciquismo* and the Revolution: Carrillo Puerto in Yucatán', in D. Brading, ed., *Caudillo and Peasant in the Mexican Revolution* (Cambridge University Press, 1980).

186  Notes to Chapter 2

20. By neo-pluralism I mean a pluralism which involves only the relatively affluent members of a society. For a discussion of theories of pluralism and neo-pluralism in developed democracies see P. Dunleavy and B. O'Leary, *Theories of the State: The Politics of Liberal Democracy.* (Macmillan, 1987).
21. Dale Story, *Industry, The State and Public Policy in Mexico* (University of Texas, 1986).
22. See the various chapters in Silvia Maxfield and Ricardo Anzaldua Montoya, eds, *Government and Private Sector in Contemporary Mexico* (University of San Diego, 1987).
23. R.D. Hansen, *The Politics of Mexican Development* (Johns Hopkins, 1971).
24. The classic statements that Mexican politics fits an authoritarian typology are found in E. Stevens, *Protest and Response in Mexico* (MIT Press, 1974) and S.K. Purcell, *The Mexican Profit-Sharing Decision: Politics in an Authoritarian Regime* (University of California, 1975).
25. The most notable account of this process is to be found in Nora Hamilton, *The Limits of State Autonomy: Post-Revolutionary Mexico* (Princeton University Press, 1982). See also W. Pansters, 'Paradoxes of Regional Power in Post-Revolutionary Mexico: the rise of *Avila Camachismo* in Puebla 1935–40', in W. Pansters and A. Onwered, eds, *Region, State and Capitalism in Mexico* (CEDLA, 1989)
26. Jean Meyer's *The Cristero Revolt* (Cambridge University Press, 1984) is an obvious exception.
27. Cosío Villegas, *La Succesión Presidencial*.
28. G. Almond and S. Verba, *The Civic Culture*, discuss the political attitudes of Mexicans in the early 1960s.
29. H. Aguilar Camín, *Despues del Milagro* (Cal y Arena, 1988).

## 2 DÍAZ ORDAZ AND THE STUDENT MASSACRE AT TLATELOLCO

1. 'Student Violence and Attitudes in Latin America', INR Working Draft. Mid-November 1968. (Lyndon Baines Johnson Library).
2. *Pensar en 1968* (Cal y Arena, 1988) p.97.
3. See, for example, the shift in perspective between (on the one hand) Robert Scott *Mexican Government in Transition* (University of Illinois, 1964) and P. Gonzalez Casanova *Democracy in Mexico* (Oxford University Press, 1970, first published in Spanish with ERA; 1965) and, on the other, R.D. Hanson *The Politics of Mexican Development* (Johns Hopkins, 1974) and S.K. Purcell *The Mexican Profit-Sharing Decision: Policymaking in an Authoritarian Regime* (University of California, 1975).
4. See, for example, Cal y Arena, *Pensar en 1968*; E. Stevens' *Protest and Response in Mexico* (MIT, 1974); E. Zermeno, *México: Una*

*Democracia Utopica: El Movimiento estudantil en 1968* (Siglo XXI, 1978); J. Scherer, *Los Presidentes* (Grijabo, 1986); Jose Cabrera Parra, *Díaz Ordaz y el 68* (Grijabo, 1980); and J.A. Hellman, *Mexico in Crisis* (2nd edn, Holmes & Meier, 1983).
5. S. Loaeza, *Classes Medias y La Politica en Mexico* (Colegio de Mexico, 1988) p.324.
6. J. Gunther, *Inside Latin America* (Hamish Hamilton, 1942) p.46. For a more scholarly account of the Avila Camacho fiefdom see W. Pansters 'Paradoxes of Regional Power' in W. Pansters and A. Onweed, *Regions, State and Capitalism in Mexico*. (Cedla: Amsterdam, 1989).
7. D. Cosio Villegas, *La Sucesion Presidencial* (Joaquin Mortiz, 1975).
8. Scherer, *Los Presidentes*. Cabrera ( in *Díaz Ordaz y el 68*) largely agrees.
9. OCI no. 1063/64. 1 April 1964.
10. Several contributors to *Pensar en 1968* stressed the way in which social conservatism contributed as much as political authoritarianism to the student radicalism of that year.
11. See, for example Scherer, *Los Presidentes*.
12. Ibid. p.19.
13. Ibid. p.17.
14. Ibid. p.16.
15. 19 February 1984.
16. A. Michaels, 'The Crisis of *Cardenismo*', *Journal of Latin American Studies*. vol. 2, part 1 (May 1970). D. Cosio Villegas, *La Sucesion Presidencial*.
17. White to Eisenhower, 29 August 1955.
18. Scherer, *Los Presidentes*, p.51.
19. 'Communist Cold War Efforts in Mexico, Central America and Caribbean' Department of the Navy, 3 March 1958.
20. Rae to Lloyd, 11 March 1958, FCO 371, File AM 1015.
21. Noble to Lloyd, FCO 371, File AM 1015.
22. H. Aguila Camín, *Despues del Milagro* (Cal y Arena, 1988).
23. Cook to Lloyd, 24 September 1958. FCO 371, File AM 1015/23.
24. I. Roxborough, *Unions and Politics in Mexico* (Cambridge University Press, 1984); E. Stevens, *Protest and Response in Mexico*; A. Alonso *El Movimiento Ferrocarrilero en México 1958–68* (Era, 1972). See also the British Foreign Office file FCO 371, AM 218.
25. See D. Mares, *Penetrating the International Market: Theoretical Considerations and a Mexican Case Study* (Columbia University Press, 1987) and S. Sanderson *Agrarian Populism and the Mexican State: the case of Sonora*. (University of California, 1981).
26. Cosío Villegas *La Sucesión Presidencial;* A. Sánchez Gutiérrez 'Mexico 1950–54: The political consolidation during the transition towards a stable development' (unpublished M. Phil thesis, University of Oxford; 1986).
27. Elisa Seruín, of INAH, is currently researching the Henriquista movement.

28. *Foreign Relation of the United States 1954*, pp. 1361–5. Memo from Ambassador White. Also White to Eisenhower, 29 August 1955.
29. Noble to Lloyd, 13 May 1958. AM 1015/4.
30. Loaeza, *Clases Medias*, p.197.
31. M. Morley, *Imperial State and Revolution*. (Cambridge University Press, 1987). However the British Embassy believed that López Mateos was seriously embarrassed when Cárdenas shared a platform with Castro in Havana on 26 July 1959. On 16 October 1959 Ambassador Noble wrote that "President López Mateos is known to be annoyed and seriously angry with Cárdenas" as a result of the latter's continuing support for Castro. (Noble to Lloyd, AM 1015/11).
32. On one of which see Loaeza, *Clases Medias*.
33. See, for example, Loaeza, *Clases Medias*. pp. 79–86.
34. A. Lajous, *La Contienda Presidencial 1988: Los Candidatos y Sus Partidos* (Diana, Mexico, 1988) pp. 56–7.
35. See, for example, Noble to Lloyd, 25 April 1958. FCO 371, AM 1015/9.
36. Loaeza, *Clases Medias* and A. Alvarado, ed., *Electoral Patterns and Perspectives in Mexico* (University of San Diego, 1987).
37. CIA Memo, 22 June 1962.
38. Loaeza, *Clases Medias*, p.327 and p.352.
39. The date was 24 November 1960.
40. FCO 371, AM 1015/9. State Department intelligence report, 30 August 1957.
41. Ibid states that 'Privately Velázquez has said that neither labor nor the PRI desires a conflict with the Church, but that the party would object strongly to Church participation in party politics'.
42. Page 195.
43. Loaeza argues this in *Clases Medias*, pp. 394–403.
44. Quoted in ibid, p.396.
45. 'It is increasingly evident that a PRI split may be inevitable and if López Mateos does not wish to be squeezed out, he may be forced to make a choice'. Mann to Sayre, 8 January 1962.
46. Ibid.
47. 1 April 1964.
48. Memo by Wallace Stuart 'The Popular Socialist Party and Vicente Lombardo Toledano, 8 May 1965.
49. 'Plans for Peasant Uprising in Linares, Nuevo Leon' CIA Intelligence Information Cable, 22 April 1964.
50. J. Reyes del Campillo, 'El Frente Electoral del Pueblo y el Partido Comunista Mexicano (1963–64), *Revista Mexicana de Sociologia*, July/September 1988.
51. This theme comes out in several contributions to *Pensar en 1968* (Cal y Arena, 1988).
52. J. Zepeda 'Los caudillos en Michoacán; Fransisco J. Mugica y Lazaro Cárdenas' in C. Martinez Assad *Estadistas, Caciques y Caudillos* (UNAM, 1988).

## Notes to Chapter 2

53. For a recent discussion of political society in Michoacán see J. Gledhill in *Bulletin of Latin American Research*, vol. 7, no. 2.
54. P. Agee, *Inside the Company:* a CIA Diary (Harmondsworth: Penguin, 1975). p.532.
55. Cosío Villegas, *La Sucesión Presidencial*.
56. Tad Szulc, *Fidel: a critical portrait* (Coronet, 1989) p.395.
57. Loaeza, *Clases Medias*.
58. See M. Wionczek, 'Electric Power: the uneasy partnership' in R. Vernon, ed., *Public Policy and Private Enterprise in Mexico*. (Harvard University Press, 1963).
59. S.K. Purcell, *The Mexican Profit-Sharing Decision*.
60. Loaeza, *Clases Medias*.
61. 1 April 1964.
62. For a discussion of the importance of patronage to the Mexican system see R.D. Hanson, *The Politics of Mexico's Development*.
63. Studies include Sanderson, *Agrarian Populism;* T. Ugalde, *Power and Conflict in a Mexican Community* (University of New Mexico, 1970); Carlos Loret de Mola, *Confesiones de Un Gobernador* (Grijabo, 1978); and J. Gledhill in *Bulletin of Latin American Research*.
64. C. M. Assad and A. Areola, 'El Poder de los Gobernadores' in S. Loaeza and R. Segovia, *La Vida Politica Mexicana en la crisis* (Colegio de Mexico, 1987) p.33.
65. FCO 371, AM 1015/9, Noble to Lloyd, 25 April 1958.
66. The classic account of this process is in P. Smith *Labyrinths of Power: Political Recruitment in Twentieth Century Mexico* (University of Princeton, 1979).
67. J. Taylor, 'Annual Report for 1951'.
68. See, for example, E. Marquez, 'Political Anachronisms: The Navista Movement and Political Processes in San Luis Potosí 1958–85', in A. Alvarez, ed., *Electoral Patterns and Perspectives in Mexico*; R. Bezdek, 'Electoral Opposition in San Luis Potosi; the Case of Nava', in K.F. Johnson, *Mexican Democracy: a critical view* (3rd edn, Praeger, 1984) and C.M. Assad, in Loaeza and Segovia, *La Vida Politica*.
69. G. Santos, *Memorias* quoted in *Proceso*, 'El Juego Sucio de la Sucesión Presidencial', 8 September 1986.
70. Bezdek (in Johnson *Mexican Democracy*) quotes Reyes Heroles as saying 'that Nava had won the gobernatorial election'. (p.251).
71. Loaeza, *Clases Medias,* p.371.
72. R. Escalante, *The State and Henequen Production in Yucatán 1955–1980*. (Occasional Paper, Inst. of Latin American Studies, London, 1988).
73. For discussion of this notion see John Bailey, *Governing Mexico: the statecraft of crisis management* (Macmillan, 1988) pp. 107–11; Gonzalez Casanova, *Democracy in Mexico*; Ugalde, *Power and Conflict*.
74. *Proceso*, 29 June 1987, is another source on this period.

## Notes to Chapter 2

75. Loret de Mola *Confesiones*, p.65.
76. The figure is provided by C.M. Assad and A. Areola, 'El Poder de los gobernadores' in S. Loaeza and R. Segovia, *La Vida Politica*, p.109. For a particular case, see Sanderson, *Agrarian Populism*.
77. *Latin America*, 19 July 1968.
78. N. Cox, 'The Partido Accion Nacional' (Mimeo, 1987).
79. Quoted in Ugalde p.159. See also Blanca Torres, 'The Mexican PAN: A case study of the party in Yucatán' (B.Phil, Oxford, 1971).
80. Ibid.
81. 7 April 1966 and 6 May 1966.
82. J. Carpizo, *El Poder Presidencial* (Siglo XXI, 1972).
83. Memo by Wallace Stuart, 'The Popular Socialist Party and Vicente Lombardo Toledano', 8 May 1965.
84. See the comments by Gilberto Alvarez in *Pensar en 1968* (Cal y Arenas, 1988).
85. This also comes out clearly in *Pensar en 1968*.
86. R.A. Camp, *The Making of a Government: Political Leaders in Mexico* (University of Arizona, 1984).
87. Loaeza, *Clases Medias*, p.129.
88. P. Cleaves, *Professions and the State* (University of Arizona, 1987).
89. Zermeño, *Mexico: una democracia utópica*, p.69.
90. Cleaves, *Professions*, p.31
91. Scherer, *Los Presidentes*, p.16.
92. The insurgency question will be considered again in the next chapter; however, *Proceso*, 11 February 1985, carried an interview with two former urban guerrillas, arrested in August 1966.
93. Aguilar Camín, *Despues del Milagro*, p.121.
94. Paul Alvarez Garin in *Pensar en 1968*, p.113.
95. Agee, *Inside the Company*, p.556.
96. Aguilar Camín, *Despues del Milagro*, p.97.
97. R.A. Camp, *Intellectuals and the State in Twentieth Century Mexico*.
98. Carlos Monsivaís, *Pensar en 1968*, p.102.
99. Cabrera, *Díaz Ordaz*.
100. Ibid.
101. Gilberto Guevara *Pensar en 1968*, p.61.
102. Ibid, p.62.
103. *Proceso*, 5 December 1988.
104. L.A. Whitehead, 'On the Governability of Mexico' in *Bulletin of Latin American Research*, vol. 1, no.1, October 1981.
105. *Latin America*, 8 March 1968 and 26 April 1968; *Daily News*, 19 July 1969.
106. *Latin America*, 26 April 1968.
107. *Latin America*, 10 May 1968 and 12 December 1969.
108. *Cancer Ward* (Penguin, 1971) p.568.

## 3 FROM COUNTER-INSURGENCY TO ECONOMIC CRISIS: THE ECHEVERRÍA PRESIDENCY

1. J. Scherer, *Los Presidentes*, p.20.
2, C. Martinez Assad, in R. Segovia and S. Loaeza, eds, *La Politica Mexicana*.
3. See C. Loret de Mola, *Confesiones de Un Gobernador*, and L. Suárez, *Echeverría en el Sexenio de López Portillo*.
4. Loret de Mola, *Confesiones*, p.21.
5. *Latin America* accepted Echeverría's version of events at the time. So did J.A. Hellman, *Mexico in Crisis*. (2nd edn., Holmes & Meier, 1983).
6. 11 August 1972.
7. Suárez, *Echeverría*, p.264.
8. *Los Presidentes*, pp.60–73.
9. Suárez, *Echeverría*, p.265.
10. *Latin America*, 21 March 1975.
11. Suárez, *Echeverría*, p.272.
12. Krause's appreciation of Reyes Heroles included the following passage. 'He did more to oppose populism from within than without. When president of the PRI during the Echeverría presidency, he several times – *sotto voce* – limited the excesses of the President. Towards the end of the succession, when Don Luis dreamed the sweet dream of re-election, Reyes Heroles firmly discouraged him'. 'Reyes Heroles; cambiar para conservar', p.170 in E. Krauze, *Por Una Democracia Sin Adjectivos* (Joaquin Mortiz, 1986).
13. G. Zaid, *La Economía Presidencial* (Vuelta, 1988) pp. 37–8.
14. P. Smith, *Labyrinths of Power*; J. Bailey, *Governing Mexico; the Statecraft of Crisis Management* (Macmillan, 1988). Bailey, normally an extremely cautious commentator, nevertheless believes that 'Echeverría sought a personal confidant who was a competent administrator and a weak politician. Echeverría's likely project was to extend his influence into the successor's terms, to create a *minimato*'. (p.38).
15. For example Scherer, *Los Presidentes*.
16. Loaeza, *Clases Medias*. See also Samuel Schmidt, *El Deterioro del Presidencialismo Mexicano: Los Años de Luis Echeverría* (Eclamex, 1986).
17. Saul Trejo Reyes, *El Futuro de la Politica Industrial en México* (Colegio de México, 1987).
18. Alan Knight, 'The Political Economy of Revolutionary Mexico', pp. 288–318 of C. Abel and C. Lewis, *Latin America: Economic Imperialism and the State*. (ILAS, London, 1985) p.306.
19. John Heath, 'An Overview of the Mexican Agricultural Crisis', pp. 129–64 of George Philip, ed., *The Mexican Economy* (Routledge, 1988).

20. S. Sanderson, *The Transformation of Mexican Agriculture* (Princeton University Press, 1986).
21. R. Looney, *Economic Policymaking in Mexico; Factors underlying the 1982 Crisis* (Duke University Press, 1985).
22. Dale Story, *Industry, The State and Public Policy in Mexico* (University of Texas, 1986).
23. For a study of Mexican policy toward foreign investment see R. Ramírez de la O, *De la Improvisación al Fracaso; La politica de inversión extranjera en México* (Oceano, 1983).
24. W. Van Ginnekin, *Socio-Economic Groups and Income Distribution in Mexico* (Croom Helm, 1980).
25. E.V.K. Fitzgerald, 'State and Capital Accumulation; Mexico 1940–82' p.215 in C. Anglade and C. Fortin, eds, *The State and Capital Accumulation in Latin America; Brazil, Chile and Mexico.* (Macmillan, 1985); Schmidt, *El Deterioro de Presidencialismo.*
26. J. Brannon and E. Baklanoff, *Agrarian Reform and Public Enterprise in Mexico; The Political Economy of Yucatán's Henequen Industry* (University of Alabama, 1987).
27. R. Looney, *Economic Policymaking.*
28. M. Basáñez, *La Lucha por la Hegemonía en Mexico* (Siglo XXI, 1980) provides evidence that high-level figures within the system were calling for a leftward readjustment in policy to follow Díaz Ordaz.
29. R. Enríquez, 'The Rise and Collapse of Stabilising Development' in G. Philip, *The Mexican Economy* (Routledge, 1985) Schmidt, *El Deterioro del Presidencialismo Mexicano.*
30. R. Miliband, *The State in Capitalist Society* (Weidenfeld & Nicolson, 1969).
31. For a study of what was a rather similar situation in Peru see Richard Webb, 'Government Policy and the Distribution of Income in Peru' in A. Lowenthal, ed., *The Peruvian Experiment; Continuity and Change under Military Rule* (Princeton University Press, 1975) and D. Gilbert, 'The End of the Peruvian Revolution: a class analysis', *Studies in Comparative International Development* 15 (1) (1980) pp.15–38.
32. On the Mexican case see S. Trejo, *El Futuro de la Politica Industrial,* Ch.3.
33. Although Echeverría did advocate some degree of urban decentralisation, very little was done. See I. Aguilar-Barajas and N. Spence, 'Industrial Decentralisation and Regional Policy 1970–86: the conflicting policy response' in George Philip, ed., *The Mexican Economy* (Routledge, 1988).
34. D. Gilbert, 'The End of the Peruvian Revolution', *Studies in Comparative International Development.*
35. G. Zaid, *La Economía Presidencial,* p.20.
36. C. Tello, *La Politica Economica en México 1970–76* (Siglo XXI, 1979).
37. P. Cleaves, *Professions and the State; the Mexican Case.* (University of Arizona, 1987).

38. C. Clapham, *Third World Politics* (Croom Helm, 1985).
39. R.D. Hansen, *The Politics of Economic Growth in Mexico* (Johns Hopkins, 1974).
40. This is clear from several contributions to *Pensar en 1968* (Cal y Arena, 1988).
41. Paul Luke, 'Debt and Oil-Led Development: The Economy Under López Portillo' in G. Philip, ed., *The Mexican Economy*.
42. Tello, *La Politica Economica*. p.199.
43. Brannon and Baklanoff, *Agrarian Reform*, p.119.
44. Tello, *México 1970–76*, p.192.
45. P. Ward, *Welfare Politics in Mexico; Papering over the Cracks* (Allen & Unwin, 1985).
46. G. Philip, 'Pemex and the Petroleum Sector' in Philip, *The Mexican Economy*.
47. Tello, *La Politica Economica*, p.188.
48. M. Basáñez, 'Viente Años de Crisis en México' (Unpublished, 1989). Part 2.
49. M.Basáñez, *La Lucha Por La Hegemonía en México*. (Siglo XXI, 1981). Echeverría did in fact, set up a new tripartite body in 1971 to discuss various themes with labour and the private sector. However the private sector did not feel that its expressed views carried any weight. See I. Morales et al, *La Formación de la Politica Petrolera en México, 1970–86* (Colegio de México, 1988) p.44.
50. Luke, in Philip, *Mexican Economy*, and Fitzgerald in Anglade and Fortin, *State and Capital Accumulation*.
51. Enriquez, in Philip, *The Mexican Economy*, p.30.
52. L.A. Whitehead, 'Mexico: From Bust to Boom' *World Development* 1980, p.846.
53. 'Mexico's Toughening Policy Toward Foreign Investment' CIA Intelligence Memorandum, November 1973, p.5.
54. George Philip, *Oil and Politics in Latin America; Nationalist Movements and State Companies* (Cambridge University Press, 1982).
55. Whitehead in *World Development*.
56. Whitehead, ibid.; Fitzgerald in Anglade and Fortin, *The State and Capital Accumulation;* and Tello, *Mexico 1970–76* are among the most persuasive of those broadly sympathetic toward Echeverría. For more hostile treatments see W. Chislett, 'The Causes of Mexico's Financial Crisis and the Lessons to be Learned' in G. Philip, ed., *Politics in Mexico* (Croom Helm, 1984), Enriquez in Philip, ed., *The Mexican Economy*, and G. Zaid, *La Economía Presidencial*.
57. Whitehead, op.cit. p.847.
58. Zaid, *La Economía Presidencial*.
59. A. Riding, *Inside the Volcano*, p.105.
60. L. Meyer, 'Debilidad de la Fuerza' in *Excelsior*, 25 January 1984.
61. *Pensar en 1968*, p.171. Schmidt, *El Deterioro del Presidencialismo Mexicano* lists nineteen different insurgent groups. (pp. 136–8).

## Notes to Chapter 3

62. See the article by James Goodsell in *Christian Science Monitor*, 16 December 1974.
63. *Guardian*, 1 July 1974.
64. *Vision Letter*, 1 February 1975.
65. Riding, *Under the Volcano*, p.106.
66. See his article in *Excelsior*, 12 December 1974.
67. A number of Soviet diplomats were expelled from Mexico in 1971 after an apparent discovery by the authorities that some Mexican guerrillas had received military training in North Korea.
68. Consider several contributions to *Pensar en 1968*.
69. *Visión*, 15 July 1975.
70. M. Basañez et al., *La Composición del Poder: Oaxaca* (INAP, 1987) p.101.
71. 11 November 1977.
72. Basañez, *Lucha por la hegemonía*, p.118.
73. Ian Roxborough, *Unions and Politics in Mexico; the case of the automobile industry* (Cambridge University Press, 1984).
74. G. Zaid, 'La Venganza de Fidel', pp. 38–9 of *La Economía Presidencial*.
75. For a discussion of unionisation within Pemex see Peter Cleaves, *Professions and the State; the Mexican Case* (University of Arizona, 1987).
76. For an analysis of this incident see the CIA's declassified report 'Mexico; Government Gets Tough on Labor Dissidents', 4 August 1976.
77. Scherer, *Los Presidentes*, pp. 127–9.
78. Ibid., pp. 134–6.
79. The word 'orchestrated' is Riding's *Inside the Volcano*, p.310.
80. Made in Suárez, *Echeverría en el Sexenio de López Portillo*, p. 278–9.
81. L. Arizpe, 'The State and Uneven Urban Development in Mexico' in G.Philip, ed., *Politics in Mexico* (Croom Helm, 1985).
82. B. Moore, *Social Origins of Dictatorship and Democracy: Lord and Peasant in the Making of the Modern World* (Beacon Press, 1966); S.P. Huntington, *Political Order in Changing Societies* (Yale University Press, 1968).
83. For a discussion on a series of incidents in 1957–8, see D. Mares, *Penetrating the International Market: Theoretical Considerations and a Mexican Case Study* (Columbia University Press, 1987); S. Sanderson, *Agrarian Populism and the Mexican State* (University of California, 1981).
84. Riding, *Inside the Volcano*, p.195.
85. Mares, *Penetrating the International Market*.
86. Sanderson, *Agrarian Populism*.
87. Basáñez, *Lucha por la Hegemonía* believes that Echeverría deliberately sought to accentuate his rural support in order to strengthen him in his difficulties over labour politics.
88. R. Michaels, 'The Crisis of *Cardenismo*', *Journal of Latin American Studies*, vol. 2 (1970).

89. Daniel Levy, *University and Government in Mexico; Autonomy in an Authoritarian System* (Praeger, 1980), suggests that Echeverría was far less controlling of university politics than was Díaz Ordaz. For a rather different emphasis see 'Mexico: conflict on the campus' (*Latin America* 11, August 1972).
90. This is very much the thesis of Samuel Schmidt,*El Deterioro del Presidencialismo Mexicano*.
91. See also the discussion in L.A. Whitehead 'On "Governability" in Mexico', *Bulletin of Latin American Research*, vol.1, no.1 (October 1981).
92. Whitehead, *ibid.*, states that 'the authorities resorted to forms of popular mobilisation evidently intended to intimidate the private sector'. (p.43).

# 4 LÓPEZ PORTILLO: FROM BOOM TO BUST

1. Paul Luke, 'Debt and Oil-Led Development: The economy under López Portillo, in George Philip, ed., *The Mexican Economy* (Routledge, 1988) provides a recent and well-balanced treatment. More ambitious is Robert Looney, *Economic Policymaking in Mexico: Factors Underlying the Crisis*. (Duke University Press, 1985). Polemical but well-argued is G. Zaid *La Economía Presidencial* (Vuelta, 1987). See also G. Bueno, 'Endeudamiento Externo y lo en México (1976–82)', *Foro Internacional* 93 (1983).
2. M. Basáñez and R. Camp, 'La Nacionalización de la Banca y la Opinión Publica en México', *Foro Internacional* 98 (1984).
3. These admissions are discussed in *Proceso*, the first on 5 December 1988, the second on 30 January 1989.
4. P. Smith, *Labyrinths of Power: Political Recruitment in Twentieth Century Mexico* (Princeton, 1979).
5. Alan Riding, *Inside the Volcano* (I.B, Tauris, 1987) p.321.
6. Krause, *Por Una Democrácia Sin Adjectivos*, p.170.
7. A good place to start is with Krause's chapter 'Jesus Reyes Heroles; cambiar para conservar', in *Por Una Democracia*.
8. M. Basáñez, 'Viente Años de Crisis en México' (Mimeo, 1979) p.47.
9. *Daily News*, 18 July 1977.
10. J. Teichman, *Policymaking in Mexico: From Boom to Crisis* (Allen & Unwin, 1988).
11. Scherer, *Los Presidentes*
12. 7 January 1977.
13. A good example is the book by Rolando Cordera and Carlos Tello, *México: Disputa por la Nación* (Siglo XXI, 1982). Tello was a leading adviser to López Portillo; Cordera is a major figure in the left-opposition.
14. Scherer, *Los Presidentes*.
15. Scherer, ibid.

16. Quoted in ibid, p.152.
17. *Proceso*, 12 December 1988.
18. A. Hernández Medina et al., *Como Somos Los Mexicanos* (Crea, 1987).
19. N.E. Cox 'Partido Accion Nacional' (Mimeo, 1987) and S. Loaeza, 'La Iglesia Catolica Mexicana y el Reformismo Autoritario', *Foro Internacional* 98 (1984).
20. J. Bailey, *Governing Mexico: the Statecraft of Crisis Management* (Macmillan, 1988) p.48.
21. A. Lajous, *La Contienda Presidencial 1988: Los Candidatos y Sus Partidos* (Diana, 1988) p.47.
22. The father of one of my former students failed to get the PRI nomination to become municipal president of a small town in Veracruz. He complained to *Gobernación* about procedural irregularities during the nominating process, and was told that it would present no problems if he ran for office as an opposition candidate. He did so, was elected, and continued to act as a PRI loyalist in every respect except the formal one.
23. David Torres, 'Reforma Politica y Preserverancia del Proteccionismo Electoral', pp.141–61 *Revista Mexicana de Sociologia* Apr-Jun 1984, and C.F. Salinas 'Tamaulipas: Mafias, Caciques and Civic-Political Culture' pp.161-181 in A.Alvarado, ed., *Electoral Patterns and Perspectives in Mexico* (San Diego, 1987).
24. Jeffrey Rubin, 'State Policies, Leftist Oppositions and Municipal Elections; the case of the COCEI in Juchatan' pp. 127–61 in A. Alvarado, ed., *Electoral Patterns*, op.cit., and M.Basáñez et al., *La Composición del Poder: Oaxaca* (INAP, 1987). On this period see also Moises J. Bailon and S. Zermeño, *Juchitán: limites de una experiencia democratica* (Instituto de investigaciones sociales, UNAM, 1987).
25. Dale Story, *Industry, the State and Public Policy in Mexico* (ILAS, Texas, 1986); L. Arreola and J. Galindo, 'Los Empresarios y el Estado en México 1976–82' *Foro Internacional;* Saul Escobar, 'Rifts in the Mexican Power Elite 1976–86', pp. 65–88 in Silvia Maxfield and Ricardo Anzaldua Montoya, eds, *Government and Private Sector in Contemporary Mexico* (San Diego, 1987).
26. L. Whitehead, 'Mexico from Bust to Boom: A Political Evaluation of the 1976–79 Stabilization Programme' *World Development*, vol.8, pp. 843–64 suggests that there was never a likelihood of such a spiral.
27. I. Bizberg, 'Politica Laboral y Acción Sindical en México 1976–82', *Foro International* 98 (1984).
28. 'Mexico; López Portillo's Political Proficiency', CIA Report, 21 July 1977.
29. Story, *Industry* p.139.
30. Arreola and Galindo in *Foro International*, p.121.
31. For a very critical discussion of the ALFA group see Maria Elena Cardero and José Manuel Quijano, 'Expansión y Estrangulamiento Financiero', pp. 221-305 in J.M. Quijano et al., *La Banca: Pasado y Presente* (CIDE, 1983).

## Notes to Chapter 4

32. George Philip, 'Public Enterprise in Mexico', pp. 28–46 in V. Ramandham, ed., *Public Enterprise in Developing Countries* (Croom Helm, 1984).
33. Ibid.
34. For general accounts of Mexican oil during this period see G. Szekely, *La Economía Política del Petróleo en México 1976–82* (Colegio de México, 1983); I. Morales et al., *La Formación de la Política Petrolera en México 1970–86*, (Colegio de Mexico, 1988). G. Grayson, *The Politics of Mexican Oil* (University of Pittsburgh, 1980) and G. Philip, 'Pemex and the Petroleum Sector' in Philip, ed., *The Mexican Economy*.
35. This particular point is well established by A. Megadelli, *Investment Policies of National Oil Companies: A comparative study of Sonatrech, NICO and Pemex*. (Praeger, 1980). See also George Philip, *Oil and Politics in Latin America: nationalist movements and state companies*. (Cambridge University Press, 1982).
36. *Latin American Economic Report*, 26 January 1979.
37. Bailey, *Governing Mexico*, p.45.
38. Luke, in Philip, ed., *The Mexican Economy*, p.59.
39. *Business Week*, 15 January 1979.
40. W. Chislett, 'The Causes of Mexico's Financial Crisis and the Lessons to be Learned', pp. 1–15 in George Philip, ed., *Politics in Mexico* (Croom Helm, 1984).
41. On these problems see, for example, M. Redclift, *Development Policymaking in Mexico: the SAM*. (ILAS Working Paper, 1981) and John Heath 'Contradictions in Mexican Food Policy, pp. 97–137 in Philip, ed., *Politics in Mexico*.
42. This point is made by Chislett in Philip, ed., *Politics in Mexico*.
43. Quoted in Bailey, *Governing Mexico*, p.50.
44. Alan Gelb, *The Oil Exporting Countries*, (World Bank, 1989).
45. George Grayson, *Oil and Mexican Foreign Policy* (University of Pittsburgh, 1988).
46. Ibid.
47. CIA National Foreign Assessment Center, *Mexico: New Activism in Central America*, 27 March 1980.
48. *Proceso*, 13 March 1989.
49. Teichman, *Policymaking in Mexico*, p.107.
50. *Proceso*, 13 March 1989.
51. Carlos Ramírez et al., *Pemex: la Caida de Díaz Serrano*. (Proceso, 1981).
52. Ibid., p. 62.
53. Joseph Kraft, *The Mexican Rescue* (Group of Thirty, New York, 1985). pp. 35–6.
54. Teichman, *Policymaking in Mexico*, p.130.
55. Kraft, *Mexican Rescue*, p.36.
56. Ibid., p. 37.
57. Ibid., p.8.
58. Ibid., p.11.
59. There are a number of accounts of the bank nationalisation. Apart from Teichman and Kraft (already cited), see Bailey, *Governing Mexico*.

60. Basáñez and Camp in *Foro Internacional* 98 (1984). See also the contemporary coverage of the issue by *Proceso*.
61. Kraft, *The Mexican Rescue*, p.46.
62. The CIA also reported that 'López Portillo's nationalisation of the domestic banks . . . (has) raised concerns that he will take equally dramatic steps in Central America'. CIA, 'Mexican Policy Toward Central America' (September 1982).

## 5 DE LA MADRID: THE LIMITS OF ORTHODOXY

1. A. Kouyoumdjian 'The Miguel de la Madrid *Sexenio*: Major Reforms or Foundation for Disaster?', pp. 78–95 of George Philip, ed., *The Mexican Economy* (Routledge, 1988) p.78.
2. For some general observations about de la Madrid's policy of cabinet appointments see Rogelio Hernández Rodríguez 'Los Hombres del Presidente de la Madrid', in *Foro Internacional*, vol. 28, no. 2 July–September 1987.
3. R.A. Camp, *'Camarillas* in Mexican Politics; the case of the Salinas cabinet' (Unpublished, 1989).
4. L. Meyer, 'Tejido de Complicidades' *Excelsior*, 1 February 1984.
5. Samuel del Villar made this clear in an interview with *Proceso*, 6 February 1989.
6. For further discussion of oilworkers under de la Madrid see George Grayson, *Oil and Mexican Foreign Policy*. (University of Pittsburgh; 1987).
7. Meyer, 'Tejido', op. cit.
8. Del Villar, 'Entre la Renovación y la Muerte' – effectively his resignation memo, written around the end of 1985 – cites examples. Carlos Jonguitud was allowed to control San Luis Potosí, just as La Quina was left in charge of the oil-producing areas.
9. Hector Dieguez, 'Social Consequences of the Economic Crisis: Mexico, the Facts' (Unpublished, 1986) p.38.
10. Miguel Basáñez, 'Viente Años de Crisis en México' (Unpublished, 1989), produces a series of social welfare measurements dating back to the early 1960s. There is no marked change in the rate of improvement of the main welfare indicators between 1970 and 1982, although there is a noticeable deterioration after 1982.
11. The popularity of the bank nationalisation is borne out by M. Basáñez and R.A. Camp, 'La Nacionalisacíon de la Banca y la Opinión Publica en México, *Foro Internacional*, no. 98, December 1984.
12. See the various contributions in A. Alverez, ed., *Electoral Patterns and Perspectives in Mexico* (University of San Diego, 1987).
13. Norman Cox, 'Changes in the Mexican Political System', in George Philip, ed., *Politics in Mexico* (Croom Helm, 1985).
14. Local studies of a weakening PRI machine include Alberto Aziz Nassif 'Electoral Practices and Democracy in Chihuahua 1985', in

## Notes to Chapter 5

    A. Alvarado, ed., *Electoral Patterns and Perspectives in Mexico* (University of San Diego, 1987); E. Krause, 'Chihuahua; de ida y vuelta' in E. Krause, ed., *Por Una Democracia Sin Adjectivos* (Joaquin Mortiz, 1986); and, on Jalisco, Jaime Sánchez, 'La Escena Politica' in *Vuelta*, November 1988.

15. Cox, 'Recent Changes' in Philip, ed., *Politics in Mexico*, p.23.
16. R.A. Camp, 'Images and Attitudes of the Mexican Entrepreneur: Political Consequences', in Silvia Maxfield and Ricardo Anzaldua Montoya, eds, *Government and Private Sector in Contemporary Mexico*. (University of San Diego, 1987), and also G. Guadarrama, 'Entrepreneurs and Politics, Businessmen in Electoral Contests in Sonora and Nuevo Leon July 1985' in A. Alvarado, ed., *Electoral Patterns*.
17. Bob Woodward, *Veil; The Secret Wars of the CIA*.
18. Cox 'Recent Changes' in Philip, ed., *Politics in Mexico*. p.22.
19. Ibid., p.29.
20. Ibid., p.29. See also Wayne Cornelius 'Political Liberalisation in an Authoritarian Regime', in J. Gentleman, ed., *Mexican Politics in Transition* (Westview, 1987).
21. H. Aguilar Camín, *Despues del Milagro* has a nice story according to which one of de la Madrid's ministers asked permission to resign on the grounds that he had been receiving bad notices in the press. De la Madrid produced a large collection of bad press reports about himself and told the minister that, if such reports were sufficient reason to resign, de la Madrid himself would have gone long since (p.122).
22. For an empirically-based attack on the 'authoritarian political culture' hypothesis see J. Booth and M. Seligson, 'The Political Culture of Authoritarianism in Mexico: a re-examination', *Latin American Research Review*, 19.1 (1984). They conclude that 'one cannot attempt to explain the authoritarian nature of the political system in Mexico as the consequence of an authoritarian mass political culture' (p.18).

    A further point would be that it is better to try to understand political cultures and sub-cultures after fully understanding how the political system actually works. Cultures may be adaptive to institutions, as well as vice-versa.

23. A poll carried in the *Los Angeles Times* on 12 August 1989 indicates that a clear majority of Mexicans support a manifest division between Church and state.
24. A point made by L. Meyer 'La Oposición en el Poder', *Excelsior*, 4 January 1984.
25. N. Cox 'Recent Changes', in Philip, *Politics,* pp. 24–5.
26. Later republished by Joaquin Mortiz, in 1987.
27. George Grayson, *Oil and Mexican Foreign Policy* (Pittsburgh University Press, 1987) and George Philip, 'Pemex and the Petroleum Sector', in Philip, ed., *The Mexican Economy*.
28. Banco de México *Informe Anual; 1985*, p.2.
29. Del Villar 'Entre la Renovación y la Muerte'.

30. Cornelius, 'Political Liberalisation' in Gentleman, ed., *Mexican Politics in Transition*, p.28.
31. Apart from Alvarado, ed., *Electoral Patterns*, see the various articles in Judith Gentleman, ed., *Mexican Politics in Transistion*.
32. See, for example, Luis Pazos, *The False Austerity Policies of the Mexican Government* (Instituto de Integracion Iberoamericana, 1985).
33. Rogelio Ramírez de la O and Joanne Curley, *The Mexican Economy: A Medium-Term Forecast, 1985–89* (Ecanal, Mexico, 1985) p.9.
34. Esperanza Duran, 'Mexico's 1986 Financial Rescue: palliative or cure?' pp. 95–110, in George Philip, ed., *The Mexican Economy* (Routledge, 1988).
35. On negotiations with the private sector prior to the Solidarity Pact see Leo Zuckermann, 'El Proceso de Toma de Decisiones de la Politica Economica en Mexico; del Crack Bursatil al Pacto de Solidaridad Economica'. (Unpublished thesis, Colegio de Mexico, 1989). Also interesting is the interview given to *Proceso*, 28 December 1987, by Bernardo Ardavin of COPARMEX. I am also grateful to Jeremy Hobbs of Essex University for certain points made during a seminar discussion at the Institute of Latin American Studies in London in December 1989.
36. *Proceso* during this period gleefully documented his inability to deal effectively with the 'Democratic Current' during 1987. It also profiled him scathingly on 5 December 1988.
37. For a recent collection which includes a fuller discussion of the 1988 elections see W. Cornelius, et al., Mexico's *Alternative Political Futures* (University of San Diego, 1989). For some excellent immediate reportage, see *Proceso*, 11 July 1988.
38. *Proceso*, 5 December 1988.
39. *Proceso*, 9 November 1987.
40. W. Van Ginnekin, *Socio-Economic Groups and Income Distribution in Mexico*. (Croom Helm, 1980). For a more political discussion see Hellman, *Mexico in Crisis*.

# CONCLUSION

1. Do Cosío Villegas, *La Sucesión Presidencial en Mexico* (Joaquin Mortiz, 1975) p.19.
2. J. Carpizo, *El Poder Presidencial* (Siglo XXI, 1978).
3. For an interesting argument along these lines see W. Olsen 'Crisis and Change in Mexico's Political Economy', *Latin American Perspectives*, vol. 12, no. 3 (1985); see also E.V.K. Fitzgerald, 'Mexico' in C. Anglade and C. Fortin, eds, *The State and Capital Accumulation in Latin America* (Macmillan, 1987).
4. I. Bizberg, 'La Crisis del Corporativismo Mexicano' (Mimeo, Mexico, 1989).

5. The phrase 'selective democracy' was used by *Proceso* to describe the system's handling of elections during July 1989.
6. F. Krause, *Por Una Democracia Sin Adjectivos* (Joaquin Mortiz, 1986), and H. Aguilar Camín, *Despues del Milagro* (Cal y Arena, 1988).
7. FO 371, An1015/12. Minute dated 2 June 1958.
8. Michael Mann, *Sources of Social Power* (Cambridge University Press, 1987) vol. 1.
9. D. Cosío Villegas, *La Sucesión Presidencial*.
10. See, for example, Lucy Conger's reports from Mexico for the *Financial Times*, for example 29 June 1989.
11. G.R. Newall and G. Rubio, *Mexico's Dilemma: The Political Origins of the Economic Crisis* (Westview, 1984).
12. G. Zaid, *La Economía Presidencial* (Vuelta, 1987).
13. R. Camp, *Intellectuals and the State in Twentieth Century Mexico* (University of Texas, 1985).
14. S. Sanderson, *Agrarian Populism and the Mexican State* (University of California, 1981) p.142.
15. M. Needler, *Mexican Politics: the Containment of Conflict* (Praeger, 1982).
16. Bob Woodward, *Veil: The Secret Wars of the CIA*, states that William Casey believed this.

# References

## BOOKS

Adler, E., *The Power of Ideology: the Quest for Technological Autonomy in Argentina and Brazil* (University of California, 1987).
Aguilar Camin, H., *Despues del Milagro* (Cal y Arena, 1988).
Alonso, A., *El Conflicto Ferrocarrilero en Mexico* (Era, 1972).
Alvarez, A., ed., *Electoral Patterns and Perspectives in Mexico* (University of San Diego, 1987).
Anglade C. and Fortin, C., eds., *The State and Capital Accumulation in Latin America* (Macmillan, 1986).
Bailey, J., *Governing Mexico: the Statecraft of Crisis Management* (Macmillan, 1988).
Bailon, Moises J. and Zermeno, S., *Juchitán: limites de una experiencia democratica* (Instituto de investigaciones sociales, UNAM, 1987).
Basáñez, M., *La Lucha por la Hegemonía en Mexico* (Siglo XXI, 1980).
Basáñez, M., et al., *La Composición del Poder: Oaxaca* (INAP, 1987).
Bauer, P., *Equality, The Third World and Economic Delusion* (Methuen, 1981).
Brannon, J. and Baklanoff, E., *Agrarian Reform and Public Enterprise in Mexico: the Political Economy of Yucatán's Henequen Industry* (University of Alabama, 1987).
Cal y Arena, *Pensar en 1968*.
Camp, R.A. *The Making of a Government: Political Leaders in Mexico* (University of Arizona, 1984).
Camp, R.A., *Intellectuals and the State in Twentieth Century Mexico* (University of Texas, 1985).
Carpizo, J., *El Poder Presidencial* (Siglo XXI, 1972).
Clapham, C., *Third World Politics* (Croom Helm, 1985).
Cleaves, P., *Professions and the State* (University of Arizona, 1987).
Cordero R and Tello, Carlos, *México: Disputa por la Nación* (Siglo XXI, 1982).
Cornelius, W. et al., *Mexico's Alternative Political Futures* (University of San Diego, 1989).
Dunleavy P. and O'Leary, B., *Theories of the State: The Politics of Liberal Democracy* (Macmillan, 1987).
Evans, P., *Dependent Development: The Alliance of Multinational, State and Local Capital in Brazil* (Princeton, 1979).
Gelb, Alan, *The Oil Exporting Countries* (World Bank, 1989).
Gonzalez Casanova, P., *Democracy in Mexico* (Oxford University Press, 1970).

Grayson, G., *The Politics of Mexican Oil* (University of Pittsburgh, 1980).
Grayson, George, *Oil and Mexican Foreign Policy* (University of Pittsburgh, 1987).
Gunther, J., *Inside Latin America* (Hamish Hamilton, 1942).
Hamilton, N., *The Limits of State Autonomy: Post-Revolutionary Mexico* (Princeton University Press, 1982).
Hanson, R.D., *The Politics of Mexican Development* (Johns Hopkins, 1974).
Hellman, J.A., *Mexico in Crisis* (2nd edn, Holmes & Meier, 1983).
Hernández Medina, A., et al., *Como Somos Los Mexicanos* (Crea, 1987).
Huntington, S.P., *Political Order in Changing Society* (Yale, 1968).
Knight, A.S., *The Mexican Revolution* 2 vols (Cambridge University Press, 1987).
Kraft, Joseph, *The Mexican Rescue* (Group of Thirty, New York, 1985).
Krause, F., *Por Una Democracia Sin Adjectivos* (Joaquin Mortiz. 1986).
Lajous, A., *La Contienda Presidencial 1988: Los Candidatos y Sus Partidos* (Diana, 1988).
Levy, D., *University and Government in Mexico: Autonomy in an Authoritarian System* (Praeger, 1980).
Loaeza, S. *Classes Medias y La Politica en Mexico* (Colegio de Mexico, 1988).
Loaeza, S., and Segovia, R., *La Vida Politica Mexicana en la crisis* (Colegio de Mexico, 1987).
Looney, R., *Economic Policymaking in Mexico: Factors Underlying the 1982 Crisis.* (Duke University Press, 1985).
Loret de Mola, C., *Confesiones de Un Gobernador* (Grijalbo, 1978).
Mann, M., *The Sources of Social Power* (Cambridge University Press, 1988).
Mares, D., *Penetrating the International Market: Theoretical Considerations and a Mexican Case Study* (Columbia, NY, 1987).
Maxfield, S. and Montoya, R.A., eds, *Government and Private Sector in Contemporary Mexico* (University of San Diego, 1987).
Megadelli, A., *Investment Policies of National Oil Companies: A comparative study of Sonatrech, NICO and Pemex* (Praeger, 1980).
Mexico, Sol Sanders, *The Chaos on Our Doorstep* (Madison, 1986).
Meyer, J., *The Cristero Revolt* (Cambridge University Press, 1984).
Miliband, R., *The State in Capitalist Society* (Weidenfeld & Nicolson, 1969).
Morales, I., et al., *La Formación de la Politica Petrolera en México 1970–86.* (Colegio de México. 1988).
Morley, M., *Imperial State and Revolution* (Cambridge University Press, 1987).
Needler, M., *Mexican Politics: the containment of conflict* (Praeger, 1982).
Newell, G. and Rubio, L., *Mexico's Dilemma: The Political Origins of the Economic Crisis* (Westview, 1984).
O'Donnell, G., *Bureaucratic Authoritarianism: Studies in South American politics* (University of California, 1973).
Parra, J.A., *Díaz Ordaz y el 68* (Grijabo, 1980).
Pazos, L., *The False Austerity Policies of the Mexican Government* (Instituto de Integracion Iberoamericana, 1985).

Philip, G., *Oil and Politics in Latin America: nationalist movements and state companies* (Cambridge University Press, 1982).
Philip, G., *The Military in South American Politics* (Croom Helm, 1985).
Purcell, S.K., *The Mexican Profit-Sharing Decision: Policymaking in an Authoritarian Regime* (University of California, 1975).
Ramírez, C., et al., *Pemex: la Caida de Díaz Serrano* (Proceso, 1981).
Ramírez de la O, R., *De la Improvisación al Fracaso: La politica de inversion extranjera en México* (Oceano, 1983).
Ramírez de la O, R., and Curley, J., *The Mexican Economy: A Medium-Term Forecast 1985–89* (Ecanal, Mexico, 1985).
Reyes, S.T., *El Futuro de la Politica Industrial en Mexico* (Colegio de Mexico, 1987).
Riding, A., *Inside the Volcano* (I.B. Tauris, 1987).
Roxborough, I., *Unions and Politics in Mexico: The Case of the Automobile Industry* (Cambridge University Press, 1984).
Sanderson, S., *Agrarian Populism and the Mexican State: the case of Sonora* (University of California, 1981).
Sanderson, S., *The Transfromation of Mexican Agriculture* (Princeton University Press, 1986).
Scherer. J., *Los Presidentes* (Grijabo, 1986).
Schmidt, S., *El Deterioro del Presidencialismo Mexicano: Los Años de Luis Echeverría* (Edamex, 1986).
Scott, R., *Mexican Government in Transition* (University of Illinois, 1964).
Solzhenitsyn, A., *Cancer Ward* (Penguin Edn, 1971) p.568.
Smith, P.H., *Labyrinths of Power* (Princeton, 1979).
Stevens, E., *Protest and Response in Mexico* (MIT Press, 1974).
Story, D., *Industry, The State and Public Policy in Mexico* (University of Texas, 1986).
Suárez, L., *Echeverría en el Sexenio de López Portillo* (Grijalbo, 1981).
Szekely, G., *Las Economía Politica del Petróleo en México 1976–82* (Colegio de México, 1983).
Teichman, J., *Policymaking in Mexico: from Boom to Crisis* (Allen & Unwin, 1988).
Tello, C., *La Politica Economica en México 1970–76* (Siglo XXI, 1979).
Van Ginnekin, W., *Socio-Economic Groups and Income Distribution in Mexico.* (Croom Helm, 1980).
Villegas, D. Cosío, *La Sucesión Presidencial* (Joaquin Mortiz, 1975).
Villegas, D. Cosío, *El Sistema Politica Mexicana* (Joaquin Mortiz, 1975).
Ward, P., *Welfare Politics in Mexico: Papering over the Cracks* (Allen & Unwin, 1985).
Whitehead, L.A. and Thorp, E., eds, *Latin America and the Debt Crisis* (Macmillan, 1987).
Woodward, R., *Veil: the Secret Wars of the CIA* (Washington, 1987).
Zaid, G., *La Economía Presidencial* (Vuelta, 1987).
Zermeno, E., *México: Una Democracia Utópica: El movimiento estudantil en 1968* (Siglo XXI, 1978).

## ARTICLES

Aguilar-Barajas, I. and Spence, N., 'Industrial Decentralisation and Regional Policy 1970–86; the conflicting policy response', in G. Philip, ed., *The Mexican Economy* (Routledge, 1988).
Arizpe, L., 'The State and Uneven Urban Development in Mexico', in G. Philip, ed., *Politics in Mexico* (Croom Helm, 1985).
Arreola, L., and Galindo, J., Los Empresarios y el Estado en México 1976–82' *Foro Internacional* (.......)
Basáñez, M., and Camp, R.,, 'La Nacionalización de la Banca y la Opinion Publica en Mexico' *Foro Internacional* 98 (1984).
Bezdek, R., 'Electoral Opposition in San Luis Potosí; the Case of Nava', in Johnson, K.F., *Mexican Democracy: a critical view* 3rd edn. (Praeger, 1984).
Bizberg, I., 'Politica Laboral y Acción Sindical en México 1976–82', *Foro Internacional* 98 (1984).
Booth, J., and Seligson, M., 'The Political Culture of Authoritarianism in Mexico: a re-examination' *Latin American Research Review* 19.1 (1984).
Bueno, G., 'Endeudamiento Externo y lo en México (1976–82)' *Foro Internacional* 93 (1983).
Camp, R.A., 'The Political Technocrat in Mexico and the Survival of the Political System', *Latin American Research Review* 20, no. 1. (1985).
Camp, R.A., 'Images and Attitudes of the Mexican Entrepreneur; Political Consequences', in Silvia Maxfield and Ricardo Anzaldua Montoya eds *Government and Private Sector in Contemporary Mexico*, (University of San Diego, 1987).
Chislett, W., 'The Causes of Mexico's Financial Crisis and the Lessons to be Learned', pp. 1–15 in George Philip, ed., *Politics in Mexico* (Croom Helm, 1984).
Cordero, Maria Elena, and Quijano, José Manuel, 'Expansion y Estrangulamiento Financiero' pp. 221–305 in J.M. Quijano et al., *La Banca: Pasado y Presente* (CIDE, 1983).
Cornelius, W., 'Political Liberalisation in an Authoritarian Regime', in J. Gentleman, ed., *Mexican Politics in Transition* (Westview, 1987).
Cox, N., 'Changes in the Mexican Political System,' in G. Philip, ed., *Politics in Mexico* (Croom Helm, 1985).
Duran, E., 'Mexico's 1986 Financial Rescue, palliative or cure?', pp. 95–110 in G. Philip, ed., *The Mexican Economy* (Routledge, 1988).
Enríquez, R., 'The Rise and Collapse of Stabilising Development', in G. Philip, *The Mexican Economy* (Routledge, 1985).
Escalante, R., *The State and Henequen Production in Yucatán 1955–1980* (Occasional Paper, ILAS, London, 1988).
Escobar, Saul, 'Rifts in the Mexican Power Elite 1976–86', pp. 65–88 in Silvia Maxfield and Ricardo Anzaldua Montoya, eds, *Government and Private Sector in Contemporary Mexico* (San Diego, 1987).
Fitzgerald, E.V.K.,'Mexico' in C. Anglade and C. Fortin, eds, *The State and Capital Accumulation in Latin America* (Macmillan, 1987).
Gilbert, D., 'The Velasco Regime in Peru: a class analysis', *Studies in Comparative International Development*, 1979.

Gledhill, J., 'Agrarian Social Movements and Forms of Consciousness' *Bulletin of Latin American Research*, vol. 7, no. 2 (1988).

Guadarrama, G., 'Entrepreneurs and Politics; Businessmen in Electoral Contests in Sonora and Nuevo Leon July 1985, in A. Alvarado, ed., *Electoral Patterns*.

Heath, J., 'Contradictions in Mexican Food Policy', pp. 97–137 in G. Philip, ed., *Politics in Mexico*.

Heath, J., 'An Overview of the Mexican Agricultural Crisis' in G. Philip, ed., *The Mexican Economy* (Routledge, 1988).

Hernández Rodríguez, R., 'Los Hombres del Presidente de la Madrid', in *Foro Internacional* vol. 28, no. 2, July–Sept. 1987.

Joseph, G., '*Caciquismo* and the Revolution: Carillo Puerto in Yucatan' in D. Brading, ed., *Caudillo and Peasant in the Mexican Revolution* (Cambridge University Press, 1980).

Knight, A.S., 'The Political Economy of Revolutionary Mexico', in C. Abel and C. Lewis, *Latin America: Economic Imperialism and the State* (ILAS, London, 1985).

Kouyoumdjian, A., 'The Miguel de la Madrid *Sexenio*: Major Reforms or Foundation for Disaster?', pp. 78–95 of G. Philip, ed., *The Mexican Economy* (Routledge, 1988).

Loaeza, S. 'La Iglesia Catolica Mexicana y el Reformismo Autoritario' *Foro Internacional* 98 (1984).

Luke, Paul, 'Debt and Oil-led Development: the economy under López Portillo', in George Philip, ed., *The Mexican Economy* (Routledge, 1988).

March, J.G., and Olsen, J.P., 'The New Institutionalism' *American Political Science Review*, 1984.

Marquez, E., 'Political Anachronisms; The Navista Movement and Political Processes in San Luis Potosí 1958–85', in A. Alvarez, ed., *Electoral Patterns and Perspectives in Mexico*.

Meyer, L., 'Debilidad de la Fuerza' in *Excelsiór,* 25 January 1984.

Meyer, L., 'La Oposición en el Poder', *Excelsiór,* 4 January 1984.

Meyer, L., 'Tejido de Complicidades', *Excelsiór,* 1 February 1984.

Michaels, R., 'The Crisis of *Cardenismo*'. in *Journal of Latin American Studies*, vol. 2 (1970).

Nassif, A.A., 'Electoral Practices and Democracy in Chihuahua 1985', in A. Alvarado, ed., *Electoral Patterns and Perspectives in Mexico* (University of San Diego, 1987).

Needler, M., 'The Significance of Recent Events for the Mexican Political System' in J. Gentleman, ed., *Mexican Politics in Transition* (Westview, 1987).

Olsen, W., 'Crisis and Change in Mexico's Political Economy' *Latin American Perspectives,* vol. 12, no. 3 (1985).

Pansters, W., 'Paradoxes of Regional Power in Post-Revolutionary Mexico: the Rise of *Avila Camachismo* in Puebla 1935–40' in W. Pansters and A. Onwered, eds, *Region, State and Capitalism in Mexico* (CEDLA, 1989).

Philip, G., 'Public Enterprise in Mexico', pp. 28–46, in V. Ramandham, ed., *Public Enterprise in Developing Countries* (Croom Helm, 1984).

Philip, G., 'Pemex and the Petroleum Sector', in Philip, ed., *The Mexican Economy*.
Purcell, S.K., and Purcell, J.F.H., 'State and Society in Mexico; must a stable polity be institutionalised?', in *World Politics*; vol. 32, no. 2 (January 1980).
Redclift, M., *Development Policymaking in Mexico: the SAM* (ILAS Working Paper, 1981).
Reyes del Campillo, J. 'El Frente Electoral del Pueblo y el Partido Communista Mexicano (1963–64)', *Revista Mexicana de Sociologia* Jul/Sept. 1988.
Rubin, J., 'State Policies, Leftist Oppositions and Municipal Elections; the case of the COCEI in Juchatan', pp.127–61 in A. Alvarado, ed., *Electoral Patterns*.
Salinas, C.F., 'Tamaulipas; Mafias, Caciques and Civic-Political Culture', pp.161–81 in A. Alvarado, ed., *Electoral Patterns and Perspectives in Mexico* (San Diego, 1987).
Sanchez, J. 'La Escena Politica', *Vuelta*, November 1988.
Spence, N., 'Industrial Decentralisation and Regional Policy 1970–86; the conflicting policy response', in G. Philip, ed., *The Mexican Economy* (Routledge, 1988).
Torres, D., 'Reforma Politica y Preserverancia del Proteccionismo Electoral', pp.141–61, *Revista Mexicana de Sociologia*, Apr.–Jun. 1984.
Whitehead, L., 'On the Governability of Mexico', in *Bulletin of Latin American Research*, vol 1, no. 1, October 1981.
Whitehead, L., 'Mexico from Bust to Boom; A Political Evaluation of the 1976–79 Stabilization Programme', *World Development*, vol.8, pp. 843–64.

## OTHER UNPUBLISHED

Basáñez, M., 'Viente Años de Crisis en México' (Mimeo, 1989) p.47.
Bizberg, I., 'La Crisis del Corporativismo Mexicano' (Mimeo, Mexico, 1989).
Camp, R.A., 'Camarillas in Mexican Politics; The Case of the Salinas Cabinet' (Unpublished, 1989).
Cox, N.E., 'Partido Accion Nacional' (Mimeo, 1987).
Dieguez, H., 'Social Consequences of the Economic Crisis: Mexico, the facts' (Unpublished, 1986).
Torres, B., 'The Mexican PAN: a case study of the party in Yucatán' (B.Phil. thesis; Oxford, 1971).
del Villar, S., 'Entre La Renovación y la Muerte' (Unpublished, 1985).

## OTHER PUBLISHED

I have also used the Mexican and international press, periodicals such as *Proceso*, and declassified US and British government documents as listed in the Notes.

# Glossary and Abbreviations

| | |
|---|---|
| *Alquimia electoral* | Literally 'electoral alchemy'; figuratively, winning elections without actually rigging the ballot. |
| *Cacique* | Power broker with clientele of his own. |
| *Camarilla* | A small group of political allies who support each other in their efforts to gain (mainly bureaucratic) office and operate the system generally. |
| Canacintra | Officially-recognised employers' confederation. |
| CCE | The employers' co-ordinating commission (founded in 1975). |
| CCI | An independent peasant confederation. |
| CNC | The official peasant confederation. |
| *Confederacion de Trabajo* | Umbrella organisation for Mexican labour movements affiliated to the system (the CTM, CROM and CROC). |
| Coparmex | The most influential independent employers' organisation. |
| CROC | An officially-recognised trade union confederation |
| CROM | A trade union confederation. |
| CTM | The most important (and officially recognised) trade union confederation. |
| *Destape* | The 'unveiling' of a presidential candidate of the official party. |
| *Ejido* | Self-managed agricultural collective. |
| FEP | Popular Electoral Front. (Attempted Popular Front-type organisation). |
| GATT | General Agreement on Tariffs and Trade. |
| *Gobernación* | Literally 'government' but reads better as 'administration'. |
| ISI | Import substituting industrialisation. |
| ITAM | Mexican Autonomous Technological Institute. |
| *Maquiladora* | 'In bond' section of the Mexican economy, exporting to the United States. |
| *Mestizaje* | A mixture of AmerIndian and Spanish blood. |

| | |
|---|---|
| MLN | National Liberation Movement. |
| NAFINSA | State-owned development bank. |
| PAN | National Action Party; a conservative pro-Catholic party. |
| PARM | Autonomous Party of the Mexican Revolution. |
| PCM | The Mexican Communist Party. |
| Pemex | State-owned oil company. |
| PMT | Mexican Workers Party. |
| PPS | Popular Socialist Party. |
| *Presidenciable* | Eligible for selection as President. |
| PRI (earlier PNR; PRM). | The Institutional Revolutionary Party. This is the dominant party in Mexico. |
| PRT | Revolutionary Party of the Workers |
| PST | Socialist Party of the Workers. |
| PSUM | United Socialist Party of Mexico. |
| *Sexenio* | Six-year presidential term. |
| *Sinarquistas* | Conservative Catholic political movement, most influential during 1936–44. |
| SPP | Planning and Budgeting Ministry. |
| UGOCM | Independent left-wing association of workers and peasants. |
| UNAM | National Autonomous University of Mexico, the largest national university. |

# Index

Aguilar Camín 20, 54
Alemán Valdes, Miguel (President 1946–52) 22, 26, 28, 30, 37, 38, 61, 94, 102, 178
ALFA group 121, 125
Allende, Salvador 60, 68, 74, 131
Argentina 2, 60, 75–6, 127, 129, 147, 157, 168
Aspe, Pedro 153
Avila Camacho, Maximino 21
Avila Camacho, Manuel (President 1940–46) 14, 25, 37, 178

Baker, James 156, 157
Barrios Sierra, Javier 56–7
Bartlett Díaz, Manuel 155
Buendía, Manuel 138, 161–2

Cabanas, Lucio 54, 85
*Cacique*(-ismo) 10–11, 13, 40, 146, 165, 170
*Camarillas* 7, 41, 134
Campa, Valentín 40, 49, 54, 103
Cárdenas del Rio, Lazaro 14, 23, 25, 26, 30, 31, 32, 34, 36, 37–8, 55, 71, 178, 188
*Cardenismo* 15, 31, 38, 90, 174, 177
Cárdenas, Cuauhtémoc 107, 160, 162, 163–4, 173, 176, 180, 182
Carter, Jimmy 120
Casteñeda, Jorge 107, 120
Castillo, Herberto 50, 59, 85, 86
Castro, Fidel 35, 38, 53, 58, 60, 188
CCI 36
Chihuahua 42, 141, 142, 145, 147, 158, 161
Chile 49, 60, 68, 74, 81, 86, 99, 168
Christleib Ibarrola, Adolfo, 47

Church, the Catholic 2, 11, 14, 25, 27–8, 32, 33, 38, 47, 55, 61, 71, 87, 103, 106, 142, 147, 180, 188, 201
CIA 37, 48–9, 56, 69, 81, 120, 142
CNC 41, 91
CNOP 143
COCEI 109
Colima 5, 133
Communist Party (PCM) 27, 28, 48, 50, 54, 86, 87, 103, 104, 109, 110, 111
CONCAMIN 33
CONCANACO 33
Coparmex 33, 79, 157, 175
CROC 9, 45–6, 142
CROM 9, 142
CTM 9, 10, 28, 41, 61, 88, 93, 110, 111, 125, 139, 142, 146, 154, 157, 183
Cuba 35, 85, 120, 147
Cuban Revolution 25, 27, 32, 34, 36, 39, 60, 175, 179, 180

De la Madrid Hurtado, Miguel 5, 6, 107, 124, 129, 133–5, 136, 137, 139, 140, 142, 143, 144, 146, 147, 148, 149, 150, 151, 152, 153, 154, 156, 157, 158, 159, 160, 162, 164–6, 170, 171, 178, 181, 182, 201
De la Vega Domínguez, Jorge 57, 159, 163
De Mazo, Alfredo 153, 154, 160–61, 162
Democratic Tendency 87
Díaz, Porfirio 16, 58
Díaz Ordaz, Gustavo 7, 19, 20, 21, 22, 24, 34, 36, 38, 39, 40, 44, 46, 48, 50, 51, 52, 53–4, 55–6, 57, 58, 59–63, 65, 66, 67, 68, 69, 71,

210

## Index

74, 80, 81, 88, 90, 93, 94, 95, 102, 104, 105, 133, 143, 147, 159, 166, 171, 173, 175, 178, 181, 193
Díaz Serrano, Jorge   100, 113, 119, 121–22, 123, 124, 136
Durazo, Arturo   102, 136
Duvalier, 'Papa Doc'   24, 62

Echeverría Alvarez, Luis   6, 19, 22, 24, 59, 60, 61, 63, 65–71, 74, 75, 76, 77, 78, 79, 80, 81, 82, 83, 85–6, 87, 88, 89, 91, 92, 93, 94, 95, 99, 100, 102, 104, 105, 109, 111, 113, 115, 117, 118, 133, 157, 160, 171, 174, 176, 178, 182, 192, 194
Echeverría, Maria Ester Zuno de   70
Enseñada   42, 45–6
*Excelsior*   89, 93, 104–5

Federal District (DF)   51–2, 75, 76, 99, 162, 183; (1985 earthquake)   151, 183
Flores Curiel, Rogelio   67, 68
Flores de la Pena, Horacio   70, 81
French diplomacy   120
French student movement   50
Fuentes, Carlos   86

Garciá Paniagua, Javier   55, 100, 126
GATT   110, 116, 156, 175
Garcia Barragan, Marcelino   55, 68
Garza Sada (family)   37, 79
*Gobernación*   6, 22–3, 41, 43, 44, 45, 47, 66, 70, 85, 99, 100, 101, 107, 108, 143, 144, 153, 155, 159, 161, 197
Gómez Villaneuva, Augusto   55, 91, 92
Gonzalos Santos   42–3
Guadelajara   70, 162
Guatemala   30, 42
Guerrero   54, 84, 85
Guevara Niebla, Gilberto   50
Gutiérrez Barrios, Fernando   85

*Halcones*, the   67, 68
Henríquez Guzman   30
Hermosillo   42, 47
Hobbesian bargain   14–15, 16, 39, 44, 58–9, 169, 173

Ibarra, David   124
IMF   82, 127, 129, 134, 140, 154, 156
Import substituting industrialisation (ISI)   13, 72–3, 167

Jalisco,   70, 162
Jaramillo, Ruben   36, 40
Johnson, Lyndon   24, 48, 49, 147
Jonguitud Barros, Carlos   146, 170, 200
Juchitán   108, 145

Kennedy, John F.   35, 75
Krause, Enrique   105, 146

La Quina (Joaquin Hernández de Galicia)   122, 146, 165, 170, 200
Lombardo Toledano, Vicente   26–7, 28, 35, 36, 39, 49–50, 60, 87
López Mateos, Adolfo (President 1958–64)   7, 22, 24, 29, 31, 32, 34–5, 36, 37, 38, 39–40, 42, 43, 46, 57, 60, 73–4, 94, 153, 171, 176, 178, 181, 189
López Portillo, Jose   6, 55, 66, 69, 70, 85, 94, 97–102, 103, 109, 110, 111, 113, 114, 115, 116, 117, 118, 119, 120, 121–2, 123–4, 125–6, 127, 128, 129–32, 134, 135–6, 141, 149, 156, 160, 171, 175, 176, 178, 181, 182, 199
López Portillo, José Ramón   100, 124, 128
Loret de Mola, Carlos   46, 65, 66
Lugo Verduzco, Adolfo   159, 161

Madero, Francisco   16
Madrazo, Carlos   44, 45, 143
Mancera, Miguel   126, 127, 134, 139, 151, 153
Margain, Hugo   70

*Maquiladora* programme 12, 80
Martínez Domínguez, Alfonso 23, 47–8, 61, 67, 68, 69, 70, 104, 175
Mérida 42, 47, 73
*Mestizaje* 21, 63
Michoacán 37, 46–7, 174, 180
MLN 34–5, 36, 50
Monterrey 33
Monterrey group 101, 111 (*see also* Garza Sada family)
Muñoz Ledo, Porfirio 37, 100, 102, 108, 160

Nayarit 86–7, 144
Navismo 41, 42–3, 141, 190
Nicaraguan revolution 98, 120, 142, 180
Nixon, Richard 55, 63, 74
Nuevo León 33, 43

Ortiz Mena, Antonio 7, 40, 52, 61, 73
Oteyza, José Andrés de 101, 116, 117, 121, 124, 128

PAN 12, 32, 37, 42, 46, 47, 55, 73, 103, 104, 106, 126, 141, 142, 145, 151, 152, 158, 162, 170, 177, 180–1
Paz, Octavio 43, 56, 59, 63, 86, 105
PARM 108, 109, 159, 162, 163
PCM (*see* Communist Party)
Pemex 77, 88, 100, 105, 112, 113, 114, 117, 121, 134, 136–7
Perón, Juan 76, 131
Petricioli, Gustavo 134, 155
PMT 85, 86
PP (*see* PPS)
PPS 26, 28, 35, 49–50, 86–7, 106, 163
PRI 2, 4, 8, 9, 10, 20, 22, 23, 24, 27, 28, 29, 33, 41–2, 43, 44, 45, 46, 48, 56, 79, 86, 87, 90, 91, 92, 100, 108, 109, 136, 141, 142–3, 145, 151, 152, 159–60, 162, 163, 165, 168, 172, 173, 177, 179, 181, 182, 183, 188, 189
PRT 86

PST 86
*Proceso* 105, 122
PSUM 108, 151
Puebla 21, 22, 33, 37, 51

Reyes Heroles, Jesús 61, 70, 100, 104, 107, 109, 112, 130, 135, 192
Ruiz Cortines, Adolfo (President 1952–58) 22, 25, 26, 30, 38, 42, 46, 60, 94, 108, 164, 178

Salinas de Gortari, Carlos (President 1988– ) 5, 7, 129, 134, 151, 153, 154, 155, 156, 160, 161, 162, 182
San Luis Potosí 33, 41, 42, 141, 159, 200
Sansores Pérez, Carlos 100, 106–7
Scherer García, Julio 23, 24, 68, 89
Silva Herzog, Jesús 126, 127, 128, 129, 134, 149, 152–5, 161
Sinaloa 46, 91, 92, 142
Sonora 46, 92, 147, 151, 177
Soviet Union 27, 85, 179, 195
SPP (Planning Ministry) 101, 105, 122
STPRM (oilworkers union) 146

Tamaulipas 108, 109
Tello Macias, Carlos 76, 101, 115, 128, 129
Tlatelolco 19, 20, 55, 56, 58, 60, 66, 88, 93

UNAM 50, 51, 52, 53, 56, 68, 69, 99, 110, 124, 134
United States 12, 25, 81–2, 83, 113, 114, 119–20, 145, 146, 148, 156, 168, 179, 181; (Embassy) 23, 26, 33, 35

Vallejo, Demetrio 40, 49, 54, 86
Vasconcelos 31
Velasco Alvarado, Juan 74–5, 76, 131
Velázquez, Fidel 5, 9–10, 55, 70, 88, 93, 107, 126, 140, 142, 145, 153, 161, 177, 183, 188

Volcker, Paul   127, 156

Washington (*see also* United States)   15, 58, 122, 127, 142, 147, 158, 166, 178

Yucatán   25, 43, 46, 65, 73, 77